replacement o/o July 16
(Britain's Mammals)

The MAMMALS
of Britain and Europe

Anders Bjärvall and Staffan Ullström

Foreword by Ernest Neal

Translated by David Christie

CROOM HELM
London & Sydney

© 1986 Anders Bjärvall and Staffan Ullström
This edition first published in 1986 by
Croom Helm Ltd, Provident House, Burrell Row, Beckenham, Kent BR3 1AT
Croom Helm Australia Pty Ltd, Suite 4, 6th Floor, 64–67 Kippax Street,
Surry Hills, NSW 2010, Australia

British Library Cataloguing in Publication Data

Bjärvall, Anders
    The mammals of Europe.
    1. Mammals—Europe
    I. Title   II. Ullström, Staffan
    599.094   QL726

ISBN 0-7099-3268-5

Contents

Foreword

Britain has a rather restricted mammalian fauna due to a large extent to its isolation from the Continent since the last Ice Age. Also, Europe has a far greater variety of habitats including Arctic wastes, high mountains, large areas of coniferous and deciduous forests, grassy steppes and the hotter and more arid regions of some of the countries bordering the Mediterranean. In this book the British reader is given the opportunity to study the more familiar native species in the wider context of the Continental ones and to appreciate the ways in which all European mammals exploit the many niches available to them.

Over the past 50 years or so there has been an upsurge of interest in mammals. At one time their study was restricted to their external features, structural adaptations and general natural history. Later, research was extended to physiological studies, and more recently, particularly with the introduction of more sophisticated field techniques, enquiries have shifted more towards behaviour, ecology, population dynamics and aspects of economic importance.

Useful field guides to the mammals of Britain and Europe are available, but these are primarily for identification and only provide in concise form very limited information about the life styles of the animals. This volume is also valuable for identification, but it goes much further towards giving the reader interesting and comprehensive summaries of what is known of each species. It is remarkable how much the authors have been able to include subject to limitations of space and available knowledge about some of the rarer and more local species.

The book not only includes all the indigenous species, but also those which have been introduced to Europe and have survived to become part of the present mammalian fauna. Sea mammals are also described including those whales and dolphins which periodically appear in offshore waters.

The illustrations are outstanding for their artistry, clarity and accuracy and along with the distribution maps add greatly to the value of this attractive book.

Dr Ernest Neal, MBE
Former President of the Mammal Society

Acknowledgements

During the course of our work on this book we have tried to get first-hand experience of as many European mammals as possible. Some we have succeeded in studying in the field, others we have been able to observe in zoological parks, and many we have had to be satisfied with studying as museum specimens.

We have made full use of the extensive literature available – both standard works and specialist volumes – a small selection of which is listed on page 235.

During our extensive travels made together or separately in Europe we have received the best possible assistance from Javier Castroviejo in Spain, Christian Kempf and Claude Dendalatche in France, Janez Cop in Yugoslavia, Hans Roth and Luigi Boitani in Italy and also Jon Andrias in Greece. In addition we have received considerable confidential information from a number of mammalogists in other countries. Without this help the material concerning in particular central and southern Europe would have had a substantially different appearance from the way it looks now.

We have also received excellent assistance from researchers and other people with zoological skills in our home country, particularly with critical examination of the text. Thus Ingemar Ahlén has checked the bats, Ulfur Arnasson the whales, Lennart Almkvist the seals and the whales, Karl Fredga the insectivores, carnivores and others, and Hjalmar Fleischer the whole text. They have all both offered constructive suggestions for improvement to the original text and pointed out errors which we were therefore able to put right. We thank them all.

We are also grateful to our families. They have not only accepted our shutting ourselves up and working evenings and weekends, but have also been our best critics.

The work on this book has been very stimulating and has given us many satisfying experiences. We hope that we are able to pass on something of this to readers.

Sollentuna and Knivsta
AB and SU

Introduction

Almost anywhere in Europe it is possible to go out and see mammals: bats flying out from their roosting places at dusk in order to hunt, foxes or Badgers leaving their dens towards evening in order to search for food, Chamois or Ibex browsing high up on a mountain slope, seals gathering on smooth-washed rocks, and so on. Mammals can also be seen purely by chance almost anywhere and in any situation. To determine then which species is involved can be hard; indeed, it can even be difficult to identify the family or other systematic unit to which the animal belongs.

In putting together this book, one consideration has been that it should be helpful to anyone wishing to identify a mammal that he or she has seen. The mammal species occurring in Europe are therefore portrayed in words and illustrations. Information on the different species' biology, as well as facts that are of interest from a point of view of nature conservation, have also been added to the species descriptions.

Another consideration has been that all information about a species should be found in one and the same place. This has also been achieved throughout – each species is described on one page, part of a page or several pages, depending on how interesting it is – but an important point must be added to this. For closely related species, such as those within the same genus, family or sometimes order, the choice of food, for example, or the breeding biology may be identical so far as is known. To show these under each species would then involve considerable repetition. In order to avoid this, those facts that are common to all are given in the initial introduction to the various systematic units. To give one example: if one wishes to read about the Elk, the species description should be supplemented with the introductions to both the deer family and the order of even-toed ungulates.

So far as mammal systematics are concerned, absolute fact does not exist, and nor does it in fact in any systematics. Any attempt to fix orders, families and species, to decide if a certain species belongs to the one or the other genus or if two forms constitute separate species or only races of one and the same species, is of necessity based on subjective views. Even though modern mammal systematists are reasonably unanimous as regards the fundamentals, considerable disagreement prevails over a great many details.

In this book, the order used by the English systematist Gordon Corbet in *The Mammals of the Palaearctic Region* (1978) has been followed. This in turn is based on – and fundamentally diverges negligibly from – several older works. On the other hand, a couple of larger works of the 'List of the mammals of the world' type have recently been published in which the authors have tried their hand at presenting even the orders in a completely new sequence. For example, carnivores and whales have been brought forward and rodents and lagomorphs placed at the end. These works, however, have been regarded here primarily as contributions to the discussion, and personal dialogue with Corbet, who contributed to one of these works, also produced convincing argument against diverging too much from the traditional picture in a book of this sort.

The whales, however, are not treated in *The Mammals of the Palaearctic Region*. The sequence, both of suborders and of families, within this order therefore follows that used by Corbet & Hill in *A World List of Mammalian Species* (1980). In that work, however, the individual species in each genus are shown in alphabetical order following the scientific name. We consider it not particularly meaningful to do the same here; instead, a more 'current' sequence is adopted, used for example by Stonehouse & Camm in *Mammals of the Seas* (1983).

The text for each species begins with data on some of its measurements. This is followed by descriptions of identification features, distribution, habitat, reproduction, and any other points. These subject matters are dealt with in this order, generally in separate paragraphs but, for reasons of space, without sub-headings. In cases where, for example, a species' distribution and choice of habitat or choice of habitat and food are closely linked together, these are treated in one and the same paragraph. For species which are described more briefly, the text is generally not divided up into paragraphs.

Where measurement data are concerned, body length (often referred to as head + body), tail length and weight are given. Other measurement details are provided only when they are necessary in order to distinguish closely related species. The body length is the measurement from the tip of the nose to the base of the tail when the animal is lying on its back on a firm, level base. The length of the tail is measured from the base to its tip, not to the tip of the longest tail hairs. Several measurement data are taken from available literature on mammals (page 235) and, unless otherwise stated, refer to the normal variation in full-grown, sexually mature individuals. Extreme values, both above and below those given, occur in many species, especially when it comes to weight. When measurement details in the literature have been inconsistent – and they certainly

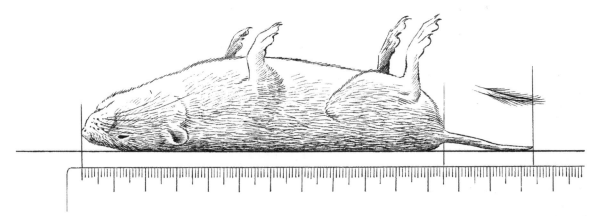

The total body length (=head+body) of a mammal is measured from the tip of the nose to the base of the tail. The animal should be lying on its back on a firm, flat surface. When measuring the tail length, any hairs projecting at the tip are not included.

are for many species — we have sought to include correct details with the help of the collections at the National Museum of Natural History in Stockholm, which were kindly made available for the purpose.

Under the hypothetical heading of identification features the first thing pointed out, to complement the illustrations, is what characterises the animal as far as appearance is concerned — what should be looked for, for instance, regarding its colour and shape in order to distinguish it from closely related species. Often, especially with small mammal species, this involves details that cannot be seen if the animal is not in the hand. Variation between winter and summer coat, as well as between different individuals, is also recorded in the text and/or illustration. The same applies to tracks and signs of various kinds, which can be significant when it comes to deciding if a species occurs in a region and sometimes also for separating different species. Finally, the more important cries and calls are described, particularly those which we humans often hear given by mammals, but this is a difficult area. Mammal calls are incompletely known: there are certainly, for example, contact calls between female and young that humans have never heard, and moreover written descriptions of calls are rather crude.

The distribution is also given in both text and illustration, the latter a map showing the range of occurrence in Europe. There are, however, no maps for the whales, which do not of course belong to the continental landmasses but to the world's oceans. Supplementary information is given in the text on occurrence, if any, in other parts of the world as well. In addition, changes in distribution are given.

The fourth hypothetical sub-heading deals with the species' habitat requirements. This is of course one of several factors which to a great degree influence distribution, but it is, at least for many species, rather poorly understood. Here, too, those cases where the population density has been shown to vary between different habitats are mentioned.

In the matter of food, the major items of the diet are given together with any others that form a subsidiary part of it. Further, whether the choice of food varies between times of the year, and whether the species in question lays up stores and how much it eats per day, are stated. On the last point, it is not unusual to come across extremely varying reports for one and the same species, many times varying to such an extent that we have felt it important to exercise a certain restraint when passing on these details.

Breeding is a wide concept that encompasses a great many details, from the initial contact between the pair during the season to the birth of the young. Indeed, even the subsequent development of the young until they are independent of their parents may be placed under this heading. The circumstances are often of a similar nature in closely related species, and in many cases breeding is mentioned – in whole or in part – in introductory descriptions of order, family or genus.

In conclusion, with the hypothetical sub-heading of incidental information, some details are supplied on those points that do not belong among any of the subject areas introduced above. Most frequently this deals with data on population density, size of home range or migrations, but facts concerning, for example, winter rest and any division into races are also provided.

What is a mammal?

The first mammal-like creatures on our earth emerged more than 150 million years ago towards the end of the geological period known as the Triassic. They were evolved from primitive reptiles in the shadow of, among others, the then numerous dinosaurs, and slowly acquired characters of the mammal. The more rapid success that came later was due to several different phenomena. When the development of the fetus began to take place within the female's body, the offspring received protection during what was formerly a very sensitive period. When reptilian scales were replaced by a coat of hair, this reduced the direct dependence on the temperature of the surroundings: the mammals acquired a uniform body heat and could occupy cooler regions which the reptiles had never reached. Most important, however, was the development of the brain: it has been said that even the stupidest mammal is an intellectual giant in comparison with a reptile. It required the whole of the Cretaceous period, 70 million years, for these characters to evolve and not until the early Tertiary, about 70 million years ago, did a division take place into basically the orders which now exist.

The mammals have evolved from reptiles which moved on all four limbs. When, during the course of evolution, elbows and knees came closer and closer in towards the body, both stability and the animal's speed increased.

All mammals are suckled. Here, the young of Wood Lemming are receiving one of their first meals.

Despite the immense size difference between a whale and a shrew, or the vastly different ways of life of a bat (which for the most part catches its food in the air), a mole (which catches it underground) and an otter (which catches it underwater), these and all other species of mammal have many characters in common.

The term 'mammal' comes from the Latin word *mamma*, which means breast: all mammal young are suckled after birth. In other words, they get their nourishment through the mother's milk. Before this, the fetus has received food, as well as the oxygen that is already necessary for life at that early stage, through the placenta. There are, however, exceptions to this latter rule. The monotremes of Australia — the Platypus and Echidna — lay eggs but their young still suck after hatching, and in the marsupials it is only bandicoots that have a placenta. In the remaining marsupials the young are born virtually as fetuses, after which they develop through sucking the mother's milk in the pocket of skin — the pouch — which the female has on the belly.

Furthermore, the mammals are almost completely clothed in hair. There is, however, one exception to this rule, too. The most important function of the coat, but far from the only one, is to be heat-insulating. It is so thanks to the fact that it retains air. In wholly aquatic species, however, this arrangement does not work, and in the whales the coat has almost completely disappeared. In these mammals it is the thick layer of blubber instead that is heat-insulating.

When we talk of a coat in a mammal, perhaps we do not always take into account the fact that this can vary between different parts of the animal, between young and old animals of the same species, and between times of the year. In arctic and temperate regions, a regular change occurs between a thick winter coat and an appreciably thinner summer coat. This change takes place through the old hairs falling out and new ones growing. In many species summer and winter coats can look fairly similar. In other species they are obviously different — the Roe Deer for example is greyish-brown in the winter, warm reddish-brown in summer — and the contrast is tremendous particularly in those species which change to a white winter coat.

This brings us to other functions of the coat, and first of all its importance in camouflage should be mentioned. This is obvious in species which change to a white winter coat: whether a hunted hare or a hunting Weasel, it must be an advantage to be as little visible as possible in both summer and winter. But why then is the Stoat not completely white but equipped with a black tip to its tail?

We do not really know, but we might imagine that this could be an advantage if the Stoat is in turn attacked by some other hunting animal, bird or mammal. The easiest thing for an attacker to determine during a whirling, rapid chase – the tip of the tail – is at the same time the least susceptible part of the Stoat's body.

Other camouflage markings are less obvious. Spotted coats are found in, among others, several species of deer, both adults and young, as well as in such carnivores as Lynx, Genet and Marbled Polecat. Here also, therefore, both hunter and hunted are involved. The common factor is certainly that the spots conceal in an extraordinarily effective way the animal that wears them, for example in the play of sunlight and shadow inside deciduous forest or in other places where the vegetation is not too dense.

Many of the colour markings of the coat – probably more than we know for certain – act as important signals to others of the species. The Roe Deer's white panels on its rear, which are dilated in anxiety and can warn other Roe, are one example of this. Other examples can be found among those species which have tail markings of various kinds. Even so barely conspicuous a marking as the Red Fox's white tail tip is considered to be an important signal to the young, making

The Stoat's white winter coat is an excellent camouflage in a snow-covered landscape. The black tail tip is perhaps a defence against attackers: it is the least susceptible part of the Stoat's body that is easiest for the attacker to fix on.

A spotted coat provides a camouflage, for example in the play of light and shade of the deciduous wood.

A tail tip of a different colour can be an important signal to the young, and make it easier for them to stay with the female in the darkness of the wood.

it easier for them to follow the female in poor light and dense vegetation.

One further function of the coat, or maybe rather of individual hairs, should perhaps be mentioned. One can usually tell the difference between the coat's fine underfur and the significantly longer guard hairs. The latter make contact at their base with nerves, and so can be said to function as sensory hairs. Some of them are developed into so-called whiskers – stiff, long and extremely sensitive owing to ample contact with the nerves. These are especially well developed in species with nocturnal habits or species which live wholly or partially underground. That they play an important role is clear from the fact that they are often still present in species where the coat has in other respects completely disappeared. Such is the case, for example, in the whales.

The colour of the individual hairs, and therefore of the coat, is determined by several factors. The ground colour comes from the keratin's own, almost beige, colour. The hair may then become darker through inlaying of pigment, or lighter through fine air bubbles getting into it. In addition, various colours and glosses may result through refractions of light in the outermost layers of the hair.

Another characteristic of mammals is that the skin contains glands. The mammary glands have already been mentioned, and in addition to these the sweat glands must be the best known to us (in man, of course, they have an important function in regulating temperature). They cannot, however, have this function in animals with well-developed coats since in these heat cannot be given off so easily from the surface of the body. In hot weather or after exertion, such species cool down instead by panting to cool the lungs. They retain sweat glands only under the paws, where in part they have another function. The secretion which they emit contains nowhere near so much volatile fluid as that

13

which comes from pure sweat glands. Instead it contains scents and fat-like substances which evaporate very slowly. One may thus draw the conclusion that these sweat glands have been transformed into what might be called scent glands and have acquired a function which is linked to the marking of territory.

Scent glands, sometimes converted from the skin's sebaceous glands, are common in terrestrial mammals and play a very big role, above all when it comes to intraspecific contacts. They can be located in very different parts of the body. The ungulates have such glands in different places on the limbs – the Chamois on all four feet; Roe Deer, Fallow Deer and Reindeer immediately above the dewclaws on the hind legs; the Roe Deer also (like Elk) immediately below the hock joint on the hind legs; and Boar at the bottom of the inside of the forelegs. In shrews they are found on the sides of the body, in some small mustelids on the belly, in bats on the breast, and in many species of ruminants on the head. In the last case they are usually sited in front of or below the eye – the ante-orbital gland – whereby the animal scent-marks by rubbing its cheek against branches etc. In the Roe Deer the buck has an additional scent gland on the forehead between the antlers.

Most commonly, however, the scent glands are in the anal region, and in many such cases the gland secretion is discharged together with droppings and/or urine, which thereby acquire importance in the matter of scent communications. This is especially important in bringing together male and female during the breeding season. Such glands are found in widely differing places among the mammals. The beaver has its castor glands with the formerly so coveted castoreum, and similar glands near the genital openings are also found in other rodents. Several species of deer have them on the tail, the European dogs

Some mammals get rid of excess heat by cooling the lungs through panting.

14

Scent glands play a very great role in communication in mammals. They can be of various kinds and, as indicated here on Roe Deer, be situated on various parts of the body.

and foxes have them in the form of so-called violet glands above the base of the tail, and the Badger has them beneath the base of the tail. In the mustelids, these anal glands are better developed than any other of their glands. This development has gone farthest in the North American Skunk, which can eject its evil-smelling secretion with great precision – an effective defence.

The mammals have essentially four limbs, which have, however, evolved in enormously different ways in connection with adaptations to a climbing, digging, swimming or flying way of life. An actual reversed development has taken place only in the whales, where the hindlimbs have disappeared and can be detected only as small vestigial legs separated from the spinal column and without function. Essentially the mammals also have five toes or fingers on each limb, but in most cases this number has been reduced.

Finally, the mammals have a lot in common as regards their internal structure. A more detailed description of this is outside the scope of this book, but several important features should be mentioned. The brain is comparatively larger and more complex in structure than in other classes of animal. The heart has four cavities and the wall between its right and left halves is unbroken. Because of this no mixing of the arterial (oxygen-rich) and venous (oxygen-impoverished) blood takes place. Only the left aortic arch remains (birds and reptiles have only the right one left). The skull is articulated with the uppermost cervical vertebra – the atlas – by two joint knobs formed by the lateral occipital bones. Birds and reptiles have only one joint knob here. In the middle ear, finally, where birds as well as reptiles and batrachians have only one auditory bone, the mammals have three: the hammer, the anvil and the stirrup-bone.

15

Marsupials
Order *Marsupialia*

This order has a wide distribution in Australia. It is also found in South America, from where one species of opossum has spread to North America. In Europe there are no indigenous marsupials, but one species has been introduced.

Red-necked Wallaby *Macropus rufogriseus*

With a body length of 60–70 cm, this species of kangaroo is not much larger than a hare. Its tail, however, is proportionately much longer, about as long as the body. The hindfeet, too, are long, about 20 cm. It is this that has given the genus its scientific name: it is made up of the Greek *makros* and *pous*, which mean respectively large and foot. Kangaroos also move quite differently from hares: they bounce on the hind legs alone, in rapid transportation. Now and then Australian animals kept in captivity in Europe have escaped. Often they have not survived, but around 1940, in two different regions in England, feral groups were established which have endured since then. They spend most of their time in shrubland and woodland but seek part of their food in more open terrain, including heaths. The single young is usually born in March–May following a gestation period of about 30 days, and thereafter spends around 280 days in its mother's pouch.

Red-necked Wallaby

Insectivores
Order *Insectivora*

Western Hedgehog *Erinaceus europaeus*

Body length 20–30 cm, tail length 1.5–4 cm, weight 0.4–1.2 kg, exceptionally up to 1.9 kg.

The spines, that is the transformed hairs of the back, separate the hedgehog on outward appearance from all other species of European mammals except perhaps the Porcupine. The latter, however, is much larger, has spines of a completely different appearance, and has a different way of life. In the hedgehog it is only the back that is covered in spines; the underside and most of the head are covered with hair. The 6,000 or so spines are all roughly of equal length (2–3 cm). Faced with approaching danger, the animal rolls itself up into a ball. The spines then stand at right angles straight out from the body and give the animal a very effective protection against natural enemies – though, unfortunately, not against motor cars!

The Western Hedgehog is found over the greater part of western Europe, and appears in forms showing a certain geographical variation. The southernmost, for example, is obviously palest below, and in the western forms the upperside of the head is considerably paler than in eastern ones. In Britain and Ireland the species is widespread and one of the most familiar of all mammals. Its natural northern limit is difficult to mark owing to a great number of attempts at introduction. These may be successful for some years, but then a hard winter can knock out entire local populations. In some parts of Europe the species has declined drastically over recent decades. The main reasons for this are road deaths, environmental pollution and impaired opportunities for finding good overwintering sites.

The hedgehog is not particularly specialised in its choice of habitat. In Britain is is often associated with cultivated country, but mostly perhaps with parks, gardens etc where proximity to man is marked. Farther south, however, the Western Hedgehog is found in very varied habitats, from open heathland to secluded wood, in both wet and dry terrain, from sea level up to at least 2,000 m in mountain regions.

On a clear night in early summer one can carefully follow a hedgehog on its food-searching and see, or perhaps rather hear, some of the food it crams into itself. Should it stop and chomp with no sound being heard other than an eager smacking of lips, a slug or earthworm may be involved; but at other times the crunching sound may reveal that it has presumably come across a large beetle. It eats most animal food of suitable size that it finds, from small insects to small vertebrates such as frogs, lizards and the young of mice and voles. The latter are probably eaten more often than not when it happens to come across a complete nest. The hedgehog also eats carrion (e.g. dead fish) as well as plant material such as acorns, mushrooms and berries.

Mating occurs in spring after the animals come out of hibernation, and can take place well into early summer. The male's courting of the female is a quite remarkable spectacle which is not difficult to see with a little care. It is a drawn-out procedure. The male walks in circles around and close to the female and the female fends off his approaches by herself turning around and around. The animals sniff each other, and the female all the while also utters a cry, a hissing reminiscent of the sound of an old steam engine that has not yet got up steam. All of a sudden the animals stop, stand for a while silently cheek to

Western Hedgehog

cheek, and then the walking and hissing begins again. This can go on for hours before mating takes place. The animals trample over a good area of ground during the ceremony, and if this takes place on a grass field or a tall-growing meadow it may afterwards appear more as if a larger mammal had lain down on the spot. After five to six weeks' pregnancy the female gives birth to a litter of two to ten young (average four to five per female) in a covered and well fitted-out nest in a pile of leaves or similar place. The young are blind at birth but equipped with an initial set of short, pliable and white spines. They leave the nest at around three weeks of age, are suckled by and accompany the female for about the same length of time, and after that lead an independent life.

The Western Hedgehog spends the winter half of the year rolled up in hibernation in a specially prepared winter nest. Its metabolism is lowered greatly. The number of breaths taken per minute reaches only about nine. In summertime a resting hedgehog takes at least double that, while one that is on the go takes 40–50 or more breaths a minute. The body temperature drops with the temperature of the surrounding air to around 6°C.

In the hedgehog a peculiar behaviour occurs which is called self-anointment. It starts with the animal very powerfully increasing its saliva production by eagerly chewing on certain objects. The saliva is spat out and then smeared over the spines. Self-anointment may occur in the young as early as their first day out of the nest. Why the hedgehog does this is not known for certain, but since the behaviour can be triggered off by the hedgehog coming in contact with

defensive ball of spines

Algerian Hedgehog

self-anointment

The Western Hedgehog spends the winter rolled up in hibernation (left). The Algerian Hedgehog (upper right) is slightly longer-legged, and has bigger outer ears than the common species. When self-anointing (lower left), the spines on back and sides are smeared with saliva.

poisonous objects — under natural circumstances (e.g. toad skin), and experimentally (e.g. cigarette ends) — one supposes that the saliva may function as a warning signal for any possible attacker with a well-developed sense of smell. In England the home range has been shown to be 15–40 ha in males, 5–12 ha in females. The animal roams through this at an average speed of 3.7 m per minute (male) and 2.2 m per minute (female).

The Algerian Hedgehog *Erinaceus algirus* is a North African species which is found in Europe in a narrow zone along the Spanish and French Mediterranean coast and on Mallorca and the Canary Islands. It stands somewhat higher on its legs and has larger outer ears than the previous species. It does not hibernate but otherwise resembles the Western Hedgehog in its way of life.

The Eastern Hedgehog was formerly regarded as a race of the common species (*E. e. concolor*). Studies of chromosome sets of the two forms, however, indicate that it should be considered rather as a separate species (*E. concolor*). It differs from the Western Hedgehog in that the underside of the neck and the breast are clearly lighter than the belly. In Europe it occurs east of an imaginary line from the Adriatic Sea to the Oder. Not illustrated.

Shrews   Family *Soricidae*

Shrews are small, velvety animals with a nose drawn out to a point. In outward appearance they resemble mice, but they belong to the insectivores order and so are far removed systematically from the small rodents. They have a very mobile nose and when the animals are active – which they nearly always are – they get scent of things by turning it incessantly in various directions. The outer ears as well as the eyes are very small and partly or completely concealed in the coat. On the sides of the body there are glands which release strongly scented secretions.

In both their outer and their inner build, shrews show similarities to their close relatives the moles. The extended nose, the stunted outer ears and the small eyes are examples of this. There are also, however, differences between the two families. An important one is that shrews' skulls lack a zygomatic arch. In this respect the family is unique among the mammals.

Within the shrew family, which has many species – more than 300 species are known from North America, Europe and Asia – what is so far as is known the world's smallest mammal species is found, the Pygmy White-toothed Shrew (page 30).

Shrews are tremendously active and have a very high metabolism. A small study of a Common Shrew in captivity for almost three months may illustrate this. During this time the animal ate a daily average of food which weighed more than half its own weight. In natural circumstances, when certainly more energy is used in seeking food, the animal requires even more – in low temperatures probably not much less than its own body weight.

The rapid metabolism and the restless life, however, leave their mark: shrews do not live long. Individuals born early become sexually mature and can reproduce as soon as their first summer. The residue of the young that survive the first winter become sexually mature in the next summer, reproduce then, after which the fully-grown shrews as a rule die during the autumn, around one-and-a-half years old.

The shrews live deep down in dense vegetation, in passages they have dug themselves, vole passages or other hollows, and as a result they are difficult to observe. They make their presence known, however, in other ways.

Several of the species are noisy: squeaking or chirping cries are often heard from their retreats. In winter it is not so rare for shrews to run on the snow cover, when they leave a track which on the one hand shows a clear impression of the tail and on the other is fairly broad in proportion to the length of the stride.

Jaws or whole skulls of both shrews and other species of small mammals can often be found and identified in owl pellets.

Finally, the fact that shrews are prey animals for both owls and other predators can in various ways reveal their presence in an area. The owls swallow small prey animals whole or break them up into big pieces. Indigestible parts – hair and parts of the skeleton – are then regurgitated in the form of what are known as pellets. Whole skulls of small mammals, shrews for example, are often found in these, well protected by a blanket of matted hair. There are several examples of shrew species that have been discovered for the first time in an area by their presence in owl pellets. Predators treat shrews in rather different ways. Many species kill them and some may eat them, but it often happens that they leave them untouched on the ground or on the snow. No doubt it is the powerful scent from the glands on the sides of the body that causes the animal to refrain from consuming its prey.

Shrews are unique among the mammals in that the cranium lacks a zygomatic arch (upper left). Their tracks on the snow are relatively broad in proportion to the length of the bound (lower left).

Least Shrew *Sorex minutissimus*

With a body length of 33–53 mm and a weight of 1.2–4 g, the Least Shrew is one of the smallest mammal species in Europe. The range extends through the northern coniferous belt, the taiga, eastwards to the Pacific coast, and westwards in a wedge which covers a large part of Finland and just reaches into north Sweden. The species is versatile in its choice of habitat and may be encountered in damp swamp edges, conifer forest with moss cover, dry pine heaths, open sandy country and in deciduous forest edges with luxuriant grassy vegetation. The density of individuals seems never to reach a high level. This, in combination with a secluded way of life, certainly makes the species very difficult to detect. In Sweden the Least Shrew was first discovered as recently as 1967, and even in 1979 it had been reported only four times.

Pygmy Shrew *Sorex minutus*

This species is slightly paler but in particular considerably smaller than the Common Shrew – body length only 42–64 mm and weight 2–7.5 g. A good distinction between the two species is that the tail in the Pygmy Shrew is pinched in at the root. In young, the tail hairs protrude as well. The middle part of the tail in particular therefore becomes almost a little bushy. The distribution embraces the greater part of Europe, but in contrast to the larger shrew the Pygmy Shrew is present in Ireland and on Gotland (Sweden). The two species often occur in the same habitat, but the relative densities can vary very considerably. On heaths, damp swampy ground and elsewhere the Pygmy Shrew is far and away the more numerous. The reason can be found in the choice of food: in habitats where earthworms are lacking, the Common Shrew decreases in numbers. The Pygmy Shrew by contrast feeds mostly on a variety of invertebrates, e.g. spiders and beetles, which it finds above ground. It is both a better swimmer and a better climber than the Common Shrew.

Laxmann's Shrew *Sorex caecutiens*

Laxmann's Shrew is small. With a body length of 48–70 mm, tail length of 31–45 mm and a weight of 3–8 g, it is between the Common Shrew and the Pygmy Shrew in size, though closer to the latter. It differs from that species in having white feet with almost silver-shining hair and a sharp demarcation between the dark brown upperside and the greyish-white colour of the underside. Further, it has a suggestion of a small bushy tuft at the tip of the tail. Laxmann's Shrew is found in Poland and north Scandinavia, although it was not discovered in Sweden until 1941; more recently the species has been found to be present here, there and everywhere in the forests of Norrland up to the low mountains. The species occurs in Finland except in the extreme western and southern parts of that country, and eastwards the range then expands over large parts of northern Asia. Laxmann's Shrew lives chiefly in coniferous habitats of various kinds. It seems nowhere to be so numerous as the Common Shrew, but locally, both in Sweden and in Finland, it can be commoner than the Pygmy Shrew.

Least Shrew

Pygmy Shrew

Laxmann's Shrew

Least Shrew

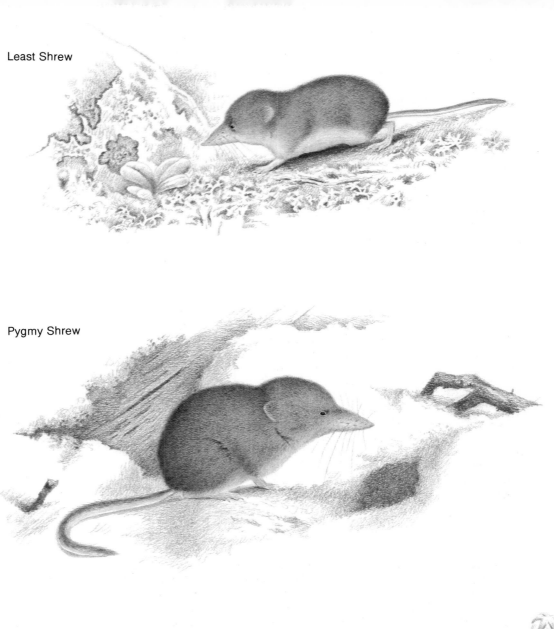

Pygmy Shrew

Laxmann's Shrew

Common Shrew *Sorex araneus*

Body length 54–87 mm, tail length 32–56 mm, weight 3.5–16 g.

The Common Shrew is in most cases brownish-black on the back and greyish-white on the underside. The back colour can, however, vary – through among other things hair loss – from light brown to almost black. Where the dark back merges with the light belly there is a light brown zone on the side which is usually well defined. The tail is bicoloured: its upperside is the same colour as the back; the underside as the belly. In one-year-old animals, i.e. those which have overwintered, the tail is often hairless and frost-bitten on its outermost part. In young individuals it is covered with short, tight-fitting hairs. The teeth in the Common Shrew, as in all other shrews belonging to the genus *Sorex* and also water shrews, are bicoloured. The base is the normal colour of teeth, and the tip is reddish-brown.

The species is found within a large continuous area which includes the greater part of Europe and in addition considerable parts of Asia. Its spread has in several places been checked by water and it is absent on many large islands lying far from land – Iceland, Ireland, Gotland, and the large islands in the Mediterranean. Further, it is absent from most of Spain and Portugal. On the other hand, it does occur on some other islands, including off the west coast of Norway.

There is hardly any type of countryside in Europe that is totally impossible as a haunt for the Common Shrew. In parts of the north there is perhaps a suspicion that it is most easily encountered in deep, perhaps even slightly damp wooded terrain, but it also occurs in quite different habitats – on grazed meadows next to the sea, in gardens, in shallow ditches, as well as both in alpine birch forest and on the mountain above the tree-line etc.

Small animals of various kinds – insects, centipedes, earthworms, spiders, woodlice – make up the main proportion of the food. The Common Shrew readily tackles carrion, while larger prey animals – particularly mice and voles – are attacked more rarely. If one catches small rodents using traps that take the prey alive, what may happen is that shrews get into the trap, kill the mouse or the vole and even begin to eat it. The Common Shrew may occasionally consume small amounts of vegetable matter, especially seeds.

In the northern parts of the range mating time falls in April–May; the species then has a litter in May–June and probably often a second one later on in summer. In central and south Europe newborn young are sometimes met with considerably later in the autumn, even in October, which may be due to breeding by young born early in the same year. It has, however, also been interpreted as meaning that a third or possibly even a fourth litter could occur in one year. The litter consists of three to ten young. They are born in a nest well put together with bits of vegetable matter and concealed in the deepest vegetation or in some hollow down in the ground. Around half of the young die before two months of age, and only 20–30% survive long enough to reproduce in the next year.

The Common Shrew climbs well, and in winter it sometimes tries to get indoors exactly as Wood Mice do. The general level of activity is otherwise lower in winter than in summer. This has been interpreted as a way of reducing both energy consumption and risk of predation. The species is not hesitant about entering water either, but is to all appearances considerably less well adapted for this than the Water Shrew. In an examination of the stomach contents of fish from a lake where there were Water Shrews, no remains at all were found of the latter species. Quite a number of fish had, on the other hand, swallowed Common Shrews. There have been a number of shrews described which repres-

Common Shrew

ent either races of the Common Shrew or separate species. They are in any case extremely closely related to the Common Shrew and cannot be distinguished with certainty from it other than by chromosome studies. One in France and some of the adjoining regions has been named Millet's Shrew (*S. a. coronatus* or *S. coronatus*), and another in southern Italy the Short-tailed or Appennine Shrew (*S. a. samniticus* or *S. samniticus*).

Spanish Shrew *Sorex granarius*

The Spanish Shrew was described at the beginning of the 1900s as a race (*S. araneus granarius*) of the Common Shrew, but differs so markedly in the matter of chromosome make-up that it is now considered a separate species. It is said also to be possible to distinguish it from the Common Shrew by the fact that it has a shorter skull. So far as is known it is found only within restricted parts of the Iberian peninsula. Not illustrated.

Alpine Shrew *Sorex alpinus*

With a body length of 62–77 mm, tail length of 60–75 mm and weight of 6–10 g, this species is distinguished, as far as measurements are concerned, in particular by its relatively long tail. The colour, too, makes it easily recognisable. Both upper- and underside are uniformly blackish-grey, while the feet are pale, on the underside almost white. The tail also is pale beneath. The Alpine Shrew is strictly confined to high mountain regions. It is found in central and east Europe, particularly in the Alps and the Carpathians, but also in the mountains of south and central Germany, the Pyrenees, the Tatra mountains as well as in high-lying mountainous districts in Yugoslavia. It lives in diverse habitats, the highest conifer woods, alpine meadows and the bare mountain moors, at levels from 200 m and up to 3,000 m above sea.

Dusky Shrew *Sorex sinalis*

The Dusky Shrew is big. The body length runs to 55–82 mm, the tail length to 41–55 mm and the weight to 6.5–14.5 g. In measurements the species is therefore bigger than the Common Shrew, but the difference is minute and is not good enough for safe specific identification. Better characters in the Dusky Shrew are the markedly broad front feet and the colour markings. The dark brown colour of the back merges without any sharp division into a greyish-brown underside which is considerably darker than in the Common Shrew. The Dusky Shrew has been known in Finland since 1949 and in Norway since 1968. It was hardly unexpected, therefore, when the first examples were captured in west-central Sweden in 1977. Outside Scandinavia the species has roughly the same distribution as the Least Shrew. It occurs eastwards through the whole taiga belt. The Dusky Shrew is met with in small discrete populations in widely varying habitats. The first discovery in Sweden, for example, was made in a rank embankment but right next to a gravel area and near buildings.

Alpine Shrew

Dusky Shrew

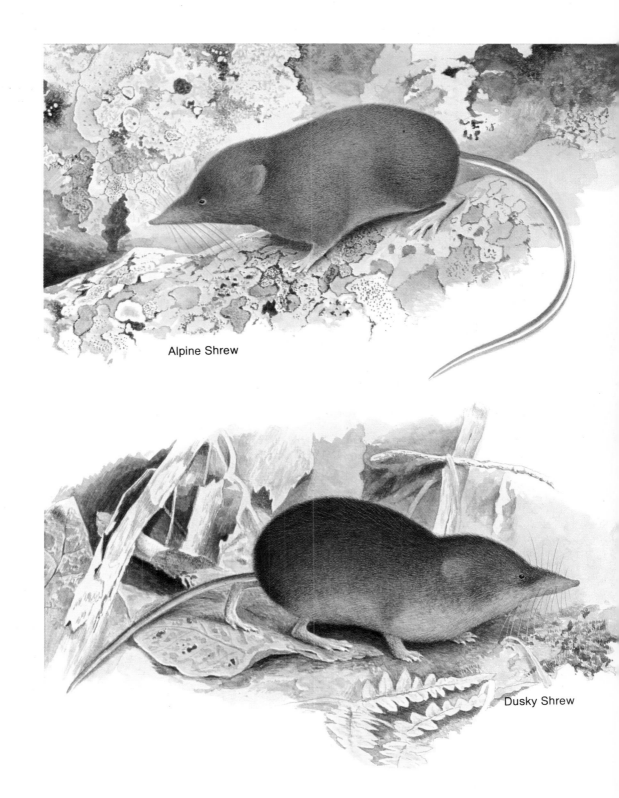

Alpine Shrew

Dusky Shrew

Water Shrew *Neomys fodiens*

Body length 63–96 mm, tail length 47–82 mm, weight 8–23 g.

The Water Shrew is clearly larger than the Common Shrew and therefore the largest of our shrew species. It is, however, easier to recognise by colour than by size: none of the other species is correspondingly black on the upperside and white or greyish-white below. The border between the colours is sharp. The scientific name of the genus is made up of the Greek *neo*, which means I swim, and *mus*, a mouse, and the species' external structure shows adaptations for living in water. The underside of the tail and the edge of the hindfeet are equipped with stiff bristles which function as a rudder and oar blades, respectively. The ear openings can be closed off. Intestine and sex organs end together, and as a result the Water Shrew is one of the few placental animals that can be said to have a cloaca.

The species has roughly the same distribution in Europe as the Common Shrew. It is absent, however, south of the Pyrenees, and also in the Balkans.

Water in most forms – lakes, rivers, streams and small brooks – is suitable haunt for the Water Shrew. This must not, however, be too fast-flowing. Nevertheless, it also moves about on land—among other things it excavates underground passages at the edge of the water. The scientific specific name alludes to this: the Latin *fodiens* means digging. When in winter the species sometimes turns up in completely the wrong environment, it may be due to the fact that the 'home water' has frozen over.

The Water Shrew catches its prey underwater, on the surface of the water or at times on dry land. Important prey animals are insects and insect larvae, worms, molluscs and small fish. In the list of prey, however, fish spawn also occurs, as well as one or two larger animals such as frogs and small mammals.

Reproduction is the same as for the Common Shrew.

The Water Shrew displays extraordinary adaptation to an aquatic life in its behaviour. It floats like a cork, swims quickly and is an expert diver. Because the coat holds a lot of air and has good supporting capacity, the dive has to start with a short leap across the surface of the water.

Miller's Water Shrew *Neomys anomalus*

This species is rather like the Water Shrew but somewhat smaller—the body length amounts to 64–88 mm, the tail length 42–67 mm and the weight 7.5–16.5 g. The stiff hairs on the underside of the tail are not so well developed as in its larger relative and the scientific specific name alludes to this: *anomalus* means different, and the tail is of a different structure. The same applies to the hairs on the edge of the hindfeet, and these details reveal that the species is not so well adapted to aquatic life as the Water Shrew. It certainly occurs in water of various kinds, but just as often only in damp terrain, e.g. swamps or well-vegetated meadows. Miller's Water Shrew is found in mountain regions in south and central Europe. The attachment to mountain districts seems to be strongest in the far west, and eastwards the species is also encountered in lower-lying terrain.

Water Shrew

Miller's Water Shrew

28

Water Shrew

Miller's Water Shrew

Lesser White-toothed Shew *Crocidura suaveolens*

The Lesser White-toothed Shrew is about the same size as the Common Shrew. Both this and other *Crocidura* species, however, differ from the Common Shrew in the teeth being uniform in colour. The body length is 53–82 mm, the tail length 24–44 mm and the weight 3.5–6 g. In appearance the species is more like the Greater White-toothed Shrew, from which it differs in being slightly smaller and in its underside being faintly yellowish. The distribution is probably incompletely known, but the Lesser White-toothed Shrew is found in a zone in south and central Europe that extends from north Portugal in the west to the Black Sea in the east. This area is very narrow around the Pyrenees, while eastwards it broadens considerably. The species resorts to the same habitats as the Greater White-toothed Shrew, but is more fond of warm places. It is said to be on the decline in Europe.

Lesser White-toothed Shrew

Greater White-toothed Shrew *Crocidura russula*

The Greater White-toothed Shrew is a little bigger than the previous species. The body length is 64–95 mm, the tail length 33–46 mm and the weight 6–14 g. It is similar to the Bicoloured White-toothed Shrew in colour, but the upperside has elements of reddish-brown and the division from the pale underside is not sharp. There are isolated, long, sparse hairs on the tail. The range covers a large continuous part of central and south Europe and extends eastwards right to eastern Asia. The species occurs mostly in cultivated areas and often in or near human habitation. As in the Bicoloured White-toothed Shrew, the young may move in a caravan behind the female.

Greater White-toothed Shrew

Bicoloured White-toothed Shrew *Crocidura leucodon*

The Bicoloured White-toothed Shrew is approximately as large as the Common Shrew—the body length is 64–90 mm, the tail length 28–40 mm and the weight 6–15 g. The body is 'bicoloured', with a sharp border between the dark brown upperside and the greyish-white underside. The outer ears are large and clearly visible outside the coat. As in the Greater White-toothed Shrew, there are isolated long, pale hairs on the tail and also on the rear part of the body. The Bicoloured White-toothed Shrew occurs within a large continuous area in central Europe. It prefers dry habitats at low levels—arable fields, meadows and gardens—and is not averse to proximity to man. If the family is disturbed in the nest when the young are small, the female removes them to a new nest by carrying them in her mouth one by one. Larger young are moved, as in the Greater White-toothed Shrew, by their taking a firm grasp with their teeth of each other's tails behind the female, who then leads the caravan away to a new place. In parts of Asia Minor, including Lesbos and some other islands in the Aegean Sea, a form of shrew is found which, when it was described, was considered a race of Bicoloured White-toothed Shrew (*C. l. lasia*). It is now thought to be a full species (*C. lasia*).

Bicoloured White-toothed Shrew

Pygmy White-toothed Shrew *Suncus etruscus*

So far as is known, the Pygmy White-toothed Shrew is the world's smallest mammal species. The body length is 36–52 mm, the tail length 24–30 mm, and within a weight of 1.5–2 g all the complicated organs and workings of the mammal body are contained. Besides its small size, the species is distinguished

Pygmy White-toothed Shrew

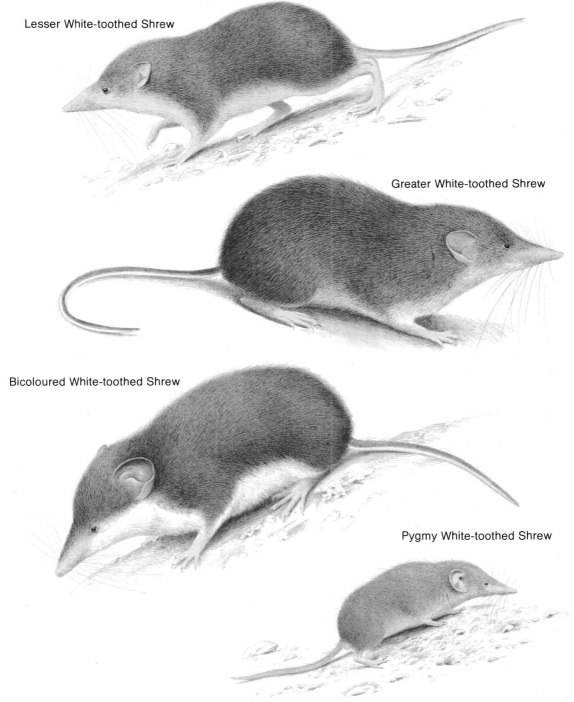

Lesser White-toothed Shrew

Greater White-toothed Shrew

Bicoloured White-toothed Shrew

Pygmy White-toothed Shrew

by strikingly large outer ears and a proportionately long tail. Further, the tip of the nose and of the tail particularly, but also the rest of the body, are equipped with sparse, greatly elongated hairs. In Europe the Pygmy White-toothed Shrew is strictly confined to the Mediterranean region, and therefore has a more southerly distribution than any other European shrew species. It is also found in North Africa and Asia. The species occurs mostly in open terrain with plenty of sunshine, and the favoured habitat appears to be cork oak woodland.

31

Northern Mole *Talpa europaea*

Body length 11–16 cm, tail length 20–47 mm, weight 65–120 g.

The moles live beneath the surface of the ground and are, together with the mole-rats, the only European mammal species that are adapted to a mainly burrowing life. The body is cylindrical. The outer ears are missing, and the small eyes are more or less overgrown by the short-haired, dense coat. The nose is drawn out to a point and equipped with a special bone that facilitates digging. The forelimbs are like small shovels—short, very powerful and fitted with strong claws for digging. The animals seldom show themselves above ground, but still reveal their presence by heaps of earth that are raised during tunnelling work—'mole-hills'. They are formed by the animals lifting up earth through vertical shafts and thereby creating the shapes of small volcanoes.

The Northern Mole occurs in large parts of central Europe, but is absent in 'fringe areas'—in the northern parts of Fennoscandia, in Iceland, Ireland and Portugal as well as significant parts of Spain, Italy, Yugoslavia and Greece. In the four last-mentioned countries, however, other very closely related species of mole are found (see below).

The Northern Mole is found in quite a variety of habitats—cultivated fields, pasturelands, gardens, deciduous wood etc. It is not at home in dry sandy areas or in very damp ground, where the tunnels can easily fall in or become impassable owing to water. In the Alps it occurs as high as 2,000 m above sea level.

Using the senses of smell and hearing, together with its extremely sensitive nose, the Northern Mole hunts animals of most kinds that get lost down its tunnels. Included in its list of prey are earthworms, insects and insect larvae and centipedes. When the Northern Mole has more food available than it needs at the time, it may lay up stores. In one of these more than 1,200 earthworms have been found weighing a total of over 2 kg. The stored animals have bitten-off heads and are kept safe tucked into the walls of the underground passages. Above ground, the species has been seen on isolated occasions attacking frogs and young birds and also tackling carrion.

Several details concerning reproduction are poorly known. Mating time falls in April in the north, but considerably earlier farther south. After a good three weeks' pregnancy the female gives birth to two to seven young in a special breeding chamber lined with moss, dry leaves etc. In the north of the range only one litter per year occurs so far as is known; in southern Europe probably two. The young leave the nest at four to five weeks of age and become sexually mature as early as their first year.

Data on the size of the territory are very variable: figures of between 200 m² and 2,000 m² are mentioned. The animal's way of running is remarkable: the front feet are moved two steps while the back feet are moved one. The species' velvet-like coat has at times been valued as a fur.

Roman Mole (*Talpa romana*) is very like the Northern Mole in both appearance and habits. Certain details in the structure of the skull, however, separate the species, and furthermore the Roman Mole's eyes are stated always to be covered by the skin. The distribution is confined to a narrow region in southwest Italy from the district of Rome down to Sicily. Not illustrated.

Blind Mole (*Talpa caeca*) is smaller than, but otherwise very similar to, the previous two species. The eyes are not always concealed beneath the skin, so the species is if anything less blind than the Roman Mole. The range includes Spain,

Northern Mole

south France, north Italy together with adjacent parts of Switzerland, Yugoslavia, Greece, as well as the Tatra region in the Carpathians, i.e. to a large extent exactly those areas where the Northern and Roman Moles are absent. Not illustrated.

Dwarf Mole (*Talpa mizura*) is one stage smaller again but in other respects is a replica of the previous three species. The distribution in Europe is probably incompletely known; the species is met with only in a few places in mountainous regions of Spain. Not illustrated.

Pyrenean Desman *Galemys pyrenaicus*

Body length 11–13.5 cm, tail length 13–15.5 cm, weight 50–80 g.

Despite the species' superficial resemblance to the shrews—the nose is elongated into an extremely mobile proboscis—the Pyrenean Desman belongs to the mole family. It excavates its own passages, but is in no way as specialised a digger as the moles proper. Instead it often moves about in water—the flattened, broad feet have webs between the toes and are edged with stiff bristles. In addition, the tail is flattened sideways in its outer section and acts as a rudder. At the base the tail is pinched and equipped with a powerful musk gland. The species is endemic in the Pyrenees and adjacent regions in north Spain. It lives chiefly along small mountain streams in long valleys at levels up to 2,000 m above sea. This should be a safeguarded environment, but the species is judged to be threatened by both pollution of the clear mountain streams and an increasing interest in hydro-power construction in the region. The food consists of small animals—freshwater worms, dragonflies, insects and insect larvae etc, but also smaller vertebrates—which are caught mainly in the water but also on land. In March–July, the litter consisting of two to four young is born.

Desman Rat *Desmana moschata*

The Desman Rat grows up to 22 cm long and is consequently considerably larger than the Pyrenean Desman, which in other respects it resembles. In fact, Desman Rat is an unfortunate name since it does not relate to a rodent but to a mole species. At the base of the tail there is, as in the Pyrenean Desman, a big gland which secretes a strongly smelling substance. The species is found in parts of southwest Russia, naturally along the rivers Don and Volga among others and as an introduced species beside the Dnieper and other rivers. It is if anything even better adapted than the previous species to an aquatic life and spends most of its time swimming: when underwater, the mobile and long muzzle is used rather like a snorkel. Not illustrated.

Pyrenean Desman

Bats
Order *Chiroptera*

The bats are adapted in such a way that they are able to fly, and in this capacity they are unique among the mammals. The wings consist of a thin flying membrane between the fore- and hindlimbs, in the majority of species also between the hindlimbs and the tail. This is held taut mainly by the greatly elongated metacarpal bones and the fingers, i.e. the hand. The scientific name of the order alludes to this. It comes from two Greek words *kheir* and *pteron*, which mean hand and wing respectively. The thumb and the claws of the hindfeet protrude outside the wing membrane.

The bats are normally nocturnal, and feed on insects which they capture in flight. This is not always achieved with the mouth, but with part of the wing membrane. The prey may then be eaten either on the wing or when the bat has landed. Inedible remains of prey animals on, or perhaps more often just below, such feeding places can provide information on choice of food.

Orientation and food-searching during flight in the dark are carried out by echo-location: the animals emit sounds within the wavelength field that lies beyond man's hearing (from 10 to over 100 kHz), and navigate with the help of the reflected echoes. We also know that many species of bats use calls to keep contact with each other. The mouth and nostrils—which emit the sounds—and the ears have evolved in special ways, and in several cases exhibit important characters for differentiating between species. For example, many species have a protuberance on the inside of the base of the outer ear called an ear flap or *tragus*, which takes many varying forms. The calls of bats can be studied with ultrasound detectors which convert the sound to frequencies that are audible to us. Along with the fact that we have discovered that many species can now be separated by call, so the detector has become an important instrument for mapping the different species' distributions and also for monitoring any population changes that may take place.

The bats are odd among the mammals not only in that they can fly, but also because their temperature is not constant. During flight the body temperature is about 40°C, but when the animal has landed and remained still for a while it can drop to nearly 30°. After finishing eating and when the droppings have been expelled, it sinks further to the temperature of the surroundings.

Their insect diet necessitates hibernation in winter, and the bats spend this in sheltered places, preferably without wide temperature fluctuations. Liquid balance is a problem during this overwintering period, and there are at least certain species that prefer places with high relative air humidity. During hibernation the animals' temperature often remains only a little above 0°C, and it may even drop a degree or so below freezing without the animals suffering. Should they, however, become colder than this, they must seek out a better place for hibernation. If this entails flying outside in the middle of winter they are unlikely to survive.

Breeding begins in late summer–early autumn, when mating takes place. The sperm is then stored in the womb for the whole winter, and fertilisation does not take place until the spring. The length of the gestation period varies with the weather conditions. If there is a setback in the weather in the spring after the egg has been fertilised, the female may fall back into hibernation, whereby the development of the fetus progresses more slowly or comes to a complete standstill, and the pregnancy is consequently prolonged.

The birth itself later is an interesting process, with at least one feature which

is unique in the mammals. When the young has emerged, so long as one pair of limbs is free (it can be born either with the head or with the back legs first), it actively takes part itself in the process. It seizes hold of the surface to which the female is attached and then flexes its body and pulls, and by so doing speeds up the course of events itself. The birth appears most often to take place during the daytime, which may be seen as a confirmation of a general rule that in mammals the young come into the world at the time of day when the species is least active. Before she is about to give birth the female clings on not only with her hindlegs but also with her thumbs, and shapes the rear part of the membrane almost into a hammock between her hindlegs. The newborn young normally lands in this, but it does not take long for it to reach the side, and then it falls. The drop is not, however, far for the young is caught up by the umbilical cord. The removal of this tie between female and young has also been observed sometimes to take place in an unusual way. The young begins to suck immediately and then, without releasing its hold of the nipple, moves its hindlegs farther and farther away from the female. By this means the umbilical cord is stretched tighter and tighter and finally draws out the entire afterbirth. Then the young crawls straight back to the female, who consumes the afterbirth, licks the young dry and finally also bites off the umbilical cord.

For the first few days after birth, the blind young clings tight to the female—even during short flying excursions. At night, however, the female is out on her own. In those species in which the females give birth in colonies, the female and young recognise each other—by smell or call—when the female returns. After about four days the young is able to see, and at three to six weeks of age it flies by itself for the first time.

During the last few decades some species of bats have decreased in numbers, at least within parts of their European range, and this may apply to more species than is actually known. There are several confirmed or suspected reasons for this. The use of pesticides to control insects can result in both secondary poisoning and poorer food supply for bats. Chemical treatment of timber in buildings can directly interfere with reproduction. Draining of ponds and other small wetlands can make living conditions worse, since the bats drink from open water surfaces in flight. Disturbance by human beings visiting mines, caves and other places where many bats hibernate together is another important adverse factor. In many places ways are now being sought to eliminate this by closing off the entrances with bars that allow only the animals to pass through. Finally, the fact that old hollow trees are not now allowed to remain standing as they once were is a further factor of detriment to the bats. This can, however, be compensated for to a certain extent by putting up bat nestboxes. Even so, in northern regions this does not make up for the natural hollow trees. A thick hollow oak is frost-free

By standing and watching bats at dusk, an observer may at some time catch sight of a Hobby for example making an attempt to take one of them.

through the winter and therefore a good site for hibernating, which a thin wooden box is not.

It has been established that bats in the wild can reach a considerable age: for example, 24 years (Greater Horseshoe Bat), 18 years (Daubenton's Bat), 13 years (Brandt's Bat), 20 years (Whiskered Bat), 17 years (Natterer's Bat), and 11 years (Common Pipistrelle).

To conclude, it may be mentioned that bats also have some natural enemies. By keeping a watch on hunting bats at dusk or dawn, one may at some time manage to see, for example, a Hobby *Falco subbuteo* appear at lightning speed and try to strike at them. In large samples of owl pellets examined, too, remains of individual bats are usually found. Furthermore, it is known that Starlings *Sturnus vulgaris* may drive out (and perhaps actually kill) bats from tree holes which the birds wish to appropriate. High average lifespan and slow regeneration, however, indicate that only to an insignificant extent are bats the victims of predation.

Slit-faced bats   Family *Nycteridae*

This family is actually mainly tropical. The very outermost part of the tail is split into two small antenna-like parts which point along the rear edge of the membrane in the direction of each respective calcar. The family consists of around 20 species, of which at least one has occurred once in Europe. This is the Egyptian Slit-faced Bat *Nycteris thebaica*, which was encountered in 1914 on the island of Corfu in Greece. It has acquired its scentific specific name from the old Egyptian city of Thebes, has an extensive distribution in Africa and also occurs in Israel. There is also a questionable report of an old discovery of a Short-eared Slit-faced Bat *N. hispida*—also an African species—from Sicily.

Egyptian Slit-faced Bat

Horseshoe bats Family *Rhinolophidae*

Most of the family's 75 known species are to be found in the tropical parts of the Old World, and in Europe there are only five species. The scientific name of the family is composed of the Greek words *rhis* (genitive *rhinos*), which means snout or nose, and *lophos*, which means comb or crust. This alludes to the complicated fold of skin which is found around the nose and which has important functions in echo-location. This 'nose leaf' is made up of a horseshoe-shaped part around the nostrils and above it two protuberances, one lower, thicker one called the sella (saddle) and one upper, narrower one called the lancet. All species within the family lack a tragus. The navigation calls are uttered through the nostrils, because the horseshoe bats fly with the mouth closed. All species apart from the Mediterranean Horseshoe Bat wrap their wings around the whole body when in a sleeping position.

Greater Horseshoe Bat *Rhinolophus ferrumequinum*

The species has a wingspan of 33–39 cm, a body length of 56–68 mm, a weight of 13–34 g. In a hanging position it is the size of a fist. The fur on the back has a faintly reddish tone and the sella is also characteristic. From in front it is actually the shape of a saddle while, seen from the side, the upper corner points diagonally upwards at an acute angle. The ears reach only just in front of the tip of the nose when folded forward. The flight is butterfly-like with irregular stages of gliding. The range includes south and central Europe, with the main concentration in the Mediterranean region, and the species occurs also in North Africa and eastwards through Asia as far as Japan. It has decreased greatly in numbers in some places: from England, for example, a reduction during the last 100 years of 98% is reported. When searching for food, it may often land and take food from the ground. Hibernation often takes place in caves, when the species gathers in larger or smaller groups, often going deep into complex tunnel systems. Loud twittering calls are heard from the summer colonies of females. The Greater Horseshoe Bat is late in reaching sexual maturity, usually not before its third autumn and occasionally not until seven years of age. Movements of more than 40 km per day are known.

Greater Horseshoe Bat

Lesser Horseshoe Bat *Rhinolophus hipposideros*

With a wingspan of 22–25 cm, a weight of 3.5–10 g and a body length of 35–45 mm, the Lesser Horseshoe Bat is small. In fact it is no longer than the endmost phalanx on the thumb of an adult human being. The upperside is dark grey-brown, but, if one has the animal in the hand, it is most easily identified by the appearance of the sella. Seen from the front this is cone-shaped, and in profile the upper corner is gently rounded off. When folded forward the ears reach about 5 mm in front of the tip of the nose. The Lesser Horseshoe Bat is found in the whole of south and central Europe and reaches farther north than any other species in its family. It is also found in North Africa and eastwards through the central parts of Asia to Kashmir. Within parts of its range the species has greatly decreased: in Germany, for example, to the point that it is thought to have almost completely disappeared. In summer the females form colonies of up to 100 individuals, but the animals usually spend the winter on their own. When

Lesser Horseshoe Bat

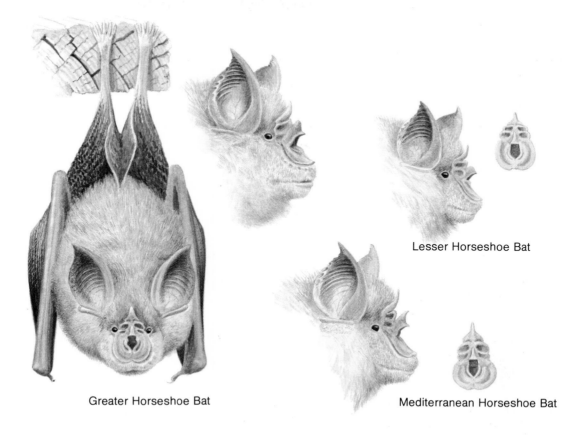

Greater Horseshoe Bat

Lesser Horseshoe Bat

Mediterranean Horseshoe Bat

hibernating in caves, the species often gets deep inside—there are caves where it is found more than 300 m from the entrance. Movements of up to 150 km between winter and summer sites are known.

Mediterranean Horseshoe Bat *Rhinolophus euryale*

The Mediterranean Horseshoe Bat has a body length of 43–58 mm and a weight of 10–18 g and it is, therefore, between the two previous species in size. In cases where measurements are not sufficient for certain specific identification, the appearance of the sella gives a good guide. Seen from in front its sides are parallel, and in profile the upper corner shoots out in a very sharp point. In addition, the lancet seen from in front has straight sides. The range is even more southerly than in the Greater Horseshoe Bat, and, as the name suggests, this bat belongs to the Mediterranean region. It also occurs in North Africa, Asia Minor and the Middle East. When it comes to habits, the species differs from the previous two species in being much more social. In summer both sexes gather at colonies which may contain up to 1,000 individuals, and the animals spend the days there very tightly packed together: there are reports of as many as 300 suspended in 1 m^2.

Mediterranean Horseshoe Bat

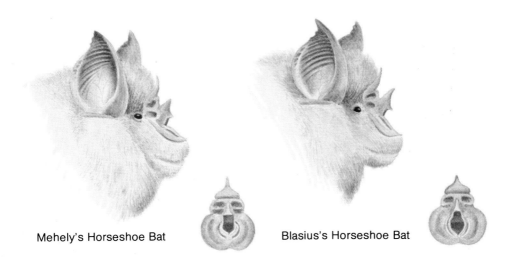

Mehely's Horseshoe Bat

Blasius's Horseshoe Bat

Mehely's Horseshoe Bat *Rhinolophus mehelyi*

This species is very similar to the Mediterranean Horseshoe Bat but it is on average slightly larger—body length 49–64 mm. In addition to this, its fur is lighter, almost pallid. The nose leaf is characteristic. In profile the sella is narrow and the upper corner drawn out to a point, though not so markedly as in the previous and the following species. Seen from in front the lancet narrows almost to a small antenna at the top. The species is found, so far as is known, patchily in the Mediterranean region from the Iberian peninsula in the west to the Black Sea coast in the east, and from there eastwards to Iran and southwards down to North Africa.

Blasius's Horseshoe Bat *Rhinolophus blasii*

Both in general appearance and in size—the body length is 44–53 mm—Blasius's Horseshoe Bat is also very similar to the Mediterranean Horse Bat. In order to separate the species, detailed examination of the nose leaf is called for. In Blasius's Horseshoe Bat the sella seen from in front appears to be drawn inwards at the middle, and from the same angle the lancet has concave sides. The species is found within a continuous area which extends from southern Greece, through Yugoslavia and up to north Italy, as well as in a few isolated places in Italy, Bulgaria and Romania. In addition, it occurs within large parts of Africa and in Asia eastwards to Afghanistan.

Mehely's Horseshoe Bat

Blasius's Horseshoe Bat

Vespertilionid bats Family *Vespertilionidae*

The vespertilionid family consists of around 280 species and is found spread over near enough the whole of the tropical and temperate parts of the world. Its scientific name comes from the Latin *vesper*, which means evening, and this of course alludes to the fact that the vespertilionids, just as the other bats, are chiefly nocturnal. The nose lacks the horseshoe bats' complex fold of skin, and the sounds for echo-location are emitted through the mouth, which is held open while flying. The tail membrane reaches either to the tip of the tail or to either of the last two tail vertebrae, which then form a little tail stump. All species have a tragus, and its size and shape is one of the most important distinguishing marks between, first and foremost, the different genera of the family. In the large genus *Myotis*, the tragus is narrow, pointed, and at least half as long as the outer ear; the genus is further characterised by, among other things, having six molars in each half-jaw behind the very prominent canine teeth. In *Nyctalus* species the tragus is small and kidney-shaped and the number of molars in each half-jaw is only five. The genus *Eptesicus* has a small, blunt tragus and the number of molars is reduced to four in the upper jaw and five in the lower jaw. The *Pipistrellus* species have five molars in each half-jaw and they also have a short and blunt tragus. The species within this genus also have a small lobe of skin on the outside of the calcar. Those species that belong to the genus *Plecotus* are most easily identified by the disproportionately large ears, but have a long narrow tragus which still protrudes when the ears are folded under the wings when the animal is at rest. The number of molars in each half-jaw is six in the lower jaw but only five in the upper jaw.

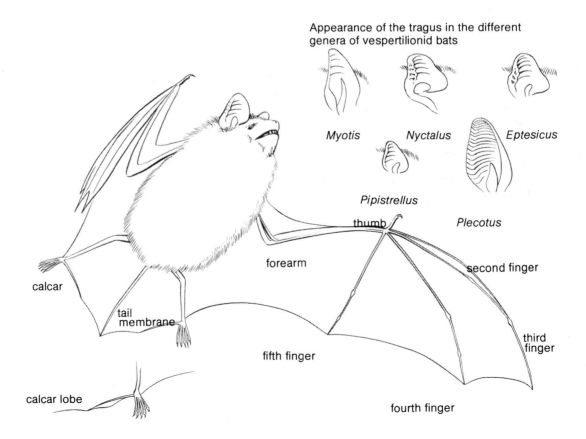

Appearance of the tragus in the different genera of vespertilionid bats

Myotis *Nyctalus* *Eptesicus*

Pipistrellus *Plecotus*

thumb

forearm

calcar

tail membrane

second finger

third finger

fifth finger

calcar lobe

fourth finger

Whiskered Bat *Myotis mystacinus*

This species cannot be separated from the following one using measurements, nor by the whiskers, i.e. a row of long hairs above the corner of the mouth which has given the species its name in both English and other languages. Even the scientific specific name comes from the Greek *mustax*, which means whisker. Identification of the species must instead be made on the basis of other characters. Those often mentioned, but which in practice are inadequate, are that the upperside is dark grey and that the ears folded forward reach approximately 2 mm in front of the nose. The tragus is shorter than half the length of the ear. Reliable distinctions, however, are that the penis is of even width, that the two back premolars in the lower jaw are of different sizes, and that the third premolar in the upper jaw is small and displaced inwards. The species occurs over almost the whole of Europe and is absent only in the southern parts of the Iberian peninsula and within minor areas in the extreme north—Iceland, Scotland, Denmark except Bornholm and south Jutland, and north Fennoscandia. Near its northern limits the species is one of the commonest bats. It is also found in North Africa and eastwards through Asia as far as the Pacific coast. The Whiskered Bat lives in meadowland in wooded districts, but also resorts to other open terrain, e.g. around buildings or near water. It may be out and about during the daytime, especially in spring and autumn, but normally has two activity peaks, one after sunset and one before sunrise. Movements of up to as much as 2,000 km are known.

Whiskered Bat

Brandt's Bat *Myotis brandti*

This and the previous species are very similar to each other and were not described as separate species until 1970. They are equally large—or rather equally small—and have a body length of 37–48 mm, a weight of 4–8 g (during hibernation) and a wingspan of 21–25.5 cm. Additionally, the feet are small and the nose, ears and wing membrane strikingly dark. Brandt's Bats, particularly old individuals, have a reddish-brown upperside, and furthermore the ears folded forward reach approximately to the end of the nose. The only characters that reliably separate the species from the Whiskered Bat, however, are that the male has a club-shaped penis and that the two back premolars in the lower jaw are of equal size. The species is found, probably continuously, from England in the west and into the Soviet Union in the east, but in many countries only a few examples have been discovered. It reaches to about 64°N in Scandinavia. Brandt's Bat lives in woodland. It often hibernates in caves, etc, when it finds its way deeper in than the Whiskered Bat, which can otherwise be found in the same place. The summer colonies, which may include several tens of individuals, are by preference located in buildings.

Brandt's Bat

Geoffroy's Bat *Myotis emarginatus*

Body length and weight in this species amount to 44–50 mm and 7–10 g respectively. In measurements it is therefore close to Natterer's Bat. It can, however, be specifically identified by the fact that the colour is reddish-brown, that the tragus is pointed and approximately half the length of the ear as well as having both front and rear edges straight, that the edge of the tail membrane is equipped with sparse stiff bristles, and above all that the rear edge of the ear has a deep, distinct notch immediately above the centre. Some unexpected patches

Geoffroy's Bat

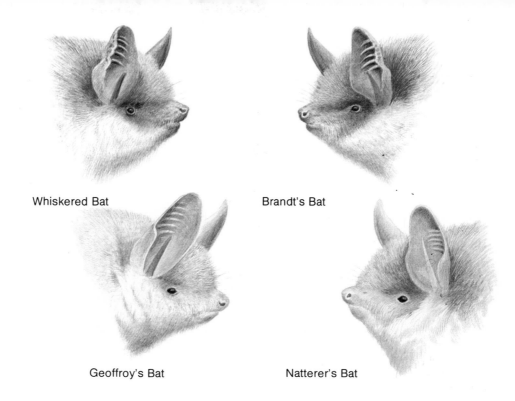

Whiskered Bat

Brandt's Bat

Geoffroy's Bat

Natterer's Bat

and gaps in the distribution suggest that this may be incompletely known, but the species is found in south Europe in a belt that extends from north Spain to the Black Sea. In addition to this it occurs in southern Asia and North Africa. The species is sociable and lives in groups which not uncommonly attract other species and can contain hundreds of individuals. They spend the winter in caves and similar places, but in summer also inhabit buildings and hollow trees.

Natterer's Bat *Myotis nattereri*

Natterer's Bat, which has a body length of 40–50 mm and weighs 7–13 g, has a thick fringe of stiff hairs about 1 mm long along the edge of the tail membrane. It is further characterised by a light, almost white underside and a sharp demarcation in front of the wings between this and the darker, grey-brown upperside. The ears are long—folded forward they reach around 5 mm in front of the tip of the nose—and the tragus is about two-thirds the length of the ear. The species is widespread in Europe, but is absent from the Balkan peninsula and the regions immediately north of there, as well as in the extreme north, about north of 60°N. It also occurs in North Africa and in Asia right across to the Pacific Ocean. Natterer's Bat lives in woods, farmland and also in the middle of towns and villages. It requires warm and calm nights to fly, but is in return then active throughout the night. The flight is comparatively slow and the species is extremely skilful in manoeuvring in small spaces. A large amount of food is caught in the air, but insects etc are also taken from leaves and twigs. In summer hollow trees, bird nestboxes and so on are made use of, whereas the winter is spent in caves and in other sheltered, damp places. Here the animals often squeeze themselves one by one into narrow cracks.

Natterer's Bat

Bechstein's Bat *Myotis bechsteini*

The long ears are a good identification mark on this species. Folded forward they reach in front of the tip of the nose with about half their length to spare, which is a better measurement compared with the two previous species than for example the body length, which is 43–55 mm, or the weight, which is 7–13 g. The ear bases, however, do not meet as they do in the long-eared bats. The back shows a faint red tone and the tragus is roughly half the length of the ear. Bechstein's Bat is found from north Portugal to the Carpathians, but is everywhere rare and probably on the decline. The species may hibernate in caves or houses. Otherwise, especially in summer, hollow trees are very important, including for the female colonies which may comprise several tens of animals. The flight is cumbersome and slow and the species is, like Natterer's Bat, active only in warm and calm weather.

Greater Mouse-eared Bat *Myotis myotis*

The Greater Mouse-eared Bat has a body length of 65–88 mm, a forearm length of 57–68 mm, a weight of 18–45 g and a wingspan of 36.5–45 cm. Among European species of bats, therefore, only the rare Greater Noctule is larger. An important specific character in addition to size is that the tragus is narrow and pointed. Old individuals have a mid-brown upperside and greyish-white underside, while young ones (less than one year old) are more uniformly greyish-brown. The species is found in the whole of south and central Europe, and also in North Africa and parts of Asia. In the north it just reaches the Baltic Sea, and it did not cross to the British Isles until the 1950s. The first Swedish record was in February 1985. The species has declined considerably, particularly in the northern parts of its range. Contributory causes of this may be changes in important habitats—light woods, parklands—or reduced supply of important prey animals, above all insects. It appears that it may be specialised in its choice of food. For example, in one investigation, the food during the whole of the active part of the year was dominated by non-flying beetles belonging to the ground beetle family Carabidae. The summer colonies, which are dominated by breeding females and can consist of thousands of animals, are located in caves or attics in buildings. The animals spend the winter in considerably smaller groups, or more often alone, and preferably in caves. They leave the daytime site late in the evening, as a rule not until it has become dark. It has been shown that the distance between summer and winter quarters can amount to more than 1,500 km.

Lesser Mouse-eared Bat *Myotis blythi* (*M. oxygnathus*)

The two mouse-eared bats are extremely similar and cannot be separated even on size, since they partly overlap in measurements: the Lesser species has a body length of 59–74 mm and a forearm length of 54–60 mm. For reliable specific identification close examination of details of body structure is needed. In the Lesser Mouse-eared the skull is shorter than 23 mm and the ear shorter than 26.5 mm. The ear is also narrower, especially in the middle (where the front edge in the Greater species bulges out). The species is found around the whole of the Mediterranean region and in many places forms colonies, particularly with the Greater Mouse-eared Bat, but also with other species of bat.

Bechstein's Bat

Greater Mouse-eared Bat

Lesser Mouse-eared Bat

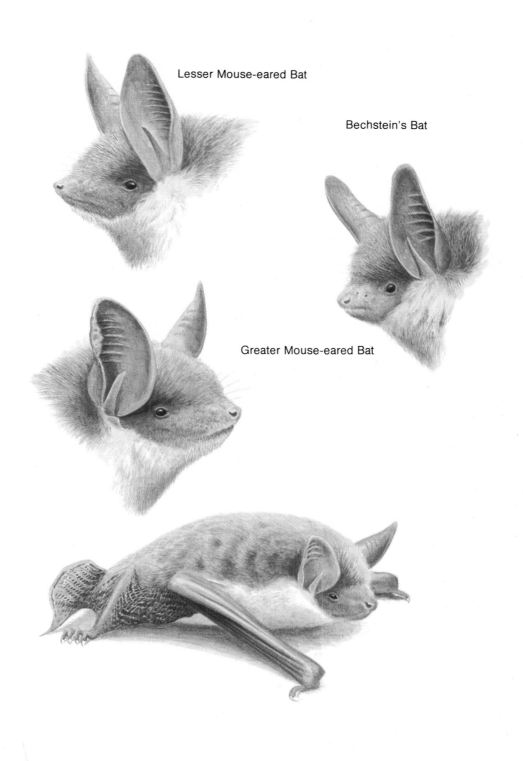

Lesser Mouse-eared Bat

Bechstein's Bat

Greater Mouse-eared Bat

Daubenton's Bat *Myotis daubentoni*

Daubenton's Bat is 40–50 mm long, weighs 6–14 g and has a wingspan of 23–27 cm. It is therefore one of the smaller species within the genus. The nose is light reddish-brown and a suggestion of a red tone is also visible on the dark back. There are, however, other characters which separate it better from the most closely related species. The ears are proportionately short, barely reaching the tip of the nose when they are folded forward, while the feet are relatively long, more than half the length of the tibia. The calcar reaches considerably more than half way between the foot and the tail, and furthermore the membrane next to and over the calcar is almost hairless. Finally, the tragus has a straight front edge but a strongly convex rear edge. The species is common over the greater part of Europe, but is absent in the extreme north and in the southeast. In Britain it is largely absent from Wales and north Scotland, while in Ireland it is found mainly in the eastern half. The range extends eastwards through Asia as far as Japan. The species is associated with water. It usually hunts up and down over small areas low above the surface, and then takes its prey from the water. If the supply of insects here happens to fail, for example as a result of strong winds, the species may resort to woodland and hunt in clearings in the wood. In summer the females form breeding groups of several hundred individuals, but the animals hibernate alone or in small groups. Movements of more than 200 km are known.

Nathalina Bat *Myotis nathalinae*

This species was not described until 1977. It is on average slightly smaller than Daubenton's Bat, but in other respects is so similar that the two cannot be separated in the field. For reliable specific identification, microscopic examination of details in the appearance of the teeth and of the sex organs is required. The species is known from a few places in Spain, France, Switzerland and Poland, but no doubt can also be found elsewhere. Not illustrated.

Long-fingered Bat *Myotis cappaccinii*

The Long-fingered Bat, too, resembles Daubenton's Bat but it is a shade larger—body length 47–53 mm and weight 8–15 g. Other characters, however, are better for distinguishing the species. The Long-fingered Bat is more light grey on the upperside, has proportionately even larger feet which besides are furnished with isolated long bristles, and in addition the membrane over and adjacent to the tibia is hairy. The species is found across the Mediterranean—though the distribution is, so far as known, not continuous—and formerly reached up to Switzerland and Austria, from where it has now disappeared, however. As in Daubenton's Bat, a large proportion of the feeding takes place over water and the species often lives in low-lying damp terrain. It readily utilises caves, both during the summer and for hibernation, and forms colonies either with just its own species or with a sprinkling of other species of the genus *Myotis* as well as those of other genera.

Daubenton's Bat

Nathalina Bat

Long-fingered Bat

Pond Bat

Pond Bat *Myotis dasycneme*

The Pond Bat is 55–64 mm long, weighs 10–20 g and has a wingspan of 30–33 cm. This makes it one size larger again than the previous *Myotis* species. As in Daubenton's Bat, the membrane across and around the tibia is almost hairless, but the species has proportionately longer ears: folded forward they reach 3–4 mm beyond the tip of the nose. The border between the dark brownish-yellow upperside and the greyish-white underside is particularly well marked along the neck. The range is northeasterly and extends from north France/Holland in the west to the Yenisei in the east, but in many areas the species is known only from isolated localities. On the whole it is rare: the world population totals perhaps no more than 7,000 individuals. It is absent from Britain and Ireland but occurs in Denmark, while in Sweden it has recently been found again in the south after many years with no records (which may indicate that the species exists, but is not being discovered, elsewhere). It feeds to a large extent low over the water, and a trained observer is said to be able to distinguish this species from Daubenton's Bat by the fact that it raises its wings high above the body when making a turn, whereas Daubenton's Bat moves them more in the horizontal plane. Summer colonies of up to 100 have been met with, in such places as hollow trees and attics, but the winter hibernation—when the animals are usually active—is generally spent alone in mines, caves, cellars etc. Movements of more than 300 km between summer and winter refuges are known.

Daubenton's Bat   Long-fingered Bat   Pond Bat

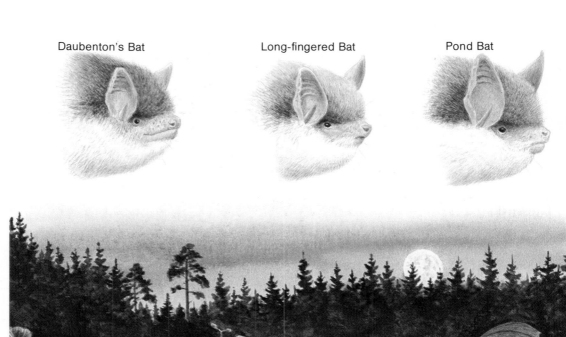

Common Pipistrelle *Pipistrellus pipistrellus*

This is Europe's smallest species of bat. The body length is only 33–52 mm, the tail length 26–36 mm, the weight 3–8 g and the wingspan 19–25 cm. It is almost inconceivable that a mammal with all that is required for flying can weigh only slightly over 3 g, which the species does at the end of the winter hibernation. Apart from its small size, it is identified by the fact that the wings are proportionately narrow (the fifth finger is at most 43 mm), that the hair on the back is uniformly coloured and has a faint reddish tinge, that the calcar is equipped with a large lobe of skin, and also that the first small premolar in the upper jaw is visible from the side but partly concealed by the canine tooth. A rapid ticking call is heard from flying animals, and if one has a colony in the attic or somewhere else in the house one is likely to have to put up with all kinds of squeaking calls that come mainly from the young. The species is found to a large extent over the whole of Europe south of 60°N, and is in many places the commonest species of bat. It occurs also in North Africa and in Asia east to the Altai. It has successfully adapted to very diverse habitats, from pure woodland to densely built-up areas. Because of this it is easily studied, and many of its habits are comparatively well surveyed. In one investigation the animals were found to leave the daytime site around half an hour after sunset, and fairly independently of factors which could be thought significant, such as cloudiness, wind strength, rain and moonlight. During the gestation period in May–June, they returned some time between midnight and dawn. At the end of June, when the young had been born, the pattern changed, however, and the bats showed two activity peaks, one after dusk and another before dawn. The time they spent away from the colony varied between two-and-a-half and five hours per day. Hunting animals often operate in groups of 10–20 individuals, while the overwintering colonies usually consist of several hundred individuals. They can, however, become much larger: an oft-reported cave in Romania has been estimated to harbour over 100,000 animals. In summer these no doubt range over a large area, since it has been established that marked individuals can migrate over 1,000 km.

Nathusius's Pipistrelle *Pipistrellus nathusii*

This species is very like the Common Pipistrelle but is a shade larger. The body length amounts to 44–57 mm, the tail length 33–40 mm and the weight 6–9 g. Also, the fifth finger is around 45 mm, which makes this species a little broader-winged than the Common Pipistrelle. The calcar has only a negligible lobe of skin, and the first premolar in the upper jaw is larger than in the Common Pipistrelle and is not concealed either by the canine tooth in front or by the large molar behind. The species has a continuous distribution only in central and eastern Europe, and to the west its occurrence is, so far as is known, more fragmented. In Britain it has been discovered a few times, in southern England, although ultra-sound detectors may show that it occurs more regularly (as has happened elsewhere in parts of north Europe). This species has, as the previous one, adapted to changing habitats, but it does not live in houses to the same extent and in many places is described as being dependent on trees. Movements of more than 1,500 km between summer and winter quarters are known.

Common Pipistrelle

Nathusius's Pipistrelle

Kuhl's Pipistrelle

Savi's Pipistrelle

Kuhl's Pipistrelle *Pipistrellus kuhli*

This species, too, is very like the Common Pipistrelle but is paler in colour and somewhat larger—the body length is 40–47 mm, the tail length 30–40 mm and the weight 5–9 g. As far as size goes, it is therefore close to the previous species. It is identified by the wings having a sharply outlined pale rear edge, particularly the part between the foot and the fifth finger, and by the fact that the first premolar in the upper jaw is small and displaced inwards so that from the side it is completely concealed by the canine tooth and the large molar behind. The species is found in the Mediterranean region, the northernmost limit being the Loire valley. It also occurs over the whole of Africa and in southwest Asia. It lives in built-up areas, including large towns.

Savi's Pipistrelle *Pipistrellus savii*

In this species the hair on the back is dark with pale tips, and the contrast between this back colour, the white chin and breast together with the black face is a good identification mark of the species. It is otherwise approximately equal in size to the two previous species: the body length is 43–48 mm, the tail length 34–39 mm and the weight 6–10 g. As in Kuhl's Pipistrelle, the first premolar is small and inwardly displaced so that it cannot be seen from the side; sometimes it may be missing altogether. Savi's Pipistrelle has an even more limited distribution in the Mediterranean region than the previous species and, apart from a few occasional discoveries in south Germany, the northern limit reaches the Alps. It is also found in North Africa, including the Canary Islands, and in Asia across to the Pacific coast. In the Alps it is met with at up to 2,600 m above sea level, and it shows a special liking for precipitous and craggy terrain, but also occurs in flatter areas at lower levels such as in towns and villages. Colonies of more than ten or so individuals are unknown in this species, and it appears usually to hibernate alone.

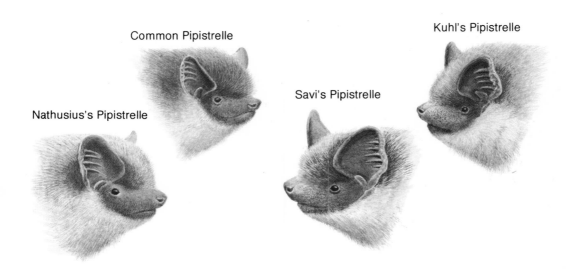

Nathusius's Pipistrelle

Common Pipistrelle

Savi's Pipistrelle

Kuhl's Pipistrelle

Leisler's Bat *Nyctalus leisleri*

This species resembles the Noctule but it is smaller—the body length is 54–64 mm, the weight 11–20 g, the forearm length 39–47 mm and the wingspan up to 34 cm. Further, the colour is more brown or even grey-brown than yellow-red and the hairs, especially on the back, are clearly bicoloured: their base is much darker than the outer part. From east Europe and eastwards to central Asia the distribution is continuous, whereas the picture in west Europe appears more fragmented. This may perhaps be due to the fact that the species has disappeared from certain regions here, but the actual range in west Europe is no doubt also incompletely known. Like the Noctule, Leisler's Bat is mainly a forest dweller, but in certain areas it also resorts to buildings. During the 1970s, for example, it was encountered several times in central London. The females' breeding groups consist of hundreds of individuals, and migration movements occur (perhaps they are even common). Distances as great as in the Noctule are not known, but there are recoveries more than 400 km from the place of marking.

Noctule *Nyctalus noctula*

The Noctule is 69–85 mm long, weighs 15–40 g, has a forearm length of 46–55 mm and a wingspan of up to 40 cm. It is therefore one of the largest species of bats in Britain. Besides the size, the dark yellow-brown or red-brown colour is also characteristic. The hair is uniformly coloured. Of the remaining characters, it is worth mentioning that the ears are black, short and wide, and that the tragus is short and wider at the top, in other words club- or mushroom-shaped. The species often shows itself in full daylight, when it flies high and steadily and utters a squeaking call which is fully audible to human ears. When it hunts at lower altitude, however, the calls are so high on the scale that we cannot hear them. The northern limit of the range coincides approximately with 60°N, and to the south the species is found over large parts of Europe, the temperate parts of Asia eastwards to Japan and North Africa. The Noctule is at home in forest of different types, but is adaptable and can for example manage to live in small clumps of trees in otherwise built-up areas. It is often found in deciduous woodland areas in agricultural country, generally with food-rich lakes and streams. In summer the males are solitary or occur in small groups, while the females form colonies which can consist of more than 100 individuals. The home range can then have a radius of 1.5–2.5 km. Hibernation, however, is social and in still larger groups—up to 1,000 animals. In regions with a mild climate the species hibernates near the summer quarters, but it generally flees from harder winters. From east Europe there are recorded instances of migratory movements of over 1,600 km, and the speed has been found to be between 20 km and 40 km per day.

Leisler's Bat

Noctule

Greater Noctule

Greater Noctule *Nyctalus lasiopterus*

This is Europe's largest species of bat. It differs from the Noctule mainly in the long forearm, 62–69 mm. There is a real difference in its weight, 41–76 g, while the body length of 78–102 mm indicates some degree of overlap between the two species. The Greater Noctule is rare and no colonies are known in Europe. It is found only as isolated individuals in widely separated localities in south and central Europe, from north Spain in the west to south Russia in the east, but it is doubtless present, as yet undiscovered, in some places.

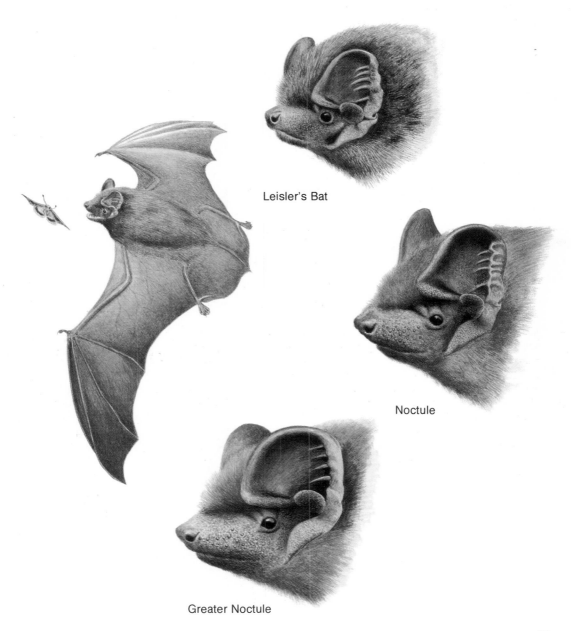

Leisler's Bat

Noctule

Greater Noctule

Northern Bat *Eptesicus nilssoni*

As the Northern Bat is considerably smaller than its nearest relative the Serotine—the body length is 48–70 mm, the weight 8–14 g, the forearm length 38–46 mm and the wingspan up to 27 cm—it is easier to confuse with several of the other smaller species. It is identified mainly by the hair on the back being dark with light tips, which makes the back almost 'shine like gold', by the sharp division of colour between the dark hindneck and the pale breast, and by the final vertebra in the tail projecting 2–3 mm outside the tail membrane. The Northern Bat is found over almost the whole of Scandinavia and even reaches northwards some distance beyond the Arctic Circle. The density, however, varies a lot between different areas. In Sweden, for example, the number of flying individuals per km² has been estimated at five to ten in Uppland, while on Gotland the figure is around 40; thus, here and there it is common, and the fact that it was not found on Öland before the end of the 1970s is surely due mainly to the difficulty in identifying bats in the field without ultra-sound transformers. Elsewhere the species is found within a large part of northeast Europe, more patchily within central Europe, and farther eastwards through Asia to the Pacific Ocean. It does not have particularly rigid habitat requirements, but lives in woodland, farmland, villages and also in mountainous regions, where—especially in the Alps—it may reach as high as over 2,000 m above sea level. The hunting flight is often divided into one period around dusk and one around dawn.

Serotine *Eptesicus serotinus*

The Serotine has a body length of 58–80 mm, a weight of 15–35 g, a forearm length of 48–55 mm and a wingspan of 34–38 cm, and is therefore close to the Noctule in size. It differs from that species, and from the *Nyctalus* species in general, in that the last and a part of the next-to-last tail vertebrae protrude past the membrane and form a small tail (about 6 mm), and in that the tragus has a different appearance: it is scarcely half the length of the ear, blunt, and, because the front edge is slightly concave and the rear edge convex, the sides are parallel. The flight also is distinctive: slow, fluttering level flight alternates with steep, rapid, vertical dives. The species is found in the whole of south and central Europe, with the most northerly outposts in southeast England and in Denmark. It is spreading in Denmark, and was encountered for the first time in Sweden in 1982. In addition it is found in North Africa and in Asia south of 57°N as far as Korea. The Serotine prefers woodland—mostly groves and parkland terrain—but also turns up within built-up areas. The scientific generic name alludes to this. It is a compound of the Greek words *epten* and *oikos*, which mean respectively I fly and house, and can therefore be translated as 'one who flies around the houses'. Both summer and winter residences may be situated in tree holes as well as buildings, though the winter site, especially in east Europe, is also often in caves. The species was formerly called the 'late-flying bat', and the scientific name means just that—'late'—but it leaves its day site at or immediately after sunset, in other words if anything earlier than several other species.

Northern Bat

Serotine

Parti-coloured Bat

Parti-coloured Bat *Vespertilio murinus*

The specific name *murinus* actually means mouse-like, but this species is no more so than many others. It is medium-sized—the body length is 55–66 mm, the weight 11–24 g and the wingspan up to 33 cm—and one of the best identification marks is the appearance of the fur. The hairs on the upperside have dark brown bases and silvery-white tips, which gives the back a frosty look. Furthermore, the ears are broader than they are long, the tragus small and kidney-shaped, and the ears, face and wing membrane very dark. The border between the upperside and the almost white underside is very sharp along the neck. The species has a flight display, primarily in autumn, during which it utters a rapidly repeated (around four times per second) squeaking or chirping cry, quite audible to the human ear. The Parti-coloured Bat has an extensive and continuous distribution in central and east Europe. It occurs patchily down to the Mediterranean Sea, and in the Scandinavian peninsula it reaches to about 60°N, but in Britain it is only a vagrant. It is found in woodland and farmland, but also in rocky and mountainous areas, and perhaps it is this latter fact that has caused it to adapt well to living in towns and villages. There it chooses a daytime retreat under roofing tiles, in ventilation cavities, in cracks in walls etc, the winter refuge being in attics, cellars and other more sheltered places. The species is hardy and in autumn often continues to be active even when the temperature has dropped almost to freezing point. The distance between the summer and winter quarters may exceeed 850 km.

Serotine

Northern Bat

Parti-coloured Bat

Hoary Bat *Lasiurus cinereus*

A North American, long-distance migrant species which may lose its way and is then very occasionally encountered in northwest Europe, where it has been found in Iceland and the British Isles. Its habit of migrating long distances is no doubt also one of the reasons why it is the only species of bat that occurs in Hawaii. It is identified by the heavily mottled or barred upperside. Further, the tail membrane is covered with hair, and this character has even given the genus its scientific name. This is made up of the Greek words *lasios* and *oura*, which mean hairy and tail respectively.

Common Long-eared Bat *Plecotus auritus*

The most prominent characteristic of this species is the enormously long ears. They are 29–38 mm, which compares with the body length of 37–52 mm. The tail length is 34–51 mm, the weight 5–12 g and the wingspan 23–29 cm. It is the ears, too, that have given the scientific name to both the species and the genus. The latter is composed of the two Greek words *pleko*, which means roughly I plait together, and *otos*, which is the genitive form of ear, and therefore alludes principally to the fact that the bases of the ears meet on top of the head. Also, the tragus is long—almost half the length of the ear—and important differences between this and the following species are that it is transparent and at no point broader than 5 mm. At rest, when the ears are laid down against the body, the tragus continues to stand upright. A further difference from the following species is that the hairs on the back have a shade of brown in them; young, however, are more grey. The hunting flight is characteristic. It is slow, perhaps to and fro in front of a wall or in circles around a tree, and is interrupted now and again by the animal hovering and grabbing something edible from a leaf or branch. The Common Long-eared Bat is found over the greater part of Europe, but is absent both from parts of the Mediterranean region and in the far north (beyond approximately 64°N). It is widespread in Britain and Ireland. Outside Europe it is found in North Africa and eastwards through Asia as far as the Pacific. It lives in various kinds of not too secluded woodland, in parkland areas and in gardens. Both the daytime retreat in summer and the sleeping site in winter are often located in buildings: under roofing tiles, behind window shutters or in attics. The species is therefore susceptible to restoration work in older houses. A bat flying freely in an open attic is almost certainly a Common Long-eared Bat. Hollow trees are also important; and for hibernation caves, mines and other underground open spaces are used as well. In a colony studied in southern England, the one-year-old females bore no young; of the two-year-olds around 75% gave birth, while the rest did not reproduce until three years old. Some females have young only every other year, but it has also been shown that one female can bear young every year for 11 years in succession.

Common Long-eared Bat

Grey Long-eared Bat

Grey Long-eared Bat *Plecotus austriacus*

This species is very like the previous one. It is on average slightly larger—the body length is 40–52 mm, the weight 7–14 g and the wingspan 25.5–30 cm—but of more help in specific identification is that the fur is always greyish, without brown tones. Also, the tragus is not transparent and is at least 6 mm broad at its widest point. The species is found in the whole of south and central Europe, including the south coast of England, and elsewhere in North Africa and in Asia eastwards to the Himalayas. It lives in farmland. In western Europe resting and hibernating sites are often in buildings, while caves appear to play a greater part farther eastwards.

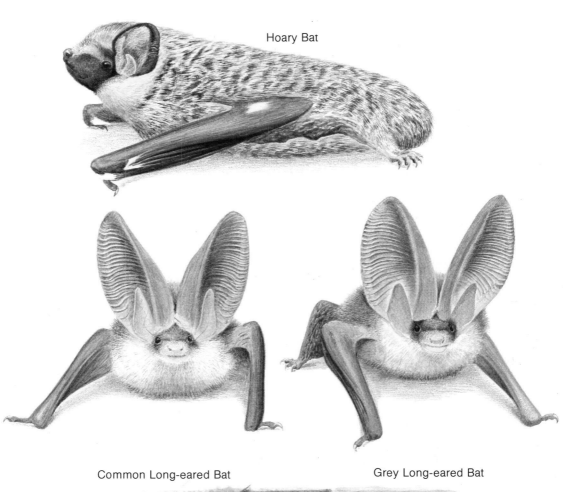

Hoary Bat

Common Long-eared Bat

Grey Long-eared Bat

Barbastelle *Barbastellus barbastellus*

A small or medium-sized species—body length 40–60 mm, tail length 41–54 mm, weight 6–13 g, wingspan 24.5–28 cm—which is most easily recognised by its short, broad ears meeting on top of the forehead. In addition, the ears are black—as incidentally is the whole face—and, owing to the fact that the nose is short and the mouth small, the Barbastelle has a face that looks like a pug's. The fur is dark but the hairs on the back, especially those on the hind part, have pale tips which make this area appear 'frost-bitten' in much the same way as in the Parti-coloured Bat. The species has acquired its slightly peculiar name from the French *barbastelle*, a diminutive form of the word for beard, and this refers to the fact that the lips are encircled with sparse down. The range covers the greater part of central Europe but is a little discontinuous down towards the Mediterranean region, where the species is found mostly at higher levels. There are reports of decreasing numbers from several west European countries. It occurs north to 59°N, but here it is rare, although reports from south Sweden have increased thanks to ultra-sound detectors. In Britain this species is found in England, but it is very local and elusive. Elsewhere it occurs in North Africa and in Asia east to the Caucasus. The daytime retreat in summer, when the animals are solitary or found in small groups, is located in small and cramped holes in buildings, cracks in walls, hollow trees etc, while the winter, when the colonies may contain thousands of animals, is spent preferably in cellars, caves and mines. Two spells of hunting per night appear to be the rule, and movements of up to 290 km are known for this species.

Schreiber's Bat *Miniopterus schreibersi*

The best identification feature on this species is the wings, which are broad at the base but otherwise strikingly long and narrow. Their outer part has a very particular structure. The longest finger—number 3, counting the thumb as number 1—is greatly extended and at rest the tip is folded an extra time against the rest of the wing. The flight silhouette, and also incidentally the method of flight, is in no small way reminiscent of that of a Swift *Apus apus*, owing to the long wings. In other respects the species is medium-sized—body length 50–65 mm, weight 8–11 g—and is characterised by its ears being very short and by the crown having short, almost slightly curly fur which differs markedly from the considerably longer-haired back. In Europe the species is found only in the extreme south, the northern limits being central France and southernmost Czechoslovakia, but elsewhere it occurs in the whole of Africa and eastwards through Asia, across Indonesia to north Australia. It is unusually susceptible to disturbance and is reported to be declining in several countries. It lives in rocky terrain and makes use of caves, ruins etc, both in summer and in winter. The summer colonies in particular can be very large—reports from Asia include ones of around 40,000 individuals—and the species also often keeps company with bats of other species. Seasonal flights between summer and winter areas do occur, but seem not to be particularly long (so far as is known, 300 km at the most) despite the fact that the species is a skilled flier.

Barbastelle

Schreiber's Bat

Free-tailed bats Family *Molossidae*

This family consists of around 80 different species and is found mainly in tropical regions. Only one species occurs in Europe.

European Free-tailed Bat *Tadarida teniotis*

The long, thick tail, about a third of which projects outside the membrane, is the character borne in mind when giving this species its English name. In other languages it is named after an equally good character, the wrinkled or folded lips. As for the rest, the species is very large—body length 82–87 mm, tail length 46–57 mm and weight 20–50 g. The ears are big, joined on the top of the head, and hang forward in flaps over the face to a level with the muzzle. The species has a characteristic flight call, transcribed as 'tsick-tsick-tsick', and often hunts at high altitude in company with Swifts. It is found in the Mediterranean region, the northern limits being the southern slopes of the Alps, and has a widespread distribution particularly in the Iberian peninsula. In addition, it occurs in North Africa and eastwards through Asia to the Pacific Ocean. It lives in mountainous regions, where, both in summer and in winter, it makes use of crevices, caves and mines but also buildings. It is often active in mild weather, even in winter time.

European Free-tailed Bat

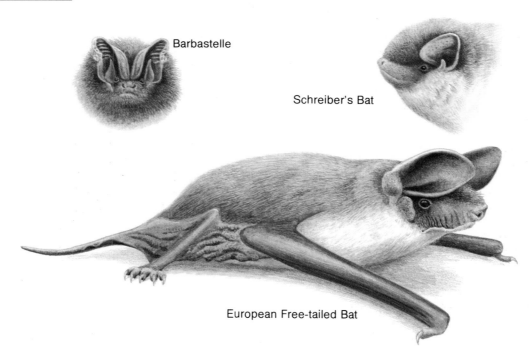

Barbastelle

Schreiber's Bat

European Free-tailed Bat

Primates
Order *Primates*

Magot or Barbary Ape *Macaca sylvana*

Body length 60–70 cm, weight 5–10 kg.

The Magot is the only wild species of ape in Europe. Since it is moreover found in only one place in our part of the world, namely the Rock of Gibraltar, it can hardly be confused with any other species. Its identification features otherwise include the long limbs and the fact that it can grip with both hands and feet. As a result, it is a skilful climber. Furthermore, it has no tail.

Its presence on Gibraltar is considered not to be endemic, despite the Magot's ancestors having been found over large parts of south and central Europe during the warm periods of the Pleistocene, i.e. around 200,000 years ago. They disappeared, however, when it became cold again, and the Magot's subsequent return is thought to be due if anything to human assistance. In any case, the stock has since been augmented several times with animals introduced from North Africa, where the species occurs in both Morocco and Algeria. An old name for this region is the Barbary Coast, hence the species' alternative English name.

The specific name *sylvana* comes from the Latin word for woodland. This, however, is slightly misleading. The species is to be found in mountainous regions, where, at least on the Rock of Gibraltar, it lives mostly in short scrub.

The food is very varied and is made up of both vegetable and animal matter. Among the former may be mentioned seeds and fruits, shoots, buds and leaves. The animal part consists mostly of insects and other small animals.

There is no fixed breeding period and the females come into season about once a month throughout the year. The majority of young are nevertheless born during the summer. The young is supported for a long period by the female, becoming independent after about one year and sexually mature after three or four.

Lagomorphs
Order *Lagomorpha*

Rabbits and hares   Family *Leporidae*

Rabbits and hares, together with the pikas, form the order of lagomorphs. The pikas are nowadays found only in North America and Asia, but they have existed in Europe and one species, the Sardinian Pika *Prolagus sardus*, probably still survived on an island off Sardinia into the 1700s.

Our rabbits and hares have very long ears and long, powerful hindlegs. The back feet have four toes equipped with claws, the front ones have five. The hindlegs are so long in proportion to the front legs that they have to be moved simultaneously whenever the animal moves. This explains the well-known rabbit tracks: the small front paws one after the other and then, in front of them, the larger back paws side by side.

The front teeth lack roots and grow throughout life. They are semicircular in shape and very long. Those in the upper jaw reach back almost to the wall of the cerebral cavity, and those in the lower jaw extend past the cheek teeth practically to the end of the jaw. They are completely coated with enamel, but the enamel is considerably thicker on the front than on the back. Because of this the back part of the teeth is more hard-worn, which results in their becoming chisel-shaped. A bitten-off sprig shows a sharp section surface, as if it were cut with a knife. The cheek teeth of the upper jaw are located outside those of the lower jaw. When chewing, the jaw is therefore moved in a sideways action.

Most of the food that rabbits and hares eat passes through the alimentary canal twice. This is not due to rumination of the usual kind, but to the fact that a part of the animals' own excrement is eaten (refecation). By this means the rabbits and hares increase their chances of assimilating both proteins and B-vitamins which have been built up by bacteria in their own blind gut. Experiments show that the recirculated droppings in Mountain Hares can contain three or four times more proteins than the food that was first taken in.

Rabbits and hares are important prey animals for a large number of predators, both mammals and birds. Several of the medium-sized mustelids hunt them, the fox does so frequently, and the Golden Eagle takes hares both in its breeding territories in the wooded and mountainous districts in the north and in its lowland wintering areas. Only about every fifth young hare reaches adulthood but, that being so, it should be noted that a number of other causes of death also play a large part.

The hare's front teeth are semicircular in shape and very long. Since the enamel is thicker on the front than on the back, they wear down almost to a chisel shape.

Man's imagination has invented a product of cross-breeding, resulting in the front body of a hare and the rear body of a Capercaillie Tetrao urogallus.

Hares figure more than any other animal in folk tales and superstitions. The hare is associated with the moon, it is the witch's servant, and it slyly milks the peasant's cows, not to mention products of the human imagination such as the result of crossing a hare with a Capercaillie *Tetrao urogallus*.

Brown Hare *Lepus europaeus*

Body length 48–70 cm, tail length 7–12 cm, length of ear 8.5–10.5 cm, weight 3.5–7 (9.8) kg.

The Brown Hare's winter coat may occasionally be a shade lighter than its summer coat, but on the whole the species looks the same throughout the year. The coat is yellowish-grey, darker above and lighter, almost white, below. The sides, especially at the front, have an almost rusty-yellow tone. The ears are longer than the Mountain Hare's, reaching just beyond the tip of the nose when folded forward. The tips of the ears are black, and the small tail black above and white below. A Brown Hare bounding rapidly away conveys a more variegated impression than any of the other hares or the Rabbit. Small young often have a white streak on the forehead, which usually distinguishes them from young of Mountain Hare. At sign of danger the Brown Hare emits a shrill scream.

The species occurs over the whole of Europe apart from north and central Fennoscandia, Iceland, west and south Ireland, and also Sardinia and the Iberian peninsula (where it is replaced by the Cape Hare). It is found within large parts of western Asia and also in the Middle East and parts of east Africa. It has been introduced in Northern Ireland and southern Sweden. It did not, then, make its own way across the land bridge that existed during the Mesolithic period between Denmark and the southern tip of Sweden, and so must presumably have been a late immigrant to western Europe. It is still very local in Ireland, but in Sweden it has spread since 1858, both spontaneously and as a result of further introductions, to large areas of the south. Outside its natural range, the Brown Hare has been introduced in Australia, Argentina, and in the Swedish districts around the Great Lakes in North America.

The densest populations of this species are found in open country, preferably with elements of lush bushy vegetation, and the species does not flourish in pure woodland habitats. Land-use is of great importance in how the hares are dispersed. Pasture holds more hares than hay-making areas, but the hares avoid direct contact with grazing animals. A density of around 20 cows per hectare seems to keep the hares away altogether. That the hayfields are of such little attraction is believed to be due to the fact that only for short periods is the vegetation there of suitable nutritional quality and sufficiently short. The latter factor can be important for the hare's visual facilities among other things.

A wide assortment of grasses and plants of open country form the Brown Hare's major food. Fields with cereal, clover, alfalfa, beets and potatoes are visited frequently and, especially in winter, the species eats buds and bark from bushes and trees, including fruit trees. In the winter it also digs for green plants under the snow, and is easy to attract to feeding stations with hay.

The Brown Hare begins breeding early in the year. When the females are in season, one or several males can then be seen following the female's trail. If the male is a long way behind, he uses his sense of smell and finds his way with his nose to the ground. Fighting between two males, or between a male and a female not yet ready for mating, can lead to the animals rearing up and boxing. One or two tufts of fur left behind at such places indicate that this is not just for show. In the central and southern parts of the range the first litter is born as early as February, and the female then has time for a further two, in some cases even

Brown Hare

three, more litters. The size of the litter averages just under three, and normally varies from one to five. The first litter of the year is the smallest and as a rule consists of only one or two young. The gestation period of 40–46 days is slightly shorter than in the Mountain Hare. Directly after the birth, the female transports the young to another place, a behaviour which probably makes it more difficult for predators to find them.

Breeding and pregnancy fall during the time of the year when the food supply is at its shortest, and, at least locally, this can mean competition for food. Larger hares then chase off smaller ones. Females are on average heavier than males, which has been interpreted as an adaptation for their greater food requirements during pregnancy.

Cape Hare *Lepus capensis*

The Cape Hare is a form of hare so close to the Brown Hare that it was formerly regarded as only a race of that species. Nowadays, however, it is considered to constitute a full species. It replaces the Brown Hare in the Iberian peninsula, and is also found in Mallorca. It has a wide distribution in both Africa and Asia. It lives in extremely varied habitats, is smaller but a shade taller than the Brown Hare and is slightly different in colour. The breast and the outside of the thighs are tinged with reddish-brown, the nape of the neck and the back have a faintly spotted appearance, while the belly, the insides of the legs and the paws are all-white. The Cape Hare seems usually to have only one young.

As recently as 1979, Spanish biologists described a form of hare which has been found in the mountain regions in northwest Spain as a new species (*Lepus castroviejoi*). It lives in isolated, high-lying habitats dominated by broom and heather. Provided that the classification holds true, that it really is a separate species that is concerned, it could perhaps be given the English name of 'Bush Hare'. Not illustrated.

Cape Hare

Mountain Hare *Lepus timidus*

Body length 46–61 cm, tail length 4–9 cm, length of ear 6–9.5 cm, weight 2–5.8 kg.

In most places (but not Ireland) the Mountain Hare's colour changes with the seasons. The winter coat, which in the north is all-white with black ear tips (known as Blue Hare) but in the south greyer (Heath Hare), is changed during the spring for a brownish-grey summer coat. This lacks the Brown Hare's brownish-yellow or perhaps even rusty-yellow elements, and is thus considerably less contrasty. The change of coat is governed directly by the effects of the climate (the light) and is certainly well adapted for the snow conditions in the habitats where the species lives. In the spring, the back becomes brown while the sides remain white. As a result, the squatting hare has the same colour pattern as a rock protruding a little through the melting snow. The tail stump is all-white, both above and below, throughout the year. The paws are large. In winter the hares frequently run along old tracks, whereby proper pathways are created. By pressing the hand in such a track one can get a good idea of how well the hare is supported, even on fairly light snow. Traces left from some of the winter's meals are easy to recognise, particularly shrubs, fallen branches or felled trees which have been turned into white 'skeletons' through heavy gnawing of the bark. The Mountain Hare utters a shrill scream when danger threatens, and also screams in association with mating. It is also occasionally reported to have a hooting cry, although this is certainly incorrect. Such reports are perhaps due to confusion with the display call of Tengmalm's Owl *Aegolius funereus*.

The Mountain Hare is found in a small area in the Alps, with a few offshoots, and within an appreciably larger area stretching from Ireland and Iceland in the west, eastwards through north Europe and Asia as far as the Japanese archipelago in the Pacific Ocean. It has been introduced in northern England. Through geographical isolation, forms have evolved in several places that are so divergent that they are regarded as separate races. The *Alpine Hare*, for example, is smaller, has longer ears, and has slightly different habitat requirements; among other things, in summer it lives at levels of up to 3,000 m above sea.

The Mountain Hare is at home mainly in woodland. It occurs from the upland birch forest in the north to the beechwoods farther south. The distribution coincides well with regions where woodland cover is reasonably good. It seems to have a certain preference for areas with a regular scattering of deciduous wood. In winter at least, its tracks are densest in deep, damp valleys, around the deciduous borders of the forest edge and in shrubbery around watercourses. Especially in areas where the Brown Hare is absent, the Mountain Hare may occupy entirely different habitats, including open ground of various kinds. Mountain walkers, for example, sometimes come across it high above the tree-line in pure alpine habitat.

Fine twigs, up to 7 mm in diameter, or bark of sallow, willow, aspen, rowan and birch, plants of various kinds together with sprigs, e.g. bilberry, bog bilberry and heather, form the Mountain Hare's principal food. Of particular importance are the protein-rich leaders of the birch. In addition, the species may also tackle completely different food: e.g. the previous year's shoots of young pines, where it eats the needles after first having bitten off the shoot itself. On the other hand, it does not eat fir or spruce. In winter, a Mountain Hare consumes around 0.5 kg of food per day. This energetic feeding results in a hare producing around 400 individual droppings per day. They consist mainly of the ligneous part of the food.

In the south of the main range, the females come into season as early as February, but farther north not until March–April. The young, which are

Mountain Hare

63

covered in fur and open-eyed, are born after a gestation period of around 50 days. The litter normally consists of two to five young, exceptionally up to eight. Renewal of mating takes place within 24 hours, sometimes only an hour or so after the birth. The female Mountain Hare has time to produce up to three litters per season in the south of the range, but only two farther north. The young suck once a day, and then only for a minute or two. They mix the mother's milk with greenstuff after only a couple of days, and are already capable of successfully coping with searching for food on their own a week or so later.

The Mountain Hare is most active during the night, and in winter may move up to 4 km per night in wooded habitats in some areas. It spends the day in a sheltered den, but usually one with some view over the surroundings. It has been found that in winter it may burrow down and take up a daytime retreat beneath the snow, and it is less active during and immediately after periods of snowfall. It is a good swimmer. Hybrids with the Brown Hare—as a rule fully capable of reproducing—are known from several places where the two species live together. A bacterial disease called tularemia or hare plague can cause very high mortality—up to 80–90%—in the hare populations. The introduction of captive-bred hares has proven to give poor results: the mortality is very high.

Hybrid between Mountain Hare and Brown Hare. As a rule such hybrids are fully capable of reproducing.

moulting

Mountain Hare in winter coat

Rabbit *Oryctolagus cuniculus*

Body length 34–50 cm, tail length 4–8 cm, weight 1.3–2.5 kg.

The Rabbit is a burrowing animal that lives colonially in and in association with underground hollows and passages. Its scientific generic name is formed from the Greek *orukter*, which is a digging tool, and *lagos*, which means hare, and in appearance it most recalls a small Brown Hare or a Mountain Hare in summer coat. The comparatively much shorter ears, however, lack the black tip which is present in these species. In addition, the legs are shorter: a frightened Rabbit scampers away much closer to the ground than the hares. When it flees, the tail is pointed straight up and its white underside becomes a flashing signal to the rear. A very rapid beating on the ground with the hindfeet serves as a warning signal when danger threatens. In many populations, including those in Britain, occasional all-black individuals occur.

The Rabbit is thought to have originated in the western parts of the Mediterranean region. As early as ancient times it spread from there to other parts of south Europe, and during the Middle Ages to central Europe. The spread took place both naturally and through introductions. On some isolated islands Rabbits were released as food for seafarers and victims of shipwrecks. These Rabbits have in some places evolved over the centuries into forms which differ so much from the ancestral form that they can no longer interbreed with them. In this connection, one could in fact argue how many species of rabbit exist in Europe. Well-known introductions outside Europe include that made in 1859 in Australia. The range to the north is limited by the species' habitat requirements (see below), but also no doubt by its susceptibility to severe winters.

Sand or other substrate which is easy to dig into is a necessary prerequisite for the Rabbit's existence. As regards the habitat above the ground, its demands

Rabbit

then are not so strict. Important haunts in Britain include open meadows and other grassland, both coastal and inland, scrub and woodland edge, and especially dunes and grassy sea cliffs. The species tends to avoid coniferous woodland and heather moors.

Plants of various kinds, crops such as cabbage, root vegetables and germinating cereals, together with bark and buds from coniferous as well as deciduous trees are the most important food. One consequence of this is that the species can cause damage on a large scale, both in gardens and in forest plantations, not to mention on farmland.

'Breed like rabbits' the saying goes, and the species indeed has a high reproductive capacity: three to six litters per year with three to 12 young per litter, which is well above the other lagomorphs—almost on a par with certain species of small rodent. The young, which are born in a special breeding chamber, differ from young of other lagomorphs in being both naked and blind at birth. When the female leaves them, she scratches over the entrance hole. The young are able to see at around ten days of age; they suck for about three weeks, but only once a day, and early-born females can reproduce as soon as their first summer.

The Rabbit is active mainly at night. So far, the most effective weapon in combating over-dense Rabbit populations with their consequent damage is a viral disease introduced from South America, myxomatosis. The first time it appears in an area, it knocks out at least 99% of the Rabbits. Owing mainly to increased powers of resistance in the surviving animals and their offspring, the effects of later outbreaks, however, are not so powerful. Controlled attempts to cross-breed Rabbits with Brown Hares have given only negative results (the two species' chromosome counts differ: the Rabbit has 44, the hares have 48).

Rodents
Order *Rodentia*

The members of the rodent order are characterised mainly by the structure of their teeth. There are two large front teeth in each jaw. In addition to this, in each half-jaw there is a row of three to five cheek teeth separated from the front teeth by a broad gap (called the diastema). As the front teeth get worn down, so they grow continuously from open roots. They are coated with enamel, which is yellowish, only on the front. They are therefore more hard-worn on the back and become chisel-shaped at the tip. The order contains a tremendous number of forms and has occupied almost all terrestrial and some freshwater habitats. It comprises well over 1,500 different species, which makes it the largest order among the mammals.

Red Squirrel *Sciurus vulgaris*

Body length 19–28 cm, tail length 14–24 cm, weight 200–480 g.

Because the Red Squirrel lives close to man in many places, the species is perhaps better known in appearance—at least on the Continent—than any other species of rodent. The 'long, shaggy tail', the ears with (especially in winter) ornamental tufts, the many smacking or chattering calls together with the species' habit of sitting upright on its hindlegs, for example when it is eating, are familiar characters. The belly is greyish-white, while the rest of the body changes from warm red-brown in the summer to grey in the winter. The change is most marked in the northern parts of the range. Colour variants—e.g. almost all-black—are common in some areas, but rare in Britain and Ireland. The scientific generic name is formed from the Greek words *skia* and *oura*. They mean, respectively, shadow and tail and allude to the fact that the squirrel sits, so to speak, in the shadow of its own tail.

The Red Squirrel is found in wooded regions over the whole of Europe except in Iceland and on some islands, including those in the Mediterranean. In parts of Great Britain it has almost completely disappeared concurrently with the range expansion of the Grey Squirrel, which was introduced from North America.

The species belongs originally in coniferous forest, but is also found in deciduous wood and, in proximity to man—even in densely built-up areas—has adapted to living in parks, gardens etc.

The Red Squirrel is mainly vegetarian, with a fairly wide choice of food. Seeds of spruce and pine make up most of the food, which can also include berries, fungus, nuts, acorns and green vegetable matter. Fungus is laid up during the autumn (in tree forks etc) and can thus form part of the food the year round. Claims that the Red Squirrel often plunders birds' nests are probably exaggerated. Analysis of the contents of 1,600 stomachs revealed remains of birds (eggs or young) in only four. Nevertheless, the Red Squirrel is regarded by many bird species as a threat and is intensely pursued by them.

The female Red Squirrel can give birth at any time during March–September. During years of poor food supply the population is in many places very sparse, and it is doubtful whether breeding then takes place at all. In other years each female may have up to three litters, with as many as eight young in each. The young are born in a very well-constructed nest (a drey)—usually a covered, spherical twig nest in a dense conifer, but at times in such places as hollow trees. The nest chamber itself is lined with beard lichen and moss. As a

Red Squirrel

rule there are several (less well-built) nests in the vicinity of the breeding drey. When the young of the first litter leave the nest they are in winter coat, while the female has changed to her summer coat. This is possibly a way for the inexperienced young to cope with setbacks in the weather in spring.

The Red Squirrel is a skilful climber, scampering quite easily head first down a tree trunk, and also moves with well-balanced leaps from one tree to another. On the ground it moves in long leaping bounds. The tracks are easy to recognise, both by their appearance and because as a rule they begin and end at the foot of a tree. The Red Squirrel is a good swimmer. During periods of poor weather it may sometimes spend several days resting inside the drey.

Persian Squirrel *Sciurus anomalus*

This species is smaller than the Red Squirrel—the body length is around 20 cm, the tail length 13–17 cm—but is similar in colour. The belly, however, is yellow, not white. It lacks ear tufts, and a diagnostic specific identification character is that in each upper half-jaw there are four cheek teeth (the Red Squirrel has five). The range extends from Iran to Asia Minor, and in Europe the species is found at least on the island of Lesbos in the Aegean Sea. Not illustrated.

In squirrel tracks, the back paws—which are the larger and have five toes—are placed in front of the front paws—which are very much smaller and have only four toes.

Grey Squirrel *Sciurus carolinensis*

Body length 23–30 cm, tail length 19.5–25 cm, weight 350–800 g.

This species is bigger and more robust than the Red Squirrel. The coat is grey above and white below—the grey in winter almost silvery-white but in summer with tinges of brown, including on the paws and in a stripe along the side. The tail hair is bicoloured. This makes the tail, especially in winter, appear to consist of a darker core surrounded by a lighter outer layer. Melanistic and albinistic individuals are frequent.

The natural range includes parts of eastern North America. From 1876 the species was introduced from there to many places in the British Isles, where it found itself very much at home. During the 1920s in particular it spread rapidly, and after the first 100 years it is now found in suitable habitats— deciduous and mixed woodland with at least 25% deciduous elements—over the greater part of England and Wales, where it is now one of the best known of all mammal species. In addition, isolated populations are found both in Scotland and in Ireland.

The food consists mainly of vegetable matter such as acorns and beechnuts, hazelnuts and seeds of other trees and bushes, green plant material, fungi and roots. Insects, birds' eggs and other animal matter form part of the food, but in insignificant proportions.

One-year-old females have only one litter per year, but older females can have two. The majority of litters are born in January–March and May–July, and the average litter consists of close on three young.

Within the area that the Grey Squirrel has colonised the Red Squirrel has almost completely disappeared. This decline has, however, taken place on the whole without direct relation to the larger species' expansion. Instead the major causes are habitat changes and epidemic diseases, but, when the population density in the Red Squirrel has decreased heavily, its renewed growth seems to be hampered by the presence of the Grey Squirrel.

Grey Squirrel

European Souslik *Spermophilus citellus*

Body length 19–22 cm, tail length 5.5–7.5 cm, weight 240–340 g.

The sousliks are squirrels which have not adapted to living in trees but live on, or rather beneath, the ground, often in colonies. Their outer ears have almost completely disappeared. The European Souslik originally belongs to open steppes in southeast Europe and Asia, but the species has adapted to cultivated steppes and occurs northwest as far as Czechoslovakia and bordering parts of Poland and East Germany. From several regions, however, the species is reported to have difficulty in making out in a modern agricultural landscape and to have decreased heavily during the 1970s. The most important habitat requirement is a substrate in which it can burrow; thus the European Souslik may sometimes inhabit for example road and railway embankments. Seeds of various kinds, including corn, make up the major part of the diet. Surplus food is transported in cheek pouches and is laid up in underground stores. With the help of these stores, the sousliks build up the fat reserves late in the autumn which provide nourishment during the winter sleep. This begins in October/November, and the animals come out again in March. The mating season comes shortly afterwards, and in April–June the litter, normally of five to eight young, is born deep down in an underground nest burrow.

Spotted Souslik *Spermophilus suslicus*

With a body length of 18–25 cm, the Spotted Souslik is quite as large as the European Souslik, but it has a shorter tail, only 3–4 cm. The tail is also less bushy. The species is, however, most easily recognised by the fact that its coat is spangled with whitish-yellow spots on an otherwise quite dark background. The European distribution is more easterly than that of the above species, but the Spotted Souslik is found from the central Asian steppes westwards to within easternmost Poland and northeast Romania. Habitat choice, habits etc are like those of the European Souslik. It appears, however, that the Spotted Souslik can sometimes become so numerous around certain crops that it causes serious damage.

European Souslik

Spotted Souslik

European Souslik

Spotted Souslik

Alpine Marmot *Marmota marmota*

Body length 50–58 cm, tail length 13–16 cm, weight 4–8 kg.

After the European Beaver and the Porcupine, the Alpine Marmot is Europe's largest species of rodent. It is heavy and compact in build. The head is large, the legs are short and it has a rolling gait. Its colour is predominantly greyish, sometimes with tinges of brown. The upperside is darker, the underside paler. Alpine Marmots live colonially in extensive underground tunnel systems. The species is watchful, and when disturbed it sits dead still on its hindlegs and sniffs the air or keeps a look-out. When danger threatens, others of its species in the area are warned with a sharp whistling signal, at which all animals swiftly dive down into their underground burrows. In other situations, too, the animals communicate with a great number of high-pitched piping or whistling calls. The scientific name *Marmota* has a somewhat odd background. It is derived from the Latin *muris* and *montis*, genitives of the words for mouse and mountain respectively, and therefore means 'mountain mouse'.

The species is a relict from forms that inhabited the plains areas of central Europe during the Ice Age. During the period following the Ice Age they then adapted to the rising temperatures by occupying higher and higher altitudes. The natural distribution is restricted to parts of the Alps. During the 1800s, the population was very heavily persecuted, mainly for its fat which was used in the manufacture of cosmetics and was considered to have healing properties. From the turn of the century numbers have recovered, and the species has also been successfully introduced in the Pyrenees, the Carpathians and the Black Forest.

The species is found on alpine meadows above the tree-limit, i.e. at altitudes of from 1,000 m and up to about 2,500 m above sea level. Here it also occurs on steep, rocky hillsides with fairly sparse vegetation. Grasses and plants form the major part of the food. The species may sometimes also dig for roots.

Mating takes place after hibernation, in April–May. The female does not become sexually mature until about two or three years of age, and gives birth to a litter of two to six young per year.

For six or seven months during the winter the Alpine Marmots hibernate, often several animals together, in a particularly well-equipped chamber. This is insulated with dry grass and the entrance hole is stopped up. During this time the animals live on deposited body-fat reserves. The body functions are substantially depressed and their temperature may drop to below 5°C.

The Bobak Marmot *Marmota bobak* is closely related to and also very similar to the Alpine Marmot, both in appearance and in habits. Up to the beginning of the 1900s it was found in steppe regions in easternmost Europe, but it is reported to have disappeared from there nowadays.

Alpine Marmot

Siberian Chipmunk

Siberian Chipmunk *Tamias sibiricus*

A mainly ground-dwelling rodent up to 22 cm long, which has a long tail and is endowed with five distinct stripes along the back which make the species easy to recognise. The genus *Tamias* occurs in North America, with about 15 species. The only representative in the Old World is found across the entire Siberian taiga, westwards to the White Sea. In addition, it has escaped from captivity— and appears to flourish—in a number of middle European countries, e.g. France, West Germany and Austria. The species is best known for its habit of laying up large stores, mostly nuts, before the onset of winter. Not illustrated.

Alpine Marmot

Bobak Marmot

Flying Squirrel *Pteromys volans*

Body length 13.5–20.5 cm, tail length 9–14 cm, weight 95–170 g.

Small, slender and shy are three common epithets attached to the Flying Squirrel, which is by no means so easy to observe at first hand as the Red and Grey Squirrels. Its most distinctive characteristic is, of course, that it can fly, or more accurately glide, since its flight is one that heads inexorably downwards. Its flight is either from tree to tree or from the highest to the lowest parts of the same tree. The supporting 'wing' surface consists of a broad fold of skin stretched out from the body between the fore- and hindlegs. The coat is light grey, and the very large eyes betray the species' mainly nocturnal habits.

The most westerly discovery has been in north Finland, very near the border with Sweden. From here and from the Baltic states, the range extends through the whole of the taiga across to Sakhalin and Japan.

The most important habitat, however, is not pure coniferous forest but mixed forest, above all old ones. Here the species makes use of old woodpecker holes in big aspen trees, both as a nesting hole and as a larder for the food reserves which are laid up for the winter. Such a store can hold up to 5 litres and usually consists of alder and birch catkins together with fine twigs. During the rest of the year, too, the food consists mostly of vegetable matter—buds, shoots, leaves, seeds, nuts and berries—but, when the opportunity is offered, the Flying Squirrel may plunder birds' nests of both eggs and young.

The Flying Squirrel is not so prolific a breeder as the Red Squirrel. It often manages two litters—in different nest holes in April–May and June–July, respectively—but the number of young per litter is normally only two or three.

The species does not hibernate, but in severe cold may occasionally sleep off for a couple of days. During the depths of winter its activity is otherwise centred around the laid-up supplies. In parts of Finland, mainly north of 65°N, the population density has decreased in recent decades. The principal reason for this is modern forestry practices of removing old hollow trees.

Flying Squirrel

European Beaver *Castor fiber*

Body length 70–100 cm, tail length 30–40 cm, weight up to 35 kg.

The European Beaver is our largest species of rodent, and much bigger than any of the other aquatic species. It lives beside shores of watercourses and lakes, in excavated burrows or constructed lodges. It may stop up running water with a dam—which can be up to 150 m long—which controls the water level at the lodge. Around the beaver dam trees and bushes are also found in abundance, and these are felled and gnawed in two with powerful bites. The European Beaver shows a series of adaptations to an aquatic life. Its tail, which is flattened and on its outer part hairless but covered with scales, acts as a rudder; the hindfeet, which have very well-developed webs, give the animal acceleration while swimming; nasal and ear openings are shut off on submerging, and the outer ears are almost completely concealed in the fur. When swimming, it may give a warning signal by slapping its tail loudly on the surface of the water. If it keeps still, it can remain under the water for up to 15 minutes. The European Beaver can gnaw underwater, thanks to a special lobe of skin with which it can close the mouth behind the front teeth. Furthermore, it has a special coat. The underfur is extremely dense; and the guard hairs are long and are flattened towards the tip, as a result of which they retain an extra layer of air outside the underfur when they are flattened against the body. The coat is looked after very carefully, with the help among other things of a double claw on the second toe of the hindfoot which functions almost as a pair of tweezers. Other important features regarding the species' appearance are that the front teeth are big, chisel-shaped, and covered with yellowish-red enamel on the front. Those in the upper jaw are shorter and more curved than those in the lower jaw. In addition, external sexual characters are lacking. Sexual organs, rectum, two oil glands which are probably important for the care of the coat, together with two beaver-castoreum glands all discharge into a common so-called cloaca.

By the time the European Beaver received protection in Sweden in 1873, after a long period of decline caused by heavy hunting but also by changes in the landscape and other factors, it was already too late. Records show that the last animal had apparently been shot two years earlier and, even if some isolated individual perhaps survived longer than this, the species was in practical terms extinct in the country. And so it remained for about 50 years until, in 1922, re-introductions were begun using animals captured in southern Norway. Up to 1939, 80 or so individuals had been released and the majority had adapted well: the population was then estimated at around 400 animals. It was still increasing up to 1961/62, at a fairly slow rate: the number then was probably around 2,200. Thereafter the population figures available indicate a tripling of the stock during the rest of the 1960s, and an increase to around 40,000 animals up to 1980. That being so, however, from 1973—in other words after 100 years of protection—some hunting was permitted, mainly in order to limit the damage to woodland. In Norway a similar but not quite so dramatic increase has taken place, and the species was of course never completely exterminated there. By contrast, it was eliminated in Finland, but when re-introduction started there two different species were used, the European and the Canadian Beavers *C. canadensis*. Of these, the latter got on best and the former is now found only within a restricted area in western Finland (150–200 individuals). The European Beaver also occurs in some places in south and central Europe: indigenously in the Rhône delta and on the Elbe, and as a re-introduced species in other places in France and Germany but also in Austria and Switzerland. In the Soviet the species has a widespread distribution, but here, too, the population has been much persecuted and has been restored with the help of re-introductions.

European Beaver

Water that does not freeze solid during the winter and shores with plenty of deciduous trees are probably the European Beaver's most important habitat requirements. If these are fulfilled, anything from streams a metre wide to large lakes is suitable. On fast-flowing watercourses, the European Beaver avoids the stretches with rapids and resorts to the slowest-running sections.

The food is made up of vegetable matter, and in various studies it has been shown that a total of around 300 plant species may be on the menu. In summertime this involves mostly herbaceous plants and grasses, which are gathered both on land and in the water. Aquatic plants may also form part of the food during the rest of the year, but bushes and trees become more and more important towards the autumn. At this time, too, many species are included— aspen, willow, birch, rowan etc, on isolated occasions even coniferous trees. The beaver often gnaws bark from trees or bites off leaves and fine twigs, but it also fells whole trees. A single animal is said to be able to fell a tree about 25 cm thick in just under four hours. Parts of the tree are used as building material, but twigs and branches are stored in the water near the lodge and provide a larder for the coming winter. At that time the European Beaver eats in a special food chamber immediately above the water's surface inside the lodge.

The mating period falls in February, and at the beginning of June the young, usually one to four per litter, are born in a special breeding chamber in the lodge or burrow. The family is then deserted, not by the previous year's young but by those that are two years old. They have stayed at their birthplace, but now move out in order to find their own territories.

Because of its odd ways of life, the European Beaver influences its surroundings in many different ways. Felled trees provide food for other vegetable-eaters directly, but also, through shoots from stumps and roots, indirectly. Since the tree-felling is focused mainly on certain species of tree and can be very extensive—in one winter one family can clear at least 300 trees of more than 4 cm in diameter at chest height—the wood around the beaver water changes character. The dam governs the behaviour of the water, e.g. the spring flood, creates habitats for ducks and waders, produces aquatic plants which can be exploited by other mammals such as Elks, encourages some fish species but does not favour others, and even provides drinking water during dry summers to animals of various species. Through the raised water level the beaver dam can, however, cause damage to the environment, most often to forest, sometimes to farmland and now and then to roads etc. In particularly serious cases, one may even speak of 'beaver-infected water', and it is this damage and the wish to prevent it that are now the principal motives behind hunting. Formerly, i.e. up to their eradication, it was instead the fur and the flesh but above all the castoreum that man wanted to get his hands on. The latter was credited with remarkable properties, and was considered capable of curing most things—all kinds of fever, stomach pains (when it was mixed with vinegar), epilepsy, impotence, labour pains as well as toothache—and therefore it was expensive: in the mid 1800s, castoreum from a beaver cost as much as a farm-hand's annual income. The European Beaver itself uses the castoreum for marking out its territory and possibly also for other contacts between individuals. Maybe this was what man bore in mind when using the substance in the perfume industry.

The beaver skull has a front-heavy appearance. The front teeth are covered with enamel on the outer side, and those in the upper jaw are shorter and more curved than those in the lower jaw.

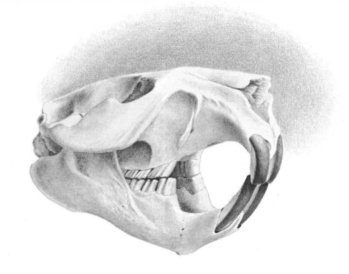

Lemmings and voles   Family *Muridae*

Subfamily *Microtinae*

The species within this subfamily vary in size, from the Common Vole at around 15 g to the Muskrat which is near on 100 times heavier. For all that there are a great many common characters. The outer ears are small and usually concealed in the fur, and the genus *Microtus* (and thus the whole subfamily) has acquired its name from the Greek words *mikros*, which means little, and *otos*, which is the genitive form of ear. In addition, lemmings and voles have a rather round body structure, a blunt snout, short legs and a relatively short tail (between one-fifth and one-half of the body length, shorter in the lemmings, longer in the Muskrat). The hindfeet have five toes; the front feet have only four fully developed ones.

Lemmings and voles are vegetarians. The cheek teeth—three in each half-jaw, both above and below—are equipped with sawtooth-like lobes of enamel which in some cases reveal important characters for distinguishing between species. There are also important differences between the three genera with the most species. Those species belonging to the genus *Clethrionomys* all show red or reddish-brown tinges in the fur. In addition, their cheek teeth have roots. This means that the teeth do not grow continuously but get worn down, usually at one to one-and-a-half years. In the *Microtus* species, on the other hand, the cheek teeth have open roots and grow throughout life. This applies also to the *Pitymys* species, the pine voles, which in addition are short-haired and have small eyes and small ears, all adaptations to a burrowing, more subterranean existence. The pine voles otherwise resemble the *Microtus* species, but can be identified by the appearance of the first cheek tooth in the lower jaw.

Several species construct tunnel systems beneath the snow in the winter. When the snow cover disappears, the remnants of these tunnels are left behind on the ground as long sausage-shaped strands of the previous year's grass.

Norway Lemming *Lemmus lemmus*

Body length 130–155 mm, tail length 15–19 mm, weight up to 130 g.

With its variegated pattern of black, yellow and yellowish-brown, the Norway Lemming is unmistakable and easy to identify, whether one sees it slipping hastily into a burrow or simply comes across a dry skin or fragment of skin of the species. During years when populations of small rodents are poor, such remains are often all that is seen of the species. When the numbers then increase and there is a 'lemming year', it is easier both to see and to hear than any other species of small rodent. Many individuals at this time behave inquisitively, some even a little aggressively, with loud hissing and squeaking calls. During and immediately after such years, the immensely abundant piles of droppings, sometimes washed together by the meltwater almost into drifts, are also very characteristic. The Norway Lemming leaves a small trotting track behind it in the snow. In this it differs from all other mammals of pretty much the same size in the same habitat, which all move by hopping.

The Norway Lemming occurs only along the Scandinavian mountain chain, south to southernmost Norway and east to the Kola peninsula. In those years when the species is abundant, this range may be extended by animals migrating from the mountain moors, willow and birch regions far down into surrounding coniferous forest. Reports from Finland show that in such years the species' southern limit of distribution can shift more than 200 km southwards.

Most of the plant species of the ground layer are included in the Norway Lemming's food, but variations between different seasons are wide. Mosses apart from bog moss are important during the winter, while grass, sedges and herbaceous plants predominate during the summer.

The breeding behaviour varies widely between different years. When conditions are at their most favourable, the female can become sexually mature at around 20 days of age (the male develops somewhat more slowly) and in one year gives birth to up to six litters with between two and 13 young in each. Litters may then be born in winter beneath the snow. When conditions are less favourable, breeding takes place only during the summer (June–August), the litter size decreases, and at least the late-born young do not become sexually mature until the following year.

Fluctuations in the population, with peaks about every fourth year, are more pronounced in the Norway Lemming than in any other species of small rodent. In peak years the population density reaches 100–250 individuals per hectare. During some of these peaks extensive migrations take place, when large numbers of animals make off, moving a long way from the home ranges. During these migrations most of the animals die, but those that get through may re-occupy areas or, at least for a time, even colonise new ones. In matters of behaviour, colour pattern and calls, the Norway Lemming is anything but discreet. It may seem that this should increase the risk of being taken by predators, but that does not appear to be so. Instead it seems that the Norway Lemming is an inferior prey compared with other small rodents. It is more difficult to take because it is aggressive, and it is possibly also less appetising. In support of the latter theory is on the one hand the fact that Norway Lemmings that have been swallowed but only partially digested are often regurgitated, particularly by birds of prey but also for example by dogs, and on the other that Norway Lemmings that have been killed are more often than other species left unconsumed at nests where there is a surplus of food. The species' striking colour is probably chiefly a warning signal.

During years when small rodent populations are high, remains of Norway Lemmings are abundant in the pellets found in the mountain regions. After the snow melts, the winter nests are left behind as balls of dry grass and moss, often against a rock, sometimes beside or even up in a bush.

Norway Lemming

Snowy Owl pellet

winter nest

Wood Lemming *Myopus schisticolor*

The Wood Lemming weighs up to 45 g, is 8–11.5 cm long, and has a 10–15 mm-long tail. It is therefore appreciably smaller than the Norway Lemming. It is slate-grey in colour, darker, almost blue-grey in the summer, lighter in the winter. Full-grown adults and young in the nest have a rusty-brown patch on the lower back, a patch which is, however, lacking in individuals that are not sexually mature. The species is very shy and retiring. It was for long thought that it was of isolated occurrence in Scandinavia, and it was not found at all in Finland during the period 1911–35. The range is, however, now known to be continuous from southeasternmost Norway northwards through Scandinavia and east through Finland and the Soviet. Damp spruce and fir forest rich in moss is the principal habitat. During peak years, when the species may become so abundant that at least locally the term 'mass presence' may be used, it is also found in other habitats. The food consists mainly of moss, especially broom, house and wall moss. The species' breeding biology is remarkable. A genetic alteration (mutation) in one of the sex chromosomes, the X-chromosome, has resulted in certain females giving birth only to female young. This in turn leads to the sex ratio in Wood Lemming populations becoming distorted: they consist of three to four times more females than males.

Northern Red-backed Vole *Clethrionomys rutilus*

This species resembles the Bank Vole, but is distinctly lighter red and has a bushy and considerably shorter tail, only 20–40 mm. Its range takes over in the north approximately where the Bank Vole's peters out, and in Europe it is a wholly arctic species. The circumpolar range also extends through northern Asia and North America. The alpine birch forest is probably the most important habitat in arctic Europe, but the species descends well into the coniferous forest and is also encountered above the tree-limit. Like the Bank Vole, the Northern Red-backed Vole gathers part of its food high above ground level, and it is also known for its habit of entering houses in some autumns, in the same way as some species of mouse do.

Wood Lemming

Northern Red-backed Vole

Grey-sided Vole

Grey-sided Vole *Clethrionomys rufocanus*

The Grey-sided Vole also resembles the Bank Vole. The fact that it averages slightly larger—body length 110–135 mm, weight up to 50 g—is of little help in the case of a lone individual, but the reddish-brown on the upperside is restricted to a narrow band along the middle of the back. Below this band the sides of the body are grey. The tail is 25–40 mm and the Grey-sided Vole, like the Northern Red-backed Vole, is thus shorter-tailed than the Bank Vole. The range extends from the southernmost mountain regions in the Scandinavian peninsula, where there may be several isolated populations, northwards through the whole mountain chain, and then east across the arctic and subarctic regions through the whole of Asia. When walkers in the Scandinavian mountains see a predominantly grey vole—in other words not a lemming—scamper beneath a tussock on the alpine moor or a stump in the birch forest, more often than not it is this species that is concerned. It also descends to the coniferous forest. The food includes a great many shoots and buds of various berry-bearing shrubs and also—since the species is an able climber—leaves and bark of both dwarf birch and other lower-growing bushes and trees.

Northern Red-backed Vole

Grey-sided Vole

Bank Vole *Clethrionomys glareolus*

Body length 80–135 mm, tail length 35–72 mm, weight 14–40 g.

Fully-grown Bank Voles have a reddish-brown back merging obscurely into grey sides. The greyish-white or greyish-yellow belly on the other hand is more clearly demarcated. The tail is distinctly bicoloured. Young (up to four to six weeks) are greyish-brown on the back, but differ from Field Vole and other *Microtus* species in having much more conspicuous outer ears. Colour variations, particularly individuals that are black above and pale below, occur in East Germany and elsewhere. The cheek teeth in the Bank Vole, as in other species in the genus, have considerably more rounded corners to the triangles than do those of the *Microtus* voles.

The range extends over the whole of Europe except the most peripheral parts—the extreme north and the Kola peninsula roughly north of the Arctic Circle, Iceland, and also the Mediterranean region apart from the Riviera. The species was absent from Ireland but has suddenly begun to appear, in all probability after having been brought there by man. To the east, the Bank Vole is found as far as Lake Baikal.

'Wood vole' would be a much better name for this species, since woods of various kinds are its primary haunt. These are mainly deciduous and mixed woods, but pure coniferous forest is also used in Scandinavia, where the species has been shown to be most numerous in areas with trees six to 30 years old. In addition, luxuriant undergrowth is a factor that favours the species, and in dense bushland for example it may be found a long way from the nearest wood. In the Alps it is found at up to 2,400 m above sea level.

The food consists almost entirely of vegetable matter: plants, seeds and fruits, leaves, grass, moss, roots, fungi etc. In spring–summer up to 60% may consist of green plant material. The species is an able climber and in many places seems to prefer the leaves of trees before the plants of the ground. It can sometimes cause damage to young trees by gnawing bark. It readily eats hazelnuts, leaving a shell with a neat small hole edged with close radial marks from the front teeth of the lower jaw. During years when nuts are in good supply, it may store them in underground hiding places, holes in trees or old bird nests. The behaviour of hiding away food is triggered off as the amount of daylight decreases. Occasionally the Bank Vole also eats insects and other small animal matter.

Breeding usually takes place between April and September/October, but the season can be prolonged even beyond the turn of the year, for example if the supply of food is good. Thus, there are reports from Germany of breeding throughout the winter following autumns with a bumper crop of beechnuts. The female becomes sexually mature at a good one month of age, the male at two at the earliest, but high population density may slow down reproduction, or even halt it altogether. The litter size varies between one and ten. The nest, which is a well-made small ball of moss, leaves and feathers, is usually placed beneath the surface of the ground but sometimes in a stump or thick bush.

In suitable habitats there are usually between ten and 80 Bank Voles per hectare, and somewhere near the upper value is the limit at which reproduction ceases. The size of the home range varies with population density, habitat and other factors, but has been shown in various studies to be between 500 m² and 7,000 m².

Opposite: In both the Bank Vole and the other Clethrionomys *species, the corners of the triangles on the cheek teeth are more rounded than in the* Microtus *and* Pitymys *species.*

Bank Vole

Balkan Snow Vole

Bank Vole

Balkan Snow Vole *Dinaromys bogdanovi (Dolomys milleri)*

The former generic name *Dolomys* is made up from the Greek words *dolos*, which means deceptive-looking, and *mys*, which is a mouse. A vole that looks like a mouse in other words, and when the species was given that name it was no doubt based mainly on the long tail (around 75% of the body length), and perhaps also the rather prominent outer ears. The species is otherwise vole-like, and the cheek teeth for example are very like those of the *Microtus* species. The fur is light grey-blue. The species has a curious history. It was first encountered as a fossil in Hungary in 1898, but it was not until 1925 that a live example was found. Eventually it was found to live in the mountain regions between 10 m and 2,200 m above sea level in Yugoslavia. In more recent years, however, as the species has been looked for in order to gain knowledge of its habits etc, it has not been possible to find it. We do not seem to know much more than that the litter size is very small, only two to three young, and the gestation period unusually long, about four weeks.

Balkan Snow Vole

Northern Water Vole *Arvicola terrestris*

Body length 120–235 mm, tail length 50–146 mm, weight up to 320 g. In outward appearance can be distinguished from Southwestern Water Vole only where both species are present, i.e. in parts of eastern France and northern Spain; there, the Northern Water Vole is smaller—body length less than 165 mm, tail length less than 75 mm and weight at most 100 g.

A large, comparatively long-tailed vole that is an expert swimmer but which does not actually show any external adaptations for this. It floats high in the water. It often sits ruffled up at the water's edge eating, when it handles the food elegantly with its front paws. If disturbed, it plunges in head first, and if you yourself have disturbed it you generally hear only a little splash. The colour varies, but the animal is dark, the upperside sometimes almost black, the underside paler with tinges of rusty-brown in some individuals. The hindfeet have five pads, whereas all other species of small rodents in north Europe have six. The Northern Water Vole excavates underground passages. In cross-section they are vertically oval, which distinguishes them from the Northern Mole's which instead are slightly horizontally oval. The cast-up heaps of earth, too, are somewhat different: those of the water voles are more irregular, unequal in size, often mixed with grass, and with the tunnel opening in the outer part.

From England and France in the west, the species is found within a large area comprising middle and north Europe and extending eastwards to the River Lena and down to the Himalayas. It is absent from large parts of the southwest, where it is replaced by the Southwestern Water Vole (see below).

The species is most often encountered in or beside water, mostly marshes, ditches etc, but it also lives on drier ground such as meadows, fields and gardens. This is what lies behind the scientific generic name, which is formed from the Latin *arvum* and *colo*, which mean respectively field and I cultivate. Reports from Finland indicate that the habitat choice can vary with the time of year. Wet areas appear to be preferred in summer, and tunnel systems in drier ground are used more in winter.

The species eats plants and various kinds of vegetable matter, occasionally also animal food. It seems to be exceptionally fond of a section of pith that is situated just beneath the panicle in the stem of the reed. The animal gets hold of this titbit, located high up on the plant, not by climbing up but by cutting away the stem from below in stages. The Northern Water Vole has also adopted a couple of other slightly special habits—many perhaps would rather call them bad habits. It lays up winter stores which not uncommonly consist of potatoes or other root vegetables. Furthermore, it may set about roots and bark on planted trees, both fruit trees and young conifers.

A first litter, usually of two to five young, is born in April–May in a nest which is usually underground and connecting to the tunnel system, but which can be a tussock surrounded by water or even on accumulated floating vegetable matter. Several litters follow later during the summer, and newborn young can be found at least into September. The young become sexually mature after about two months; early-born young can therefore breed in the same year.

Southwestern Water Vole *Arvicola sapidus* replaces the Northern Water Vole in southwest Europe—in parts of France and in the Iberian peninsula. The species is comparatively longer-tailed (tail length 105–135 mm) and a shade bigger (body length up to 220 mm) than the Northern Water Vole. In areas where both species occur together (parts of eastern France) the Southwestern species tends to be the one that lives in the moister habitats. Not illustrated.

Opposite: The Northern Water Vole, like the other voles, has five toes on the back foot and four on the front foot. The hindfeet are also considerably bigger than the front ones.

Northern Water Vole

Muskrat *Ondatra zibethicus*

Body length 24–40 cm, tail length 19–28 cm, weight 0.6–1.8 kg.

There is much about the Muskrat that recalls the European Beaver. Whether an animal is seen swimming, i.e. a head with bow-waves attached, or sitting on land eating or preening, the observer may have to look for some time before realising that he is dealing with a small replica: the beaver is around 20 times heavier! The Muskrat is brown in colour, darker above, lighter below. The hindfeet are considerably larger than the front feet, and their area is further enlarged owing to the toes having dense bristles on the sides. The tail, especially in adult individuals, is flattened from the sides and in cross-section about three times deeper than it is wide.

The Muskrat is originally a North American species. In 1905 it was introduced into Europe because of its valuable fur and quickly spread to a number of countries. It reached Finland as early as 1919 and is now abundant there, and around 1950 it reached Sweden, and has since then expanded its range over a large area of the northern coastlands (during 1964–73 at a speed of a good 3 km per year). It is also found across most of central Europe. In the 1930s Muskrats occurred in Britain, but they were successfully eradicated.

The Muskrat is not especially particular in its choice of where to live: the species frequents coastal areas, large and small inland lakes and running water of various kinds. In the northern part of the Gulf of Bothnia it seems able to colonise even fairly isolated islands. Good adaptive capacities are then shown by the Muskrat, including in its nest building. In the habitat most often used—large, shallow, well-vegetated inland lakes—it builds lodge-type nests on water up to 1 m deep. On seashores and in running water these would be easily destroyed by waves or strong currents, and so here the nest is instead prepared in an excavated burrow.

The Muskrat is first and foremost a vegetarian, and as such far from specialised. In several countries the diet has been found to be made up of about 50 different plant species, in the north horse-tail and sedge of various species being among important foods. The Muskrat consumes only a small part of the plants it bites off, preferably the basal parts which are richest in carbohydrate and protein. The species does not, however, concentrate exclusively on a vegetarian diet. It is known to consume bivalves, sometimes in large quantities, and at least in some places also fish.

Breeding takes place during the period March–September. In central Europe the female normally has two litters, each of up to ten young (average almost five). Farther north she usually manages only one litter per year, but in the south as many as three.

Muskrat populations vary greatly with the seasons. The density in winter can be around three individuals per kilometre of shoreline, and rise to a peak in July of more than ten individuals. By that time, some emigration of young animals has taken place during the spring. During the autumn the population then drops, mainly as a result of predation, and normally 80–90% of the young die before the winter. The species is an important prey for several species of carnivore, for example fox and American Mink, especially during years when voles and other small rodents are in poor supply. If the Muskrat is surprised when on land, it can display an extremely fierce temper and sometimes be downright aggressive. The males have musk glands.

Muskrat

Common Pine Vole *Pitymys subterraneus*

Body length 75–106 mm, tail length 25–43 mm, weight 12–27 g.

The specific name *subterraneus* alludes to an underground way of life, and the species has small ears as an adaptation for this. Other such adaptations are its small eyes and dense, short fur. These features, incidentally, characterise the whole *Pitymys* group. The species' innermost cheek tooth in the upper jaw has four enamel lobes on the inside, which distinguishes it from, among others, the Mediterranean Pine Vole. The range encompasses large parts of central Europe, from the French Atlantic coast in the west and into the Soviet Union in the east. The limit in many places is set by the fact that the substrate is unsuitable for digging in, but the species' absence in some areas is considered to be due also to its inability to withstand competition with other species, in particular the Common Vole. It is not, however, particular in choice of habitat, and lives in meadowland and grasslands of various kinds but also open woodland. In the Alps it is met with above 2,300 m. It is possible that the fluctuations in pine vole populations take place somewhat more slowly than in the *Microtus* voles. The litter at any rate consists usually only of two or three young, and the female is provided with two pairs of nipples (the majority of other vole species have four). Chromosome studies have revealed at least three forms that are so similar to the Common Pine Vole that they cannot be distinguished either by appearance or by habits, but which must for all that be regarded as separate species. Of these, the Bavarian Pine Vole *P. bavaricus* occurs in the Bavarian Alps, the Tatra Pine Vole *P. tatricus* in the Tatra Mountains in the northwest Carpathians, and Liechtenstein's Pine Vole *P. liechtensteini* in northwest Yugoslavia.

Alpine Pine Vole *Pitymys multiplex*

This species was formerly called 'Fatio's Pine Vole' and is still sometimes known as such. If, however, one supports the view that the name should preferably say something about where the animal lives, its appearance or its particular characteristics, Alpine Pine Vole is more suitable since the distribution is restricted to alpine regions in Switzerland and northern Italy. In appearance it differs very little from the Common Pine Vole. The species is on average slightly larger—body length 90–115 mm—and its coat is a shade more yellowish-brown. The two species can, however, be distinguished with certainty only by the chromosomes: the Alpine Pine Vole has 48, against the Common Pine Vole's 52 or 54.

Mediterranean Pine Vole *Pitymys duodecimcostatus*

The colour in this species varies, but the upperside is tinged with yellow and it is considerably paler than the Common Pine Vole. Furthermore, the coat is dense and velvety and the tail short, only 19–35 mm. The innermost cheek tooth in the upper jaw has only three ridges on the inside, and those on the outside are very uneven in size. The distribution has previously been considered to include large, but discrete, areas in the Mediterranean countries. Chromosome studies have, however, shown that the Mediterranean Pine Vole is found only in southeastern France and an adjacent area in the eastern and southern part of the Iberian peninsula. The pine voles that occur in the northern and western parts of this peninsula and within an area in southern Yugoslavia and Greece are impossible to distinguish by appearance, but are nevertheless regarded as separate species. They have been named the Lusitanian Pine Vole *P. lusitanicus* and Thomas's Pine Vole *P. thomasi*, respectively.

Common Pine Vole

Alpine Pine Vole

Mediterranean Pine Vole

Savi's Pine Vole

Savi's Pine Vole *Pitymys savii*

This species is outwardly very similar to the Common Pine Vole. It is 72–105 mm long and therefore equal in size, and the fact that its colour is a shade lighter and the tail on average a little shorter, 21–35 mm, is not sufficient for positive specific identification. The innermost cheek tooth in the upper jaw is a better guide. It has only three triangles on the inside. The Mediterranean Pine Vole also has the same number, but Savi's Pine Vole differs from that species in that the ridges on the outside of the same tooth are equal in size. The range is thought to be discontinuous. The species is found in the whole of Italy and also—in what are in that case separate races—in the Pyrenees, both in France and in Spain, as well as in Yugoslavia. Those in the Pyrenees and Yugoslavia may in fact be separate species, *P. gerbii* (or *P. pyrenaicus*) and *P. felteni* respectively.

Common Pine Vole

Alpine Pine Vole

Mediterranean Pine Vole

Savi's Pine Vole

Snow Vole *Microtus nivalis*

The Snow Vole differs from other European species of voles apart from the Balkan Snow Vole in its grey coat and its pale, in old individuals almost white, tail. It is roughly equal to the Balkan species in size—the body length is 84–140 mm—but the Snow Vole has a shorter tail, 39–75 mm. In addition, its first cheek tooth in the lower jaw is very distinctive in shape, with a triangle pointing in each direction at the very front. From above it appears almost to form an arrowhead. The Snow Vole is found in south and central Europe, from the mountain regions of the border districts of Portugal/Spain in the west to the Carpathians in the east. In most places it lives immediately above the tree-line, often in areas where the ground is more than 75% covered with rock. It can, however, be found both above and below this level. On Mont Blanc it occurs above 4,000 m, and on the Yugoslavian coast of the Adriatic there are local populations at altitudes between 120 m and 560 m above sea level. The species is markedly diurnal and often active on sunny slopes. There it is seen to be skilled not only in climbing over scree but also in jumping from rock to rock.

Common Vole/Orkney Vole *Microtus arvalis*

The Common Vole differs from the Field Vole only in small details. It is a shade lighter, a little shorter-haired, almost hairless inside the ear but with a thick and short edging of hair towards the tip of the ear. For certain separation of the species, however, one must examine the teeth. The Common Vole lacks the Field Vole's extra loop on the middle cheek tooth in the upper jaw, and is distinguished from the Root Vole by the very first cheek tooth in the lower jaw having five triangles on the outside. The species is found in the greater part of Europe and farther east through Asia. It is, however, absent from a large area of the Mediterranean, from Fennoscandia except the greater part of Jutland, as well as from the British Isles except in the Orkney Islands and Guernsey. It was previously thought to occur in southern Finland; microscopic examination of, among other things, the appearance of the spermatozoa, however, indicate that this is incorrect and that it is instead the Sibling Vole that exists there. The Common Vole differs from the Field Vole in its choice of habitat. It shuns wet grassland and is rare in areas with tall grass, where the Field Vole can be numerous. On dry meadowland the two species may live side by side, but the Field Vole is then found where the grass is longest and the Common Vole where it is shortest. The species excavates and uses underground tunnels more than the Field Vole does and thus survives better in areas which are grazed. Surveys in central Europe have found home ranges of up to 1,500 m² in males and about a quarter of this in females.

Sibling Vole *Microtus subarvalis (M. epiroticus)*

Of several forms of *Microtus* that have been described during recent decades, this appears to be the only one that actually constitutes a proper species. Others have proved on examination to be races, often of the Common Vole. No external differences exist between the two species, but the Sibling or Russian Vole can be identified only by examining chromosomes or spermatozoa. It is found in southern Finland (see Common Vole), in the European part of the Soviet Union and also in southeast Europe, including Yugoslavia and Bulgaria. Not illustrated.

Snow Vole

Common Vole

Sibling Vole

Günther's Vole *Microtus socialis (M. guentheri)*

This and the following species are on the one hand similar to the Common Vole, and on the other hand so similar to each other that they were formerly regarded as one species. In several details, however, the two forms differ so much that they are now considered to be separate species. Günther's Vole is short-tailed. The tail is 20–36 mm, i.e. one-fifth to a quarter of the body length. In addition, the tail is pale and the back paws almost white. The species is found from extreme southeast Europe—Greece, Yugoslavia and Bulgaria—eastwards through Turkey and the Middle East. Not illustrated.

Cabrera's Vole *Microtus cabrerae*

In outward appearance this species differs from the Common Vole mainly in having a number of hairs on the hind part of the body which are darker and appreciably longer than the ordinary guard hairs. It is also darker on the back than the Common Vole. The skull enables identification: the forehead is almost straight in profile, whereas in the Common Vole it is convex. The species is found in Spain and Portugal and inhabits slightly lower levels and slightly damper ground than the Common Vole. Not illustrated.

Common Vole

Snow Vole

Field Vole *Microtus agrestis*

Body length 78–135 mm, tail length 18–49 mm, weight 14–90 g.

The upperside is usually dark brownish-grey, the sides paler, sometimes with a yellow cast, and the belly, the underside of the neck and the paws are grey. The tail is darker above than below. The coat is rather long, and if one sits down anywhere where the species is present and is able to see it at close quarters—which is not difficult since it is often active by day and easily becomes quite confiding—the coat can look matted or unkempt. The hair inside the ear and along the upper edge of the ear is sparse. The middle cheek tooth in the upper jaw nearly always has a small extra enamel lobe at the back on the inside. Individuals lacking this are difficult to identify specifically. Piles of droppings and feeding places where the blades of grass are carefully broken off can be found along the runways which are used in summer. The Field Vole has a low, chirping call.

The Field Vole is found over the greater part of north and central Europe, but is absent on some islands such as Iceland, Ireland and Gotland. The southernmost outposts are found in Portugal and on the French Riviera. The range extends eastwards through Asia to the River Lena and Lake Baikal.

The scientific name *agrestis* means that the species is at home in open fields, and it is indeed found in meadows and grassland of different kinds. One can find it in such habitats in extremely varied surroundings—on islands of archipelagos, seashores, the edges of ditches near cultivated land, in open woodland, e.g. upland birch forest, and also on mountain heath. In the Alps it reaches to about 1,900 m above sea level. Damp ground is not a necessary prerequisite but perhaps nevertheless a factor which favours the species. Following clearance work in coniferous forest, the Field Vole is not so common in the predominantly *Vaccinium* scrub habitat that immediately succeeds the felling as it is in later stages when the plant life is more abundant. Correspondingly, it can be fairly scarce, or even absent, in a grazed area and increase greatly if the grazing ceases.

Grass is the most important food, but during the height of summer many herbaceous plants are included. During the winter the species may gnaw bark and thereby cause damage, especially to fruit trees. A full-grown Field Vole can put away up to 30 g of grass per day.

The breeding season normally spans April to September. It can be markedly shorter in areas at higher altitude above sea level, but is prolonged during favourable weather conditions. In central Europe young may then be found throughout the year, and in the north young have been discovered in nests under the snow. The number of young in the litter averages between four and five. A small proportion of the young from one summer survive to the autumn of the next year and thus reach a maximum age of 16–18 months.

The home range used by the Field Vole varies with a number of factors, for example food availability and population density. Areas of between 200 m² and 1,000 m² have been reported in different studies, and the male's range is often about twice as large as the female's.

Root Vole *Microtus oeconomus*

The Root Vole is very similar to the Field Vole. It is, however, a shade darker, slightly bigger—body length 85–161 mm and weight up to 103 g—and in particular has a proportionately longer tail. In full-grown animals the tail is usually at least a third the length of the body, whereas in most Field Voles it is

Opposite: The Field Vole's skull can be identified by the middle cheek tooth in the upper jaw having an additional small enamel lobe on the inside at the very back (left). This lobe is lacking in the Root Vole (right).

Field Vole

Root Vole

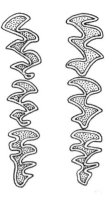

shorter than this. Nevertheless, the teeth provide the safest distinctions between the species. The Root Vole lacks the Field Vole's extra lobe of enamel on the middle upper cheek tooth. In addition, the first cheek tooth in the lower jaw has a distinctive appearance, with four triangles on the outside. The species occurs in northern North America and Siberia. In Europe the range extends in a northerly patch towards the Kola peninsula and northern Scandinavia and a southerly one to the Elbe south of the Baltic Sea. To the west and south the species is found in the Netherlands and Hungary respectively; this is not, however, a continuation of the range but, so far as is known, isolated populations, which are also found a long way down the Scandinavian peninsula. The species has been reported to be declining rapidly in the Netherlands in association with drainage projects, where the Common Vole, as the habitat dries out, takes over the Root Vole's previous domains. The major habitat difference from the Field Vole is that the Root Vole is often encountered in swamps and other wet habitats.

Root Vole

Field Vole

Common Hamster *Cricetus cricetus*

Body length 18–30 cm, tail length 28–70 mm, weight up to 500 g.

The black underside distinguishes the Common Hamster from all other small European mammals. The species is further characterised by a generally 'variegated' appearance, short tail, and also, when irritated or excited, diverse hissing and squeaking cries. In some areas all-black individuals are common. The Common Hamster lives in extensive subterranean systems reaching down to 2 m below the ground where each individual has its own tunnels, food-storing spaces and nest chambers.

The range extends from the steppes in the southern Soviet westwards into Europe in a wedge which is broad in the east but which narrows in central Europe. Towards Holland, Belgium and eastern France this range is no longer continuous. In many purely agricultural areas the species has declined tremendously in recent decades.

The steppe, then, is the original habitat. The species has adapted from this to grassland of varied types, including cultivated areas. It prefers loess and clay soils, in other words substrates that are easy to burrow into but where the underground passageways do not then cave in.

The food consists mainly of plants, both wild and cultivated. Among the latter may be mentioned as examples corn, maize, fodder plants, beets, potatoes as well as fruit and vegetables of all kinds. Insects and other small animals also form a part of the diet. During the summer and autumn, the Common Hamster transports food in its very elastic cheek pouches and lays up underground stores. One such store may often contain, for example, 5 kg of potatoes, but hiding places with up to 65 kg of food may be found. Its choice of food means that the Common Hamster is often considered a harmful animal and it is heavily culled, in some places with the use of gas.

The mating period begins in April, immediately after hibernation, and during May–August one to three litters are born, each of three to 15 young. The female is already sexually mature at about two-and-a-half months of age, which means that early-born females can reproduce as soon as their first summer.

From October/November to March/April the Common Hamster lies in hibernation 1–2 m down in an underground burrow. The winter rest is both begun and broken off when the outside temperature passes the 10°C mark, but it is not an uninterrupted sleep that is involved. The food reserves are visited from time to time and, especially during periods of mild weather, the animals often go out on short walks.

Grey Hamster *Cricetulus migratorius*

This hamster is as small as a vole—the body length is 9–11 cm—and the suffix *-ulus* in the Latin generic name is a diminutive which indicates that we are dealing with a little hamster. It is distinguished from the voles by the outer ears being more conspicuous and the eyes bigger. It has an easterly distribution. The species is found over large parts of Asia, and in Europe only in restricted areas in the extreme southeast, in Greece, Bulgaria and Romania. It lives in open arid country and is a vegetarian: in a Russian study 37 different plant species were reported to be included in the diet. During the winter its activity decreases, though not to the point that the species goes into hibernation.

Common Hamster

Grey Hamster

Romanian Hamster

Romanian Hamster *Mesocricetus newtoni*

This species is considerably smaller than the Common Hamster—the body length is 13–18 cm—and it differs also in having an almost all-white underside. *Meso* in the scientific generic name means between, which alludes to its systematic position between the two previous species. The distribution in Europe is limited to a narrow zone along the Black Sea coast in Bulgaria, Romania and adjacent parts of the Soviet. The species is so closely related to the Golden Hamster *M. auratus* that the two forms are sometimes assigned to a single species. They can interbreed but have different chromosome counts—the Romanian Hamster has 38, the Golden Hamster 44—and the offspring are sterile. The Golden Hamster originates from Syria. It is kept as a pet and in laboratories, but escapes can survive in the wild, at least for a time, and even establish feral populations.

Common Hamster

Romanian Hamster

Grey Hamster

Mole-rats   Family *Spalacidae*

A family of odd mammals which are possibly even better adapted than the moles to a life underground. The outer ears and tail are missing and the eyes are overgrown with skin. The head is large and merges into the plump body without any obvious neck. The paws are not, as in the moles, transformed into digging feet, but instead the mole-rats excavate their underground tunnels using the very powerful front teeth. Theirs is not, however, an entirely underground existence: in several studies of prey choice in different species of owls, skulls of mole-rats have been found to occur in the pellets. The food is vegetable matter and is dominated by underground plant material. Large supplies may be laid up in hollows connected to the tunnels, and locally the mole-rats may do damage to fields of, for example, potatoes and onions. Two species occur in Europe.

Greater Mole-rat *Spalax microphthalmus*

This, the most easterly of the two species of mole-rats, is 20–28 cm long and has hindfeet 25–30 mm long. The outer ear openings are small, only 1.2–2.5 mm. Its colour has a very greyish tint, but varies so much that this character is not sufficient to separate the two species with certainty. From the main range in the Soviet, north of the Black and Caspian Seas, a wedge extends southwestwards into Romania and Bulgaria. Populations north and south of the River Dniester represent different races. Some zoologists consider the difference to be so great that the forms should be regarded as full species, *S. polonicus* and *S. graecus* respectively.

Lesser Mole-rat *Spalax leucodon*

The Lesser Mole-rat is the slightly smaller species—the body length is 15–24 cm and the length of the hindfoot 19–30 mm. The external ear opening on the other hand is slightly larger than in the previous species, 2.1–3.9 mm. Unfortunately, however, the surest means of distinguishing between the species is by the skulls. In the Lesser, there are two small holes or—in isolated populations, including on Peloponnesos—distinct cavities at the back of the cranium on each side of the posterior opening. The range also differs to some extent. The Lesser Mole-rat is found from Yugoslavia and Greece, around both the Black Sea and the eastern part of the Mediterranean Sea, to Egypt and Libya.

Greater Mole-rat

Lesser Mole-rat

Mice and rats   Family *Muridae*

The species in the family Muridae vary a great deal in size but have certain common characters. The tail is long, between two-thirds and one-and-one-third the length of the body, the snout pointed, and the ears, eyes and hindfeet relatively big. The latter have five toes each, while the front feet have only four. The cheek teeth, three in each half-jaw, have rounded nodules (cusps), indicating the versatile diet.

Harvest Mouse   *Micromys minutus*

With body and tail lengths of, respectively, 80 mm and 77 mm at the most and a weight of 3–11 g in full-grown animals—up to 15 g in pregnant females—the Harvest Mouse is the smallest in the family. In addition to this, it is distinguished by the fact that sexually mature animals have warm russet-coloured backs—young are grey-brown—and that the tail can be used to grip with. The species is therefore a climber, and the nest, which is usually built of grass, is a small sphere suspended in vegetation half a metre or so above the ground. The Harvest Mouse is found in the greater part of Europe—although it is absent in the northwest as well as in most of the Mediterranean region—and farther east through Asia to Japan. It prefers dense vegetation, if possible with a good sprinkling of grass or sedge. During population peaks especially, it turns up in woodland, and it also resorts to cultivated fields, particularly in the northwest part of the range. The principal food is seeds and other vegetable matter but, especially in winter, the Harvest Mouse finds insects, which constitute an important food at that time. A female can give birth to as many as seven litters in one year, usually with two to six and a maximum of seven young in each litter.

Harvest Mouse

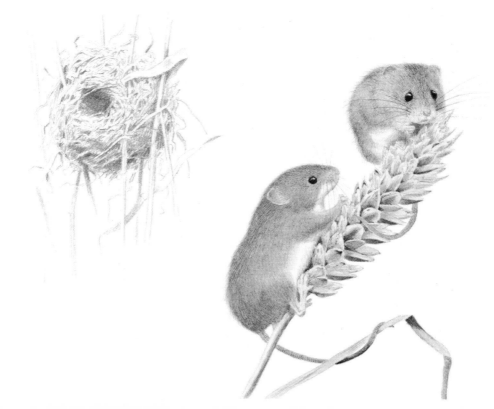

Yellow-necked Mouse *Apodemus flavicollis*

Body length 90–130 mm, tail length 90–135 mm, weight 10–45 g, length of hindfoot usually more than 24 mm, tail usually with 165–235 rings.

In the northern parts of the range—in England and Scandinavia—the species can be identified by a yellowish-brown patch or streak on the underside between the front legs. When present, this is broader than it is long. Towards the south, however, this feature becomes more and more uncommon, and in many areas in the Mediterranean region it is lacking in more than half of the population. Identification must then be based on size and the fact that the species is browner above than the Wood Mouse.

The Yellow-necked Mouse is found in the greater part of Europe but is absent from the north, as well as from parts of west Europe. It occurs eastwards approximately to the Urals, and in Scandinavia it reaches a little farther north than the Wood Mouse. In Britain it occurs only in England and Wales south of the Wirral, and even within this area its distribution is patchy.

The scientific generic name is Greek and means more or less 'away from the house'. It has been assigned to this genus in order to distinguish it from the House Mouse, which is indeed strongly associated with buildings. The Yellow-necked Mouse lives mostly in woods of various kinds, but it is also found in other, especially drier habitats—in the Balkans in maquis scrub and in east Europe also in more open terrain. In England it inhabits hilly areas at lower levels than the Wood Mouse, but in mountainous regions in many other places the opposite applies: the Yellow-necked Mouse goes considerably higher. In the Alps it occurs at above 2,000 m altitude.

The food is derived from both plant and animal kingdoms. The vegetable part, which predominates, consists of seeds, nuts, shoots and buds from a broad assortment of plants—herbaceous plants, bushes, but also trees. The animal food, which may form 10% or more of the diet, consists of all types of invertebrates including larvae and pupae. Hazelnuts are opened by making a hole at the side. The contents are then gnawed out using the lower front teeth, at the same time as the upper ones hold firmly on to the outside of the shell. Since the nut is turned in a circle, this results in an edging of upper front teeth marks around the opening in the shell. When the species has a greater supply of food than it needs at the time, it lays up stores.

The breeding season is long and, at least in middle Europe, starts as early as February. After an autumn of abundant production of beechmast, breeding may even continue right through the winter. The nest is placed under a stump or in the roots system beneath a tree, and the entrance may be sealed with a bit of moss or a dead leaf. A female can give birth in one season to up to three litters, and the young from early first litters can themselves produce young in the same season. The litter size varies between one and eight, with an average of about five. The patch between the front legs becomes visible on the young towards the end of their second week.

The size of the home range varies between a few tenths of a hectare and 2–5 ha. The population density also varies: the highest quotations are around 50 animals per hectare, but a value of between one and ten is more usual.

Yellow-necked Mouse

Wood Mouse *Apodemus sylvaticus*

The Wood Mouse has a body length of 80–105 mm and a tail length of 70–95 mm, thereby averaging slightly smaller than the Yellow-necked Mouse. Since the measurements overlap, however, specific identification must as a rule be based on other things. Points of importance are that the hindfoot is usually shorter than 24 mm and that the tail normally has 130–180 rings. In as much as there is a patch on the underside between the front legs, it is longer than it is broad. The species has a considerably more widespread distribution than the Yellow-necked Mouse, both within and outside Europe. In Europe it is actually absent only in north Fennoscandia; it is present on all larger islands, including Iceland, but in Ireland and on some other, smaller islands it was probably introduced by man. It is also found in North Africa and in Asia eastwards to the Altai mountains. The species is associated with woodland to a far lesser extent than its larger relative, and occurs near enough anywhere where it can conceal itself in dense ground vegetation. Its principal food is seeds, but animal matter, including earthworms, also forms a part. Despite the fact that the Wood Mouse and the Yellow-necked Mouse are so similar to each other that there are even examples that cannot be identified with certainty, hybrids are not known either in the wild or in laboratories where the two species have been kept together.

Krk Mouse *Apodemus krkensis*

It is doubtful whether the Krk Mouse constitutes a full species or is merely a race of the Rock Mouse. It is found only on the island of Krk in Yugoslavia, where it lives in the same habitat as the Wood Mouse. It differs from that species, as does the Rock Mouse, in having a pale grey coat lacking brown tinges. It differs from the Rock Mouse in having shorter hindfeet—22–24 mm as against more than 24 mm for the Rock Mouse. Not illustrated.

Wood Mouse

Pygmy Field Mouse

Rock Mouse

Pygmy Field Mouse *Apodemus microps*

The Pygmy Field Mouse most resembles the Wood Mouse, but is a shade smaller—the body length is 73–96 mm and the tail length 64–89 mm. The species are probably best separated by the fact that the Pygmy Field Mouse's hindfoot is 20.5 mm or less and the ear less than 15 mm, corresponding measurements in the Wood Mouse being 20–24 mm and 14.5–18 mm. The species is found in a large part of eastern Europe and is not particular as to its choice of habitat. Open terrain, however, is preferred to enclosed woodland, and there are reports from some areas of competition between Pygmy Field Mouse and Wood Mouse.

Rock Mouse *Apodemus mystacinus*

With a body length of 100–130 mm and a tail length of 102–140 mm, the Rock Mouse averages slightly bigger than the Yellow-necked Mouse. The difference, though, is so small that it is not good enough for specific identification. The species is, however, purer grey, almost never has a throat patch, and has long whiskers. The longest are on average more than 47 mm, as against less than 40 mm in the Yellow-necked Mouse. It is this that gives the species its scientific name, which comes from the Greek word for moustache. In Europe the species is found only in the extreme southeast—south of the January 0°C isotherm—and, as the name indicates, it occurs mostly in rocky terrain. It has a poorer reproductive capacity than Yellow-necked and Wood Mice.

Pygmy Field Mouse

Rock Mouse

Striped Field Mouse *Apodemus agrarius*

The Striped Field Mouse has a body length of 73–123 mm and its tail is around two-thirds as long—up to 89 mm. The species is therefore about the size of a Wood Mouse. Measurements, however, play a secondary role, since the Striped Field Mouse is easy to identify by the back stripe combined with the fact that the tail is shorter than the body. The range is easterly, but with two westerly projections, one into north Italy and the other into north Germany and Denmark. In the latter country, however, the species was thought to remain at the beginning of the 1980s only on the islands of Lolland and Falster. In southeast Finland, by contrast, reports from the same period suggest a slow expansion. In the central parts of the range the Striped Field Mouse occurs in all possible habitats, but towards the periphery it is more precise in its requirements. In southeast Europe, for example, it is associated with damp habitats, particularly river valleys. Characteristic of the diet is that the amount of animal matter is higher than in other *Apodemus* species, and this seems to apply particularly during the period immediately before breeding. It is mostly insects and insect larvae that are involved, but also other items such as worms, molluscs and small vertebrates, though these are probably more often than not found when dead. The vegetable part of the food is made up mostly of seeds and to a very small degree of green plant material. The litter consists on average of five or six young, a higher mean than in the Yellow-necked and Wood Mice. The Striped Field Mouse is also more diurnal than those two species.

Ship Rat *Rattus rattus*

The Ship Rat has a body length of 95–240 mm and a tail length of 115–260 mm. It can be distinguished from the Common Rat by the tail, which is uniformly coloured and longer than the body, but also in other ways. The whole animal is slimmer and considerably more agile, the tail is narrower, and the ears are almost hairless and relatively large—folded forward they reach at least partly over the eyes. The colour is of little help, since both species occur in brown as well as black forms. The Ship Rat probably originated from India, but as early as prehistoric times was dispersed along the old trading routes to Europe. It is now found throughout the Mediterranean region, but north of there its occurrence is first discontinuous, then sporadic, and in general the species is on the decline. It can, however, still turn up virtually anywhere, mainly owing to boat and train freight. In south Europe it occurs in cultivated areas, including those far from human habitation, but towards the north it is more and more tied to densely built-up areas and buildings. The decline here may be due to competition with the Common Rat, but also to the fact that demolition or rebuilding of old houses means that suitable retreats for the Ship Rat disappear. It has a greater bent for vegetable food, in particular fruit, than the Common Rat. The nest is above ground—in trees or buildings—and the litter size varies between one and 16, with a mean of about seven.

Striped Field Mouse

Ship Rat

Common Rat *Rattus norvegicus*

Body length 110–290 mm, tail length 85–230 mm, weight up to 600 g.

The Common Rat is clumsier and somewhat slower in its movements than the Ship Rat. It is perhaps most easily identified by its tail being shorter than the body and bicoloured—grey-brown above and pale below. Furthermore, the ears are slightly hairy and short: folded forward they barely reach the rear corner of the eye.

Just like the Ship Rat, the Common Rat is considered to originate from the east. It came to Europe from east Asia during the Middle Ages, after which it slowly replaced the Ship Rat which had at that time been present here for hundreds of years. It has been most successful in central and northern Europe, which it has almost entirely colonised, whereas it is uncommon in the Mediterranean region. In Greece, for example, it is found only in a few of the big cities on the mainland and on some of the largest islands in the Aegean and Ionian Seas.

The species is associated in the main with man, and lives mostly in and around buildings, including in sewage systems, storage areas, warehouses, barns and on refuse tips. In some areas it frequents cultivated fields in summer and autumn, and there are places where the species lives all the year round practically without any contact with human beings. The majority of such places are damp and include even marshy coastal areas with dense vegetation.

The dominant food is vegetable—grain, fruit, vegetables—but the Common Rat is omnivorous and the choice of food varies widely between different habitats. Frogs are important prey in many places, as are birds, both eggs and young. Here the species can cause serious damage, and there are instances of for example large colonies of Common Terns *Sterna hirundo* being exterminated by Common Rats. It can also kill other smaller mammals, especially mice and voles, but cannibalism—directed against sick or young individuals—has been proven only under circumstances where the animals were suffering from protein deficiency.

Pregnant females can be found all year round, at least in central Europe, but breeding shows one peak in spring and one in autumn. Farther north there is usually no reproduction in winter. Sexual maturity, which varies with, among other things, population density and food availability, begins at the earliest at three months of age, more often at four. The gestation period is about 24 days. The litter size can vary between one and 15, depending for one thing on the female's weight. In 75% of cases, however, the litter consists of four to eight young.

The species lives in social groups or colonies which develop from one pair or a pregnant female and which do not tolerate infiltrators. The mortality is high: in full-grown rats it may reach more than 90% per year.

Common Rat

House Mouse *Mus musculus*

The House Mouse's skull can be identified by the front teeth in the upper jaw having a small notch at the back.

The House Mouse has a body length of 70–100 mm, a tail length of 55–95 mm and a top weight of 33 g. It is thus close to the Wood Mouse in size. Most House Mice, however, differ from the Wood and Yellow-necked Mice in that the upper front teeth, seen from the side, have a small notch on the rear edge. The House Mouse shows great variation, particularly in the matter of appearance but also in its way of life. This has given rise to many suggestions for systematic divisions of the various forms. Seven different races have been separated in Europe of which five are given the status of full species by some authorities. They may be divided into two groups. One consists of those forms that are dependent on, or at least live in close contact with, man. These are found principally in north and west Europe and are characterised by the tail being roughly the length of the body. They are also darker, although the southernmost individuals have a pale belly. The second group contains those that live more in the wild. They are dominant in the Mediterranean region and occur mostly in open cultivated country, seldom in woodland. They are distinguished by the tail being markedly shorter than the body, and are besides consistently paler than the more northerly races. House Mice are mobile, and in particular the young of the year emigrate and attempt to colonise new areas. The majority of these attempts fail, one reason being that the species is sensitive to competition from other species of small mammal. The food choice in wild-living House Mice is concentrated mainly on seeds of both wild and cultivated plants. In several studies the amount of oil-bearing seeds has been large. A great deal of animal food remains also occur throughout, in particular insects, which can be found in a good 10% and more of stomachs. House Mice living close to man are omnivorous. Such animals may breed all the year round, and a female can produce as many as ten litters with four to eight young in each. Those living in the wild on the other hand have a breeding season limited to March/April–October. The animals become sexually mature at 35–40 days of age and the gestation period is nearly 20 days.

Cretan Spiny Mouse *Acomys cahirinus (A. minous)*

The Cretan Spiny Mouse is roughly the same size as the Yellow-necked Mouse—the body length is 91–128 mm and the tail length 92–120 mm—but specific identification is normally made using other than measurement data. Most important, and also the feature which gives it its English name, is that the hairs on the back are transformed into, if not spines, then at any rate elongated, stiff bristles. A pale streak or patch behind the ears is also distinctive, as is the sharpness of the division between the grey-brown upperside and the almost white belly. To this should be added the fact that in Europe the Spiny Mouse is found only on Crete. There it occurs in scrubby, rocky terrain, but often it both resorts to buildings and comes inside houses. It is omnivorous, and both insects and seeds form important food. The litter size is smaller than in other mice, on average only two or three, and the gestation period longer, around 36 days.

House Mouse

Cretan Spiny Mouse

House Mouse

Mediterranean form

northwest European form

Cretan Spiny Mouse

Dormice   Family *Gliridae*

A small specialised family of rodents found only in the Old World and with only five species. Their large eyes and long, well-developed whiskers reveal that they are animals of the dusk or night. They spend the day sleeping in, for example, a tree hole, an abandoned bird's nest, an empty nestbox or their own nest. The Garden Dormouse, the Forest Dormouse and the Fat Dormouse usually prepare this in a hollow of some kind, while the Hazel Dormouse builds a loose, sphere-shaped and very well-made nest with a side entrance, more often than not in a thick bush.

Dormice hibernate. Hollows beneath the ground, or in another frost-free place, are usually chosen for a wintering site, and the animals line these with dry grass, moss, dead leaves etc. Hibernation is triggered by the outdoor temperature, and in the Fat Dormouse activity may begin to decrease when it is still as warm as 18–20°C outside. The metabolism is lowered at this time, and the breathing and heartbeat slow down more and more. During hibernation the animal's own temperature matches that of its surroundings, but, should the temperature approach freezing point, there is a mechanism which wakes the animal up and saves it from freezing to death—exactly as in the Hedgehog. Waking-up is also triggered by a rise in the temperature. This can be very rapid: there is one case described for the Hazel Dormouse where the animal's temperature rose from 6°C to 36°C in 40 minutes. In mild weather, dormice may come out of hibernation and be active for short periods.

All dormice are skilful climbers. They live to a great extent in trees and bushes above the ground, and show adaptations for this way of life in their body structure. The feet are turned outwards, and of the five toes on the hindfoot—the front foot has only four—the outermost is longer than the rest and can also be moved independently. The foot is therefore well suited for gripping around a branch.

The breeding timetable is fairly similar in the five species. Mating takes place in spring once the animals have come out of hibernation, and after around three-and-a-half weeks' pregnancy the female gives birth to a litter of two to nine young. The gestation period in the Fat Dormouse is slightly longer, about four-and-a-half weeks, and as a result the young are born somewhat later, normally not until August. The young are born naked and blind; they open their eyes after about 18 days (Garden and Hazel Dormice) or 21 days (Forest and Fat Dormice), and then suck for a further week or so. For the Hazel Dormouse there are reports of two litters per year.

Because of their nocturnal habits, dormice are subject to a certain amount of predation by owls. There are several examples where the first discovery of a species in a particular locality has been in an owl pellet.

Fat Dormouse *Glis glis*

Body length 13–19 cm, tail length 11–15 cm, weight 70–200 g, immediately before hibernation even more than 300 g.

The Fat Dormouse is bigger and greyer than the other dormice and, because its tail is long and bushy, it takes on a certain likeness to the Grey Squirrel. It has, however, a more pointed snout, rounder, more outward-pointing ears, a hint of a dark line along the middle of the back, and a splendid 'black eye' in the shape of a black ring around the eye. In addition, it is of course nocturnal. It is noisy, and its calls include a harsh creaking sound if it is disturbed.

Fat Dormouse

The species is found within the greater part of south and central Europe and thus has roughly the same distribution as the Garden Dormouse. It is, however, absent from the Iberian peninsula except the extreme north. It was introduced around 1890 in England, but its dispersal here has been very limited and it is found only in Hertfordshire and Buckinghamshire. Outside Europe it occurs in Russia west of the Volga, in Asia Minor and in parts of the Middle East.

The species belongs originally in pure deciduous forest, and this is still its favourite habitat. In many places, however, it has adapted to mixed forests, parks, orchards closely associated with human habitations, and (rarely) also pure coniferous forest.

It seems generally agreed that the predominant food is vegetable—nuts, fruit, berries, seeds and bark of deciduous trees—but opinions regarding the animal part of the diet are highly divergent. In places the Fat Dormouse is alleged to be a serious predator on small breeding birds. From Germany, for example, it is reported that for this reason there have been calls to keep the species in check in nature reserves where animal life was in other respects totally protected. From Luxemburg on the other hand, the species has been reported to be purely vegetarian. In most instances in the literature, however, insects and other small animals are stated to form part of the diet.

It is not because the species nowadays provides food for man to any extent that it acquired its alternative English name of 'Edible Dormouse'. It was different, though, in Roman times. In those days Fat Dormice were kept in captivity, in large enclosures to begin with, and then in small cages where they were fattened up with acorns and chestnuts. When sufficiently fattened, the small animals were then served as 'one of the greatest delicacies on the table of rich gormandisers'.

Hazel Dormouse *Muscardinus avellanarius*

Body length 6–9 cm, tail length 5.5–8 cm, weight 15–43 g.

The yellowish-red or almost fox-red upperside distinguishes the Hazel Dormouse from all other species of small rodents. The underside is paler, the throat and breast almost white, and the tail bushy just as in other dormice. In anger or fear, the tail can become extra bushy through the hairs being spread out. The Hazel Dormouse may then also emit squeaking or whistling cries. In both the upper and lower jaws the Hazel Dormouse has four cheek teeth with transverse, almost parallel enamel ridges, a pattern that differs totally both from the zigzag-patterned enamel lobes of the voles and the nodular cheek teeth of the mice.

The species has roughly the same distribution in Europe as the Fat Dormouse. It is, however, absent from part of the Mediterranean region—in the Iberian peninsula, and in Greece apart from the extreme northeast—but on the other hand it extends very slightly farther north, where the range reaches both the North and the Baltic Seas and also includes the southern parts of Britain and Scandinavia. In Britain it is an elusive species found mostly south of a line between mid Wales and the Wash, with a few outposts farther north. Eastwards the Hazel Dormouse is found in the Soviet west of the Urals and in Asia Minor.

Hazel is not a necessary prerequisite for the species' existence, but hazel country with nuts and a mixture of dense shrubbery and open, sunny glades are all the same probably the favourite habitat. Other haunts are juniper country, swampy forest, woodland edge, at times also dense forest plantations, heathland with heather and scrub, parks and orchards. The habitat requirements therefore appear on the surface fairly loose and are probably governed by factors such as temperature and humidity. The species suffers from herbicide use, clearance of dense bush vegetation, overgrazing and strong overgrowing of areas, i.e. from factors that reduce the variety in the habitat.

Hazelnuts have already been mentioned and the food otherwise consists of fruits, e.g. acorns and beechnuts, chestnuts, juniper berries and rowan berries, but also of buds, shoots, seeds and bark. Insects form part of the diet, but apparently only on a small scale.

The Hazel Dormouse is confiding and can adapt to living in very close proximity to man. A tendency to form colonies is reported from several places.

Hazel Dormouse

Garden Dormouse *Eliomys quercinus*

Body length 10–17 cm, tail length 9–12 cm, weight 45–120 g in summer, up to 210 g in the autumn before hibernation.

The 'highwayman's mask', i.e. the black patches joining together under the ear and around the eye, together with the large ears are the first things one notices about this attractive little animal. The back is reddish-grey to reddish-brown, the belly and the paws white, and the tail long with dark upperside and bushy, white tip. The Garden Dormouse often utters squeaking and chattering calls.

The Garden Dormouse is found in the greater part of south and central Europe, but in the north does not quite reach either the North Sea or the Baltic. It reaches farthest north in the easternmost parts of the range, and the small isolated populations in southern Finland are probably relics of a more continuous distribution there during the warm period following the Ice Age. The species also occurs in North Africa.

The specific name *quercinus* alludes to its partiality for oakwoods (the genus *Quercus*) in south Europe. Farther north it lives in both mixed and coniferous forests, but also in vineyards, orchards and gardens.

The Garden Dormouse is omnivorous to a greater degree than the other dormice. It eats acorns, nuts, berries and fruits of various kinds, as well as animal food. This part consists not only of insects and other invertebrates, but also of both birds and other species of small mammals. It may plunder nests of small birds both of eggs and young. In captivity the Garden Dormouse has been seen to attack birds as large as adult Jackdaws *Corvus monedula*. In autumn it sometimes finds its way into buildings in search of food.

The female and young—probably also groups of young—may sometimes move 'in caravan' in the same way as certain species of shrews. The animals then walk one close behind the other, each one with its front paws on the animal in front.

Forest Dormouse *Dryomys nitedula*

With a body length of 8–13 cm, tail length of 8–9.5 cm and a weight of 30–60 g, the Forest Dormouse is considerably smaller than the Garden Dormouse. Its black eye markings are at least as distinct, but it is otherwise appreciably less contrasty. The upperside can vary in colour from light grey to almost reddish-brown. The ears are relatively smaller, but the tail is if anything longer and, in addition, bushy throughout its length. The species has a more easterly distribution than the Garden Dormouse, and is found in an area stretching from eastern south and central Europe to India. Habitat choice and lifestyle are as those of the Garden Dormouse, but the species concentrates on vegetable food to a greater degree than its larger relative.

Mouse-tailed Dormouse *Myomimus roachi (M. personatus)*

This, too, is a small dormouse—body and tail lengths are 9–13 cm and 7–10 cm respectively. The tail is not bushy as in other dormice, but short-haired: it therefore resembles a mouse's tail. The species is, however, distinguished from mice by its proportionately much smaller ears. In Europe the Mouse-tailed Dormouse is found only in a small area in the extreme southeast, in Bulgaria and Greece. Not illustrated.

Garden Dormouse

Forest Dormouse

Garden Dormouse

Forest Dormouse

Birch Mice   Family *Zapodidae*

The birch mice are in general reminiscent of the true mice, but they differ in having a long tail, at least 25% longer than the body, and powerful hindfeet well suited for hopping movements. This has given the family its scientific name, which is a compound of the Greek *za-*, a reinforcing prefix which means big or very, and *podos*, the genetive form of foot. A dark stripe runs down the centre of the back. The winter is spent in hibernation, which indicates that the animal part of the food—which is more difficult to come by during that season—is more important than the vegetable part. The family comprises about ten species, two of which are found in Europe.

Northern Birch Mouse *Sicista betulina*

The Northern Birch Mouse has a body length of 50–75 mm and a tail length of 76–110 mm. The tail is accordingly around one-and-a-half times as long as the body. Apart from the dark, quite broad back stripe, the upperside is uniform brown. The outermost toe on both the front and the back paws can be placed in the opposite direction to the others when the animal grips—an adaptation for climbing. The species occurs patchily in Scandinavia and eastern middle Europe, and continuously from southern Finland and the Baltic states eastwards across large areas of northern Asia. The isolated outposts in the west no doubt represent remnants of a formerly more continuous distribution here as well. The Northern Birch Mouse's scientific name comes from the Latin name for the birch tree. It does not, however, live only in birchwoods but also in other wooded terrain and is favoured by dense undergrowth and high humidity. In the Carpathians, for example, its occurrence coincides entirely with the distribution of the spruce. The summer nest is a small round ball of grass placed on the ground. In this, one litter—probably in rare cases two—of one to 11 young is born. Hibernation on the other hand, which continues from October through to May/June, is spent in hollows in trees or below the surface of the ground. During this time the animal's weight can drop by 50%. It has been shown that the home range can be between 0.4 ha and 1.3 ha.

Northern Birch Mouse

Southern Birch Mouse *Sicista subtilis*

The Southern Birch Mouse is the same size as the Northern species—the body length is 53–78 mm. It is, however, shorter-tailed, the tail length being only 60–90 mm. It is perhaps also, as indicated by the Latin specific name, slimmer or more slender-limbed. A good character is additionally that the dark back stripe is edged with pale bands, especially on the lower back. The species has its main distribution in central Asia, but it occurs westwards into Europe to eastern Austria and the Yugoslavian steppes. It prefers more open terrain than the Northern Birch Mouse and is present in cultivated fields as well as in other habitats. The number of young in the litter varies between two and eight.

Southern Birch Mouse

Northern Birch Mouse

Southern Birch Mouse

Porcupine *Hystrix cristata*

Body length 50–70 cm, tail length 5–12 cm, weight 10–17 kg.

The size and the thick spines of varying lengths—up to 40 cm—on the lower part of the back make the Porcupine difficult to confuse with any other European animal species. The spines are actually modified hairs, and on the neck and the upper part of the back the animal has fur that is certainly thick but for all that more 'normal'. The hairs on the crown and nape are, however, extra bristly and also white. They can be erected when the animal is disturbed, a threat behaviour that may be reinforced by growling calls, a rattling noise which results when the spines are shaken against each other, and a peculiar jumping movement. When immediate danger threatens, the animal may roll itself up. The toes, five on each paw, are equipped with powerful digging claws. The male has no scrotum and the sexes are difficult to distinguish by appearance. The female's teats are not on the belly but high up on the sides. The animal's movements are slow, somewhere between lumbering and dignified.

The species is found in south and west Italy. It also occurred previously within a small area in the border regions between Greece and Yugoslavia, but it is reported now to have probably disappeared from there. It is thought to have been introduced to Europe during Roman times from Africa, where it is widely distributed north of the equator.

Arid areas, preferably with sections of dense scrub, are important haunts. Locally the species utilises cultivated ground.

The Porcupine is a vegetarian, living on green plant material, fruits, roots, bark etc. When eating, it holds the food firmly with the front paws.

In Europe, mating takes place in April. After a good two months' pregnancy, a litter of one to four young is born. They are equipped with short, soft spines which both grow and harden very quickly.

The Porcupine is nocturnal in its habits and spends the day in a burrow (often excavated by the animal itself) or in dense shrubbery. It does not hibernate, but in winter may be inactive for short periods in poor weather.

Porcupine

Coypu *Myocastor coypus*

Body length 36–65 cm, tail length 22–45 cm, weight 4–8 kg.

The Coypu is between the Muskrat and the European Beaver in size and is therefore a big rodent. The head is proportionately heavy, the front teeth large and orange-yellow, and the tail is long, round, thick at the base and evenly tapering, as well as being covered with scales and sparse hairs. The front legs are short and the front paws equipped with proper claws. The hindlegs are longer and more powerful and have well-developed webs between four of the five toes, an adaptation to a mainly aquatic life. In steep river banks where the Coypu lives, it digs holes and tunnels. It seeks shelter in these, and a nest is prepared in a dry hole and lined with plant material.

The Coypu's original home is in the subtropical and temperate parts of South America. From there it has been introduced from the end of the last century to fur farms, and then escaped and established itself in the wild in many countries in Europe. The populations fluctuate widely between different years, owing to the fact that the species is very sensitive to cold winter weather.

Lakes and watercourses of slightly different kinds—mostly inland waters but also saltwater shores—form the Coypu's natural haunts. In Europe it appears to do best in clear, slow-running water, preferably surrounded by dense vegetation.

The species is a vegetarian and lives to a great extent on aquatic plants—reed, bulrush, sedge, waterweed etc. The Coypu is an expert diver and much of its food is gathered underwater. Occasionally, animal food (e.g. bivalves) is included in the diet.

The females become sexually mature at around five months of age, and thereafter come into season approximately every fourth week throughout the year so long as fertilisation does not take place. This means that litters can be born at any time, but, at least in captivity, this happens most often in the spring. The female is pregnant for around four months, and two to nine young is the normal litter size. The young are born with fur and open eyes, and can suck even in the water since the female's mammary glands are placed high up on the side.

The skin is a valued fur. It is known as nutria, a name that is sometimes used for the species. In preparing the skin, the long guard hairs are plucked out and so only the dense, fine underfur is used.

Carnivores
Order *Carnivora*

Dogs and foxes   Family *Canidae*

The dogs and foxes are medium-sized carnivores. They have long legs, are fast runners, and live mostly in open terrain. Their front paws have five toes, the innermost not coming into contact with the ground, and the back paws four. The muzzle is long. The family consists of around 38 species, five of which are found in Europe. To these should perhaps be added dogs that have run wild, which are numerous in many places in south Europe.

Jackal   *Canis aureus*

With a body length of 65–105 cm and a weight of 7–15 kg, the Jackal is between the Wolf and the Red Fox in size. It is most similar to the former, but has more of a yellowish-red tint—*aureus* means golden. It is also more slender, shorter-legged, and has proportionately smaller paws but bigger ears. Its cry is a mournful howl, which may sometimes develop into a bark. It is found in open terrain in the greater part of Greece, more patchily in the countries north of there. It is also found in large parts of Asia and in North and East Africa. It occurs singly or in small groups. In feeding ecology the Jackal is close to the Red Fox, but it concentrates on berries and fruit to such an extent that it can cause direct damage in such places as maizefields and vineyards. Otherwise it ferrets about on refuse tips and along beaches, and also hunts birds and mammals ranging in size from voles to Roe Deer. Mating takes place early in the year, and the litter is usually born in April.

Wolf *Canis lupus*

Body length 90–150 cm, tail length 33–51 cm, weight 20–80 kg (male), 18–55 kg (female).

In appearance the Wolf is most reminiscent of an alsatian, and it is in fact from the Wolf that the dog originates. The coat is grey or greyish-yellow and slightly blotchy, but the Wolf differs from a Wolf-like dog only in the matter of details: for one thing, the head is broader and looks extra big owing to the heavy ruff of hair on the cheeks. In field observations, therefore, it is the location and the animal's behaviour rather than its appearance that are crucial for specific identification. The Wolf's pawprints are about 100 mm long, but in fact so like the tracks of a large dog that they cannot be separated on isolated prints alone. Longer runs of tracks on the other hand have different characters. The dog moves a little inquisitively and not so purposefully, the Wolf on a more direct and positive course. Its length of stride is normally 110–140 cm and it walks with its feet turned slightly outwards, an important difference compared with the sometimes rather similar tracks of the Lynx. Wolf tracks differ from these in the four front pads being comparatively bigger and in claw impressions usually being visible. In addition, the Wolf is heavy: in snow it sinks about as deep as a grown man on foot. The species is social, and howling cries play a big part in maintaining contacts both within the pack and with other packs.

From having earlier been present over the greater part of Europe and almost the entire northern hemisphere north of 20°N, the Wolf population has declined drastically during the last 300–400 years. The chief cause is human persecution. It became extinct in England and Wales around 1500, but survived in Scotland until about 1740 and in Ireland until about 1770. In Europe it is found in the eastern states, in particular the Soviet, but in numbers that can be counted in thousands in Yugoslavia and Romania and at least in hundreds in Poland, Czechoslovakia and Bulgaria. It occurs also in numbers of roughly this latter size in Greece, Italy, Spain and Portugal. In Scandinavia a few scattered Wolves remain in the north; in 1977 several animals crossed into Sweden from Finland (which in turn received a significant wave of immigrants from the Soviet) and bred in the following year. These Wolves, however, disappeared as quickly as they came and the species' continued existence there seems to depend on a few individuals in west-central Sweden in the border districts with Norway. The Wolf is now a totally protected species in Norway, Sweden and Italy.

The Wolf is extremely adaptable, and was formerly found in every habitat of the northern hemisphere except pure desert. Heavy persecution has gradually driven it out, mainly into wilderness areas but also to regions with dense, and for humans almost impassable, vegetation.

Choice of prey is almost entirely biased towards large mammals. The smallest species anywhere to form the staple food is the beaver, but the deer (Elk, Reindeer, Roe Deer, White-tailed Deer) and cattle families (Bison, Musk Ox, Chamois, Ibex) play a considerably greater role. The chase can stretch over a great many kilometres and often the prey is first bitten in the rear, after which the mortal bite is directed at the neck or head. North American studies have shown that single Wolves there are not capable of killing full-grown Elks (Moose). This does not accord with the situation in Fennoscandia, where in several cases single Wolves have not only succeeded in killing Elks but have for a long time been shown to survive on this prey. The explanation for this apparent difference lies in the fact that the studies have been carried out under completely different conditions. In North America work has been in areas with dense populations of Wolves; there the pack is the natural unit, and isolated Wolves

Jackal

Wolf

123

are outcast individuals, usually animals that are too old, and these cannot cope with killing an Elk. The single Wolves that have been tracked in Fennoscandia, however, have not been outcast and old but without doubt animals in their prime but which have not had any pack to live with. Where natural prey animals are absent, predation may instead be directed against domestic animals of various kinds. In these cases the Wolf is not selective, but where wild prey are concerned the Wolf has been shown in a number of different studies to take mainly young and very old animals or individuals in poor condition. Carcases left behind are exploited by a number of carrion-eaters, and it might be asked whether or not a few Ravens *Corvus corax* here and there live mainly as parasites on the Wolf.

The female is in season from the end of January to the beginning of April—latest in the far north—and after around 63 days' pregnancy the litter is born. It consists of six young on average, but may sometimes contain as many as 11. The female stays near the young for at least two months, and during this time both she and the cubs are fed by the male, at times also by other animals in the pack. The Wolf may become sexually mature at two years of age, but rarely breeds before three.

The Wolf pack lives within a home range which varies with habitat etc from only 100 km^2 or so to more than 10,000 km^2. Here it travels at a speed of approximately 8 km per hour and covers distances of between a few kilometres and up to 70 km per day.

If one gets the chance to compare the tracks of Wolf and fox, the differences are very obvious. The Wolf has a longer stride and is heavier; despite its considerably bigger paws, it sinks deeper into the snow.

Arctic Fox *Alopex lagopus*

Body length 50–85 cm, tail length 28–55 cm, weight 3–8 kg.

The Arctic Fox is unique among European mammals in that it occurs in two different colour morphs. The commoner one is in summer brownish-grey on the face, on the upperside and on the outsides of the legs, and greyish-white below. In winter it is all-white. The other one (the 'Blue Fox') is appreciably darker, almost blue-grey, throughout the year. Genetically these forms behave in such a way that if both parents are normal-coloured, i.e. white in winter, so too are the young. If, however, a normal female pairs with a dark male, two possibilities arise. If the male lacks the capacity for normal colour, all the young are dark; if he has it, about half are dark and half normal-coloured. The white variant blends exceedingly well into a sparkling white winter landscape, but by contrast it is thought that the dark morph must be at a disadvantage there. In fact, the latter comprises only a few percent of the population in Scandinavia. Elsewhere, however, particularly in regions near the sea, it is considerably commoner and, since the proportion of white individuals in such populations decreases the nearer one gets to the water, the dark variant is no doubt an adaptation for hunting on the shores. The winter coat is long and thick, and is a better insulation against rigorous winter cold than the coat of any other carnivore species. The species also displays other adaptations to an arctic climate, including the hairy undersides of the paws. This is alluded to in the scientific specific name, which is a compound of the Greek words *lagos* and *pous*, meaning hare and foot respectively. The young are born in dens which may be hundreds of years old and are provided with dozens of exits. As a result of droppings and food remains, the den gradually comes to be covered with luxuriant vegetation of a completely different kind from that of the surroundings. The Arctic Fox rarely trots but usually moves at a gallop. In so doing, a hindfoot is often placed close to a front footprint in each group of bounding jumps. At other times the

Arctic Fox

hindfoot impressions are set wide apart, when the positioning of the paws can recall the track of a hare. The species has several different barking cries. One of these is a warning cry, another is used against intruders, including mountain walkers, that have happened to come too close to the den.

The species has a circumpolar range across the entire Arctic, and inhabits tundra and open mountains. In Scandinavia it occurs along the entire mountain chain, although with a very uneven distribution. One reason for this is that it seeks areas with hillocks or slopes composed of sand or sandy soil, the only substrate where the den can be excavated.

Norway Lemmings, and to some extent other vole species as well, not only dominate the food but, where they occur, they represent an almost essential prerequisite for breeding. In other places and during poor years for small rodents, the species is forced to turn to anything else edible—e.g. birds, including eggs and young, as well as berries—and in winter carcases killed by other larger species of carnivore are, in many places at least, something of a vital necessity for the Arctic Fox. It is on the whole adaptable. One example of this is that Arctic Foxes living on the coast in areas where the waters are tidal adopt a daily rhythm which involves hunting for food on the uncovered ebb shores.

When there are plenty of small rodents about, i.e. every third or fourth year, the Arctic Foxes breed. Then, at least some sort of hole is excavated in the den as early as March in association with the mating season, and in May/June a litter is born. This may consist of as many as 13 young, although five to ten young are most common. The litter stays around the den until the early autumn.

In Iceland it has been established that the home range can be 8–19 km². Particularly during winters following summers with good breeding success, Arctic Foxes may move long distances and may turn up in wooded country and along coastal regions of the north, far from the open mountain regions where the species really belongs.

Red Fox *Vulpes vulpes*

Body length 58–90 cm, tail length 32–48 cm, weight 5–10 kg, in extreme cases even more than 15 kg.

The reddish-brown colour and the long, bushy tail, which often has a white tip and is held only slightly below the horizontal, makes the Red Fox unmistakable. The ground colour can, however, vary from sandy-beige to pure 'fox-red'. Also characteristic are the white underside and the black on the paws and behind the ears. The normal pace is trotting, and the pawprint is 50–60 mm long. The Red Fox's nocturnal tracks wind forward with many turns and continual detours. These are often related to the search for food, but also to marking of the territory. This is taken care of with droppings placed in prominent places—rocks, stumps etc—and with urine. Both have a very pungent smell, even to the human nose. The den is a hollow with several exits in a mound of stones or a sandy embankment. Foxes also often make use of unoccupied Badger sets or parts of reoccupied ones. During the breeding period there are often prey remains lying outside, and the vegetation is worn away as a result of the young playing. Particularly during calm winter nights, during the mating season, the Red Fox utters a hoarse, slightly hacking bark that dies away, but a total of 28 different cries has been identified in this species.

Few European animal species have a more widespread distribution than the Red Fox. It occurs over the whole of Europe except Iceland and some other islands, including the Balearics. In addition, it is found in North Africa, in Asia east to Japan and south to approximately 20°N, and in a considerable part of northern and central North America. It was introduced to Australia in 1868, after which it quickly spread over the greater part of the continent. The total population in Europe (outside the Soviet) in the spring, before breeding, has been estimated at 660,000 or more foxes.

The Red Fox is tremendously adaptable and there is no habitat in Europe that does not harbour the species. It breeds in city parks and in built-up areas, as well as, in the far north, open mountains above the tree-limit. The density, however, varies a great deal with the habitat. In country with alternating clumps of woodland and open fields it may be one pair per square kilometre, while in a more impoverished environment, e.g. open mountain, it is perhaps one-fortieth of this.

A great deal of the Red Fox's adaptive capacity is based on the fact that it is an opportunist: it feeds on whatever is offered at the time. Despite this, there are certain items as regards food choice that recur in many places. Small mammals—small rodents and lagomorphs—form the major part of the diet. As far as small rodents are concerned, voles are involved more than mice, and it is clearly demonstrated that if the Red Fox has the opportunity to choose then it prefers voles of the genus *Microtus*: it seems quite simply to like them most. At certain localities it may take a great deal of prey among ground-nesting birds, not only the birds themselves but also their eggs and young, while in other places refuse tips or other rubbish play a large role. It is also very fond of sweet berries and fruits. Finally, the Red Fox is very alert to the activities of other larger species of carnivore and readily visits carcases left by them. It finds these by following either the carnivore itself or its tracks, but by so doing it exposes itself to certain risks. At any rate, both Lynx and Wolf may occasionally kill such foxes.

The mating season varies with latitude within the period December–February, the females having an oestrus period of three weeks but fertilisation being possible during only three days. After around 52 days' pregnancy the

Red Fox

young are born, from the beginning of March to the beginning of May. The whole course of events is delayed by a cold winter with heavy snow, and in fact happens later in the north than in the south. When food is scarce breeding may not take place, and food availability governs the size of the litter. This can vary between one and nine—the average is near four—and the newborn cub weighs about 100 g. The young remain in the vicinity of the den until the end of the summer, within the parents' home range for a further few months, and go their own way late in the autumn. Their mortality in the first year is high: in some areas it may reach 80%.

It has long been thought that foxes live in pairs. Studies of animals by radio telemetry, however, have shown that more complex social patterns actually exist. A male may keep company with several females, and one-year-old females may stay behind at the den and lend a hand in the raising of the following year's litter. The Red Fox can be affected by fox-mange. This is a parasite that attacks the fox's fur, which falls out in tangled knots. The affected animal tries to scratch the exposed areas, tearing holes in the skin, following which the wounds become infected. In the end the fox freezes to death. The distribution of this disease, however, is uneven. In some areas the majority of foxes are infected, in others practically none.

When the Red Fox catches a vole, it may locate it by sense of hearing and then press it hard against the ground following a leap high in the air (top). The droppings are often deposited on such places as a stump (right) and act as a territory marker. Fox-mange (lower right) is caused by a parasite that attacks the fox's coat and in the end brings about the animal's death.

hunting vole

droppings on stump

normal-coloured and 'cross' variety

fox-mange

Raccoon-dog *Nyctereutes procyonoides*

The Raccoon-dog is 55–80 cm long, has a tail length of 15–26 cm and weighs 5–10 kg. Although it may possibly be confused with the Raccoon, it has quite different markings both on the face and on the tail, besides having a much heavier coat. The outer hairs in the winter coat can be up to 120 mm long. The natural range encompasses large parts of eastern Asia, including Japan. From here the species has been introduced to the European part of the Soviet and then spread westwards. The first breeding in Finland was confirmed in 1962, and 20 years later the greater part of that country was occupied. A couple of discoveries were made in the far north of Sweden during the 1940s, and 30 years later the species had spread southwards and a few individuals had reached Götaland. The expansion is also going on in central Europe, where at the beginning of the 1980s the species reached Denmark and France via Germany. The Raccoon-dog prefers woodland, especially if it is damp and has luxuriant undergrowth. If there is water near at hand, it often seeks food on the shores. In such cases, frogs, fish etc are included in the diet, which is otherwise dominated by small rodents but also consists of insects and vegetable matter. In the more northerly parts of its range the Raccoon-dog goes into a winter sleep in a fox or Badger earth or in a den which it excavates itself. The winter rest is often interrupted during milder spells. The female is in season in February–March, and the litter consists of two to eight young, in extreme cases up to as many as ten. The species is markedly nocturnal and the scientific generic name alludes to this. It is formed from the Greek *nuktos*, genitive of night, and *ereuna*, which means seeking.

Raccoon-dog

Bears   Family *Ursidae*

The bears have the least purely flesh-orientated diet of all carnivores, and for the majority of this family of only seven species plant food plays a large part. This is reflected, for example, in the appearance of the teeth: the cheek teeth have blunt ridges and are consequently more suited to grinding and crushing than to cutting. The bears are plantigrades and have five toes on each foot.

Brown Bear   *Ursus arctos*

Body length 130–250 cm, tail length 5–15 cm, weight 100–315 kg (male), 60–200 kg (female).

With its size and shape—the thick legs, the powerful neck and the humpback—the Brown Bear is unmistakable. The coat, which is usually brown, can, however, vary between different individuals across the whole spectrum from light greyish-yellow to almost black. It may also be long-haired to a greater or lesser degree. Many young bears have a conspicuous pale neck collar. The tracks, too, are characteristic. More often than not they show impressions of all five claws on each foot, the hind footprint with its pronounced heel imprint is very reminiscent of a human footprint, and no other European animal species walks with its legs so wide apart as the bear. The droppings can vary a great deal, but the piles of droppings are usually large and their contents often easy to identify—they give the impression of having been poorly worked during the passage through the alimentary canal. The bear also leaves other signs behind it, in particular excavated anthills, overturned rocks, as well as bite and scratch marks on the vegetation. Many of these anthills are characteristic—they are attacked from above, and parts of the contents may be tossed or flung several metres to the side—but faced with signs of this kind one should always reflect on whether any other animal species could be involved. The discovery of footprints or hairs can help to determine this. A larger prey animal killed by a bear usually shows signs of violent blows. It is also flayed, entirely or partially, in a very skilled fashion and may be covered over, for example with moss. Around the corpse there are also likely to be plenty of droppings.

In Europe, where the species previously had a wide distribution, it is still found nowadays in Fennoscandia, the Soviet and as relict populations in mountain regions of southern Europe—in the Pyrenees, the Alps, the Apennines, the Carpathians and the Balkans. The populations in both the Pyrenees and the Alps consist of at most about ten animals which have managed to survive in a few, so far relatively isolated, long valleys. In addition it is found to the east in large parts of Asia, as well as in parts of North America, where in some places it is called the Grizzly. The word *arctos* has nothing to do with the Arctic, but is a Greek word for bear. Around 1975 a census in Sweden gave a total of 400–600 animals, and the annual 'bag' (since 1981, only hunting by licence has been permitted there) tends to remain at between ten and 40 bears.

The Brown Bear is a forest animal and its presence, especially in the Old World, coincides well with the distribution of the great coniferous forest regions. Old spruce forest is particularly important. Good bear habitats also contain sectors of terrain that are steep and difficult of access. A number of other habitats, e.g. bare mountain tops, cultivated land, open clearings and bogs, are visited by the bears, but in such instances it is often a case of searching for food.

The major part of the Brown Bear's food is made up of vegetable matter. In the spring it digs up roots and finds sprouting grass and plants, and in the summer green plant material of every conceivable kind predominates. Bilberries

Brown Bear

and other berries appear in the excrement as soon as they begin to ripen, and become the most important food throughout the late summer and autumn. Many bears build up their winter fat reserves on a diet almost entirely of berries. Of the animal food, ants are important particularly in the spring. Added to this are some large mammals—of wild species, e.g. Elk, and of domesticated animals, mostly Reindeer, sheep and cows—which the bear itself kills. In Fennoscandia most reports of hunting of Elks and Reindeer are in the spring. One reason for this is that they are no doubt easiest to find then, but it may also be the case that in spring it may be more difficult for the bears to find vegetable food. Sometimes hunting is by stealth, at other times by fierce pursuit which can carry on for several kilometres. The bear can derive advantage from crusted snow which will support it but not the Elk, and at least where Reindeer are concerned it is striking that the hunter is often a smaller bear.

The young are born in the middle of winter, from the end of December to February. They are then blind, hairless and weigh only 260–625 g, in other words not much more than a squirrel. The development of the fetus has been in progress for eight to ten weeks up to birth, but the female's season does not fall during late autumn but in early summer, from the end of May to July. Implantation is therefore delayed for four-and-a-half to seven months. The young normally winter in the company of the female, both as one-year- and two-year-olds, and do not leave her until the third summer. Three years is in fact probably the interval between litters. The most usual litter size is two, and the bear does not become sexually mature before five years of age at the earliest.

The Brown Bear hibernates for five to six months in the north (October/November–April) and three to four months farther south (December/January–March). It eats nothing at this time, and many body functions are very much depressed. Digestion and urine production, for example, cease altogether and the heartbeat is down to ten per minute compared with the normal 40. Since the body temperature is also lowered, from around 38° to 33–34°C, perhaps we should call the winter rest torpor rather than sleep. The Brown Bear's home range is large, but can vary very considerably with the habitat. The female's may comprise anything from 10 km² up to about 200 km², and the male's can be even greater than 2,000 km².

The Brown Bear has five toes with very powerful claws on each foot. The heelprint is usually more visible in the tracks of the hindfoot than in those of the front foot.

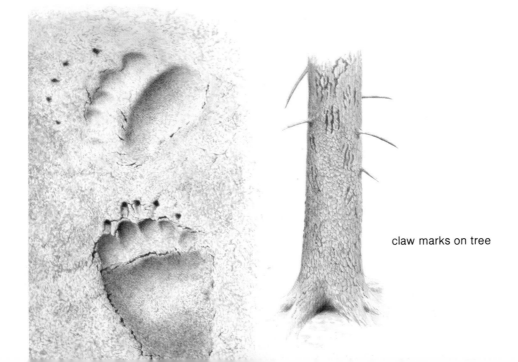

claw marks on tree

Polar Bear *Thalarctos maritimus*

The Polar Bear, which is 1.6–2.5 m long and can weigh up to 700 kg, is impossible to confuse with any other animal species owing to its size, its white or yellowish-white fur and of course also its geographical habitat. It is circumpolar, confined to high-arctic coasts and sea-ice, and tracks and droppings can be found only a few kilometres from the geographical North Pole. In Europe the main area for the species is Svalbard, but wandering animals may turn up in Iceland or in north Norway, sometimes no doubt with the help of the drift-ice. The species has been heavily hunted, but since 1976 has been protected in the Arctic through an international agreement which permits hunting only by the local inhabitants and only by traditional methods. The Polar Bear has adapted to a flesh diet more than any other species of bear. Seals, mainly Ringed Seal, form most of the food, which also consists of fish, seabirds and birds' eggs as well as carrion. There are observations of over 40 Polar Bears gathered around a stranded whale corpse. Seals are not taken in the water, but either at the breathing holes or when they are lying at the edge of some ice, at which time the bear's attack comes from the water. It can put away at least 40 kg of flesh and blubber in one meal. The young are born around the turn of the year in a hollow, more often than not on a steep slope high up on a mountainside. Mating takes place in March–April, but implantation is delayed throughout the summer. The young are poorly developed at birth, weighing 410–840 g, but grow quickly. The mother's milk contains 30% fat, a higher value than in any other species of carnivore. The species does not hibernate like the Brown Bear, but many Polar Bears doze through at least periods of poor weather during the depths of winter. They then either allow themselves to be covered with snow or dig themselves in.

Raccoon *Procyon lotor*

Body length 48–70 cm, tail length 20–26 cm, weight up to 8 kg.

The black 'highwayman's mask' and the bushy tail with black rings are the best identification marks on the Raccoon.

It belongs to the family Procyonidae, where *pro* means before and *cyon* comes from a Greek word for dog. The family belongs to the New World, and the Raccoon was introduced from North America after the 1930s, gained its liberty and quickly increased in numbers in several places in Europe. Large populations are found in particular in West and East Germany and in adjacent parts of most bordering countries.

The proximity of water is the major habitat requirement. If this is fulfilled, the species can adapt to wooded habitats of many and varied kinds. The densest populations in Europe are found in oakwoods. One reason for this may be that acorns are an important food, especially in winter, another that the animals have plenty of suitable breeding holes there.

The Raccoon is omnivorous, and the food varies greatly depending on season, locality etc. Acorns have been mentioned, and other important vegetable foods are sweet berries and fruits together with oats. It may break off small branches up in a plum tree in order to get at the much-sought-after fruits, and it gathers up oats into sheaves which it holds under one 'arm' and feeds from. Animal food taken includes insect larvae, eggs and young of ground-nesting birds, as well as mammals from small rodents up to young hares.

In March–May a litter of three to four young is born in a hollow, often high up in a tree.

In poor weather in winter the species may stay in its den for up to a week, but it only needs the sun to appear and it readily goes out, even if the weather is both snowy and cold.

Raccoon

Weasels and other mustelids   Family *Mustelidae*

This family consists of 60 or so species and is represented in all parts of the world except Australasia. The typical mustelid is small or medium-sized with a long, slender body and rather short legs. It has five clawed toes on both front and back paws, and powerful anal glands which open at the anus and give a pungent odour to the droppings.

Many, but not all, species of mustelid have delayed implantation. The period between fertilisation and implantation of the egg, however, varies greatly: in the Stoat it may amount to 11 months, while in the American Mink it is only about one month.

Only exceptionally do mustelids trot. They move with bounding leaps, which means that all four paws are placed near one another each time the animal lands. Sometimes the hindpaws are set down exactly in the impressions left by the front paws. In each set of bounds, impressions from only two paws are then visible (paired prints). At other times only a single hindpaw is placed in one front pawprint; then a triple print is formed instead.

Pawprints are not all that one can see along the routes taken by mustelids, especially those of the small and medium-sized species. Sometimes clear impressions of the animal's underside are also visible. Most obvious perhaps is that of the Otter, which may actually 'slide' long distances. This is a way of scent-marking: glands on the animal's underside release scent secretions when they are rubbed against the substrate.

Prey are usually killed with a bite on the back of the neck. Where small prey are concerned, this is often made so high up that it crushes the back part of the skull.

Both Otter and other mustelids may slide on snow-clad slopes.

Stoat *Mustela erminea*

Body length 18–31 cm, tail length 5.5–12.5 cm, weight 75–445 g. The male is about 50% bigger than the female, and there are also very wide regional variations: in England, for example, the weight of adult males varies between 200 g and 445 g, in the Soviet between 134 g and 191 g.

The all-black outer part of the tail, present at all times, is the best identification mark on the Stoat and the one that should be looked for if one catches only a glimpse of a 'weasel'. Often, however, there is no need to satisfy oneself with a mere glimpse: the species is inquisitive and may come out and show itself at close quarters if given a little time. The rest of the coat is brown above and yellowish-white below in summer. In the winter those Stoats living in the far north change their coat to white, though still with a black tip to the tail, while those in the south retain the brown upperside in winter. The two types overlap in a quite narrow zone, where various intermediate forms also occur.

The commonest tracks are the paired prints characteristic of mustelids. Very often they are slightly irregular, with short and long bounds alternating. The tracks of a small female and of a Weasel, or those of a large male and an American Mink, can be very difficult to distinguish on size alone. In comparison with the American Mink, the Stoat is, however, more 'inquisitive'. If it passes a hole of any sort, it usually cannot help diving into it.

The species is absent from the greater part of the Mediterranean region and from Iceland, but is otherwise found in the whole of Europe. It also occurs eastwards throughout Asia.

The Stoat is not confined to any fixed biotope, but occurs in all habitats from open seashores to bare mountain tops. It seems nevertheless to show a certain preference for damp ground, as well as for ditches and stone walls.

The food consists mainly of small rodents—mice and voles—but varies both seasonally and between the sexes. Particularly in the spring and early summer, when the females hunt mostly water voles and Field Voles, the males change over to larger prey, such as young of hares and Rabbits and birds. During periods when small rodents are in very poor supply, the Stoat may change to completely different food: earthworms, insects and frogs, as well as fruit and berries. The female consumes food equivalent to around two small voles per day, the male about double that.

Mating occurs during the period May–August—the old females mate first, the young ones later—and the young are born in April or May, in other words after a long period of fetal development. The litter size varies between five and 12 young, and during poor rodent years reproduction may not take place. The newborn young have fluffy pale hair, and a conspicuous brown mane which the female seizes hold of if she needs to move them. The female and the litter stay together until July/August. By then the young have learned to hunt for themselves and the family splits up.

The size of the home range varies with such factors as season and surroundings. In various studies the female's has been found to be 5–10 ha, the male's about three or four times bigger. In a Swedish study each female controlled about 1.5 km of stone wall, while the equivalent for males was around 5 km. The Stoat is an expert swimmer and climber.

Stoat

winter

summer

Weasel *Mustela nivalis*

To give measurement data for the Weasel without at the same time stating the geographical origin of the animals measured is meaningless: in terms of percentages, there is no European animal species that varies more in size. The species is smallest in the north, largest in the south. As an example, the male's total length—that is the distance from nose tip to tail tip—may be given. This is 172–227 mm in north Sweden, 215–295 mm in England and 263–382 mm in Greece. The equivalents for females are 167–194 mm, 205–255 mm and 228–285 mm. The tail length also varies widely. In Sweden it reaches 30–60 mm, in England 40–75 mm, and in Greece 70–88 mm in the female and all of 65–125 mm in the male.

If an observer accustomed to seeing the small northern form is brought face to face with the southern European one, he cannot but be amazed. Were it not for the non-black tip of the tail, he would doubtless take the animal for a Stoat. Nevertheless the two forms are today considered only geographical races of the same species. The northern one, known as the Snow Weasel (*M. n. nivalis*), is identified by its winter coat being all-white (although occasional individuals have larger or smaller remnants of the dark summer coat), by the border between the white underside and the (in summer) brown upperside being almost straight, and by the paws often having white on top. The southern form (*M. n. vulgaris*) is brown above in winter, too, and has a very irregular border between this brown and the underside, a dark upperside to the paws, and often a dark cheek patch behind the corner of the mouth. The boundary between the two forms is fairly distinct, and in Sweden overlap occurs only in a narrow belt in the south.

The Weasel is found over the whole of Europe except Iceland and Ireland. It is also present in North Africa and in large parts of Asia and North America. It is thought to have reached many islands, particularly those in the Mediterranean region, with human assistance.

It is sometimes said that the species occurs everywhere where there are voles or mice, but, even though there is a lot in this assertion, the Weasel is more specialised than the Stoat. The staple food varies greatly between different areas. In some places Field Voles and Bank Voles are favourite prey, and abandoned grasslands and clearings therefore important haunts. In other places various species of mice predominate, as well as other prey; for example, Rabbits and birds and their eggs form part of the diet.

Breeding follows a totally different pattern from that of the Stoat. There is no delayed implantation in this species, but the litter, which usually consists of one to seven young, is born after 34–37 days' pregnancy. This means that the Weasel, better than the Stoat, can quickly react to a sudden improvement in availability of small rodents. The majority of litters are born in April–May, but Weasels may sometimes be seen with small young in later summer or early autumn. Such late-born litters are either second litters or the litters of young females which were themselves born in the same year.

The size of the home range varies with prey availability. It has been established that it can vary between 1 ha and 25 ha in the male; in the female it is appreciably smaller.

Weasel

Weasel, Greece

Snow Weasel, summer

4 examples from north-central Sweden

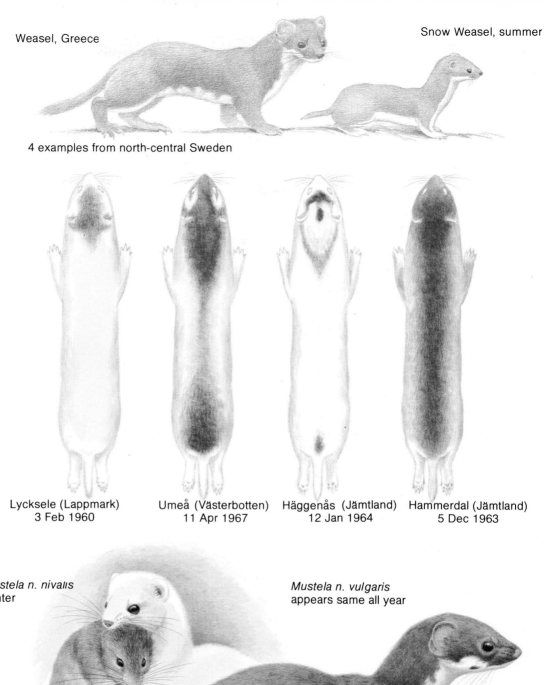

Lycksele (Lappmark)
3 Feb 1960

Umeå (Västerbotten)
11 Apr 1967

Häggenås (Jämtland)
12 Jan 1964

Hammerdal (Jämtland)
5 Dec 1963

Mustela n. nivalis
winter

Mustela n. vulgaris
appears same all year

American Mink *Mustela vison*

Body length 30–47 cm, tail length 13–23 cm, weight normally 2 kg at the most but males in captivity can weigh up to as much as 3 kg.

An encounter with an American Mink often involves nothing more than a head coming swiftly to the surface and equally rapidly disappearing, leaving no impression other than the ever inquisitive look of the mustelid. Longer observation reveals a glossy, brownish-black coat with a white mark under the chin, sometimes also a white patch on the throat. Animals that have escaped from fur farms may be totally different in colour. The tracks may be typical paired prints, but on harder surfaces there are often impressions of all four paws in each set of bounds. The small web found between the toes is visible only under near-perfect conditions. The tracks begin and end at water. The droppings are like the Otter's both in appearance and in where they are placed, but have a foul smell.

This mink originates from North America. It was introduced to northern Europe in the early 1900s as a farmed animal, but it was not long before escapes established feral populations. In other places, mainly in the Soviet Union, the species has been deliberately set down as a game species of value for hunting. The species is now widespread in Britain, particularly in eastern and southern England, and is also found in several pockets in Ireland. Other feral populations exist in Scandinavia, Iceland, eastern Europe and elsewhere.

The species is very adaptable and occurs beside water of every conceivable kind: offshore islands, large and small lakes, rivers and small streams, even those high above the tree-line.

The food varies a great deal both with season and with habitat. During the winter months it is mostly fish, which at that time are easy to come by as a result of their reduced activity and mobility when the water becomes colder. During the summer months, mammals, birds, crayfish and amphibians predominate instead. The mammals consist almost entirely of small rodents, exceptions being the occasional shrew, mole and lagomorph, and the proportion fluctuates widely with the yearly variations in the populations. In the case of birds, ducks and gulls predominate and a large part of the food taken in early summer is young birds. The American Mink is therefore no specialist but kills whatever it comes across, and there is a tendency for the male to hunt on land to a greater degree than the female. In North America, and also in parts of the Soviet Union, the Muskrat constitutes by far the major part of the food.

The mating period falls in February–April, following which fetal development is delayed for 13–50 days. The actual gestation period after that is 28–30 days, which means that the young are born some time in April–May. The litter, which normally consists of four to six young but in captivity up to as many as 17, remains together until the end of the summer.

The turnover in an American Mink population is rapid. In studies in two or three different places, all the animals have been found to disappear and to be replaced by new ones within only three years. The home range can embrace a stretch of shore of 1.5–6 km.

American Mink

paired tracks

quadruple tracks

Western Polecat *Mustela putorius*

Body length 30–46 cm (male), 29–36 cm (female), tail length 9–18 cm, weight 0.5–1.5 kg (male), 0.45–0.8 kg (female).

The best identification mark on the Western Polecat is the pale edge of the ear. This, together with the face pattern—which, however, varies regionally—gives the species a characteristic appearance. Furthermore, the coat has a distinctive lustre caused by the fact that the pale underfur shines through the darker, sparse hairs of the outer coat. The tracks resemble the Pine Marten's but the individual footprint is shorter, up to 3.5 cm compared with up to 5 cm in the marten. The bounds, too, are shorter—40–60 cm against normally 50–100 cm for the marten—and are grouped in prints of three or four paws more often than one paired print. In addition to this, the Western Polecat is a poor climber and jumper.

The species is found over the greater part of Europe, but is absent in the southeast and also in the north, where too harsh a winter climate puts a halt to its distribution. In Britain it is confined to Wales and the border country of England. It lives principally in low-lying, damp environments, where it makes use both of wooded areas and of more open terrain, and it is not at all afraid of moving about close to buildings. Now and then it may even settle down inside barns and other outhouses. In several places the species is considered to have decreased in numbers in recent times, and this is thought to be connected with the contraction of wetland areas.

In many places the Western Polecat's main food is small rodents, but the choice of prey is wide and includes everything from hares, and birds the size of hares, to lizards, insects and earthworms. The sense of smell when hunting is more important in the Western Polecat than in other mustelid species. The Western Polecat gets into poultry houses more often than any other mustelid, and it may occasionally cause mass slaughter.

The female is in season in March–June, but at least in some areas not all one-year-old animals take part in breeding. The litter, which normally consists of five to ten young, is born after 40–42 days, i.e. without delayed fetal development.

The Western Polecat has very well-developed anal glands which give off a secretion both when the animal marks its territory and—probably as a pure reflex—when it is alarmed. The secretion stinks, and the scientific specific name comes from the Latin *putor*, which means 'foul smell'.

A close relative of the Western Polecat is the Ferret. It is usually regarded as a race (*M. p. furo*) of that species, sometimes as a full species (*M. furo*), and sometimes as a race (*M. eversmanni furo*) of the Steppe Polecat, from which it differs, however, in number of chromosomes. The Ferret is a domesticated animal of unknown origin which is used, often in albino form (i.e. with yellowish-white coat and red eyes), in hunting Rabbits. Feral populations, partially mixed with Western Polecats, are found on some islands, both off England and Scotland and in the Mediterranean. The Ferret has been introduced into New Zealand in an attempt to control the Rabbit population. This, however, has not been successful: the Ferret prefers indigenous animal species and has become very widespread.

Western Polecat

Steppe Polecat *Mustela eversmanni*

The Steppe Polecat is the same size as the Western Polecat, and resembles it also in every other respect apart from the colour of its body. It is much lighter, almost beige, particularly on the back and the sides. In the past it has often been regarded as only a race of the Western Polecat (*M. putorius eversmanni*), but in the broad zone where both forms occur together they are now looked upon as separate species. The range is easterly and includes steppe and semi-desert areas in large parts of interior Asia. So far as is known, the places where it occurs in east Europe—Hungary, Austria, Czechoslovakia, Poland and East Germany—represent isolated relics of a previously more continuous distribution.

Steppe Polecat

146

European Mink *Mustela lutreola*

Body length 28–40 cm, tail length 12–19 cm, weight up to 1.5 kg.

The European Mink is glossy brownish-black with a distinct white upper lip. There may also be some white on the lower lip and in the form of a spot or streak under the chin. During the 1800s it occurred over the whole of middle Europe, but the range contracted and by the middle of the 1900s the species was found from Finland, Poland and Romania eastwards to about 75°E, in addition to a small area in France. Since then it has probably decreased still further: there were, for example, no reports from Finland during the whole of the 1970s. The reasons for this very marked decline have not been clarified, but heavy pressure from hunting on account of the valuable fur, deterioration in breeding success as a result of the effects of habitat pollution, together with competition from the American Mink may all have contributed. The species' association with water is indicated by the scientific specific name. This is a diminutive of the name for the Otter and therefore means more or less a small otter. The food is in fact collected in or beside water and consists mainly of fish, amphibians and small rodents, but also of crayfish and other invertebrate animals. There is no delayed implantation in this species, but the season falls during the late winter and the young are born in April–May, after 35–42 days' pregnancy. The home range in the summer runs to 15–20 ha.

European Mink

Marbled Polecat *Vormela peregusna*

Owing to its very distinctive colour pattern, the Marbled Polecat, which with a body length of 28–38 cm is slightly smaller than the Western Polecat, is unmistakable among European mammals. The whole underside is dark brownish-black, while the back is mottled brownish-black and white or yellowish-white. A broad, white band runs above the eyes from cheek to cheek, and the ears, relatively big in comparison with those of other polecat species, are also edged with white. The anal glands are very well developed, and if alarmed the Marbled Polecat can release a foul-smelling secretion. In Europe it is found only within a small area in the southeast: Romania, Bulgaria, Yugoslavia and northernmost Greece. From there the range extends eastwards through Asia to westernmost China. It lives in dry and open terrain, which means semi-desert and steppe regions as well as cultivated land with, for example, maizefields and vineyards. Small rodents are the most important food but other items are also taken; these include larger mammals such as hamsters, together with birds, frogs, insects etc. Mating takes place in January–February, and the litter, which normally consists of four to eight young, is born in March–April.

Marbled Polecat

Pine Marten *Martes martes*

Body length 36–56 cm, tail length 17–28 cm, weight 0.5–1.8 kg. The female is 10–25% shorter and lighter than the male, and there are reports of males weighing up to 2.2 kg.

The Pine Marten is warm brown with a long, fairly bushy tail and an irregular yellowish-white patch on the throat and breast. When on the move, the species looks considerably longer-legged than other small or medium-sized mustelids. It has many calls, including a shrill noise with a slight gurgling tone reminiscent of a cat. This is heard, among other times, from the young, both in the den and later during the summer when they move around in the home range. Despite the fact that the Pine Marten is an able climber, it moves a great deal on the ground (according to Finnish studies, up to 99% and more of the time). Usually it leaves paired prints from a bound 50–100 cm in length. If the surface is fairly hard, however, it places neither of the back paws or just one of them in the prints of the front paws. In each group of bounds there are then three or four impressions, the latter not uncommonly positioned in a way that can recall the tracks of a hare. The individual pawprint is up to 5 cm long, but the exact size can be difficult to measure since the outline is indistinct owing to the luxuriant fur on the soles of the feet.

The Pine Marten is absent from Iceland and the greater part of the Iberian peninsula, as well as from Greece and immediately north of there, but elsewhere it is found over almost the whole of Europe. In Britain a small relict population still exists in north Wales and locally in a few other areas, but the species is most numerous in north Scotland, where it has benefited from afforestation.

Even though the Pine Marten lives in open terrain in some areas, it is on the whole confined to forests. The density of populations varies widely. Russian and Swedish studies show that there are two or three times more Pine Martens in old forest than in modern forestry areas with a large element of planted, younger woodland.

Pine Marten

The Pine Marten's droppings are often placed on an elevated site and act as a territory marker.

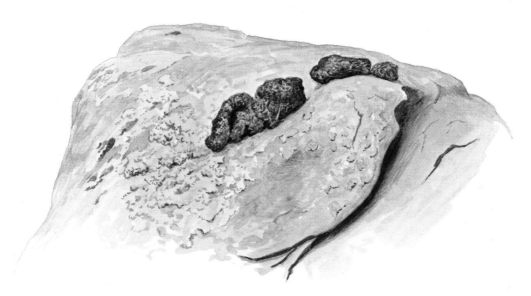

The food varies a great deal with both area and season. In winter in northern coniferous forests, it is mainly mammals (small rodents, hares and squirrels) together with birds (mostly grouse and other gallinaceous birds, but also for example Great Spotted Woodpecker *Dendrocopos major*). In the case of squirrels, there are reports from Russia that in poor rodent years the Red Squirrel can constitute more than half of the prey taken by the Pine Marten; when small rodents are more numerous, the proportion of squirrels then drops to about 10%. The Pine Marten also seeks out carcases of Elks and Reindeer, which may in fact account for up to 10% of the food. It finds a good deal of this type of food by 'parasitic tracking', i.e. following tracks of other larger species of carnivore. In Scotland, small birds—tits, Treecreepers *Certhia familiaris* etc—are important prey, and in deciduous forest areas in central and southern Europe the species may change in summer–autumn to a diet consisting almost entirely of berries and fruits. A good deal of the hunting within the marten's own home range seems to be based on the animal learning where it is successful, and then remembering this. This has been demonstrated in a Norwegian study and may doubtless apply also to other species of mustelids. What was studied was the extent to which Pine Martens preyed on nests of Tengmalm's Owl *Aegolius funereus*, a bird that normally nests in hollow trees but which may also breed in nestboxes that have been specially erected. The Pine Martens took fewer broods from nestboxes that had been in position for one to three years than from those that had been up for four to 13 years. In addition, it was more common for the brood to be taken from those nestboxes where the nest had also been plundered the year before than from those where the previous year's nesting had been successful.

The female is in season in July–August, and, after a long period of delayed implantation (five-and-a-half to six-and-a-half months), there is a true pregnancy of about 30 days. The young are born in April–May. They weigh about 30 g, and the litter normally consists of one to five young. At two to three months of age they still move with remarkable caution, and give the impression of almost clinging to the branch they are on. This is an adaptation to the den site, which more often than not is high up in a tree where the slightest mistake by a young with incompletely developed motor co-ordination can be fatal.

The home range is normally a few square kilometres, and daily movements of anything from only a few metres to 65 km are known. There are reports from Finland of Pine Martens forming part of the prey of the Golden Eagle *Aquila chrysaetos*.

*On snow, the Pine Marten usually
leaves neat paired tracks behind it.*

Beech Marten *Martes foina*

The Beech Marten is very like the Pine Marten but a shade heavier and not quite so long-legged. It is perhaps most easily identified by the throat patch, which is almost pure white and has a slightly different shape: the brown on the belly continues some distance up the breast and divides the patch into two parts, one meeting each front leg. In addition, the white underfur shows through slightly more than in the Pine Marten. The range includes the whole of central and southern Europe, and the species is also found eastwards through Asia to Mongolia. It is absent from Britain and Ireland and Scandinavia. In Denmark, the population has greatly increased since the middle of the 1950s. The Beech Marten is in no way confined to woodland like the Pine Marten, and the difference in habitat choice is evident from a French study where both the species had been trapped. Of the Pine Martens, 70% were caught in woodland and none within built-up areas; the corresponding figures for the Beech Marten were 14% and 69% respectively. The Beech Marten's special liking for buildings means that, despite its mainly nocturnal habits, it is easy to observe. Unfortunately, it is also unpopular in many places since it not only resorts to built-up areas but also gets inside buildings. In such areas it can do considerable damage to houses, mainly in the outer panelling and insulation.

Sable *Martes zibellina*

The Sable has a body length of 32–46 cm and a tail length of 14–18 cm. It is thus a little smaller than the Pine Marten, but the two species are similar to each other and can even hybridise. The Sable, however, is longer-legged and has considerably larger ears. Its lightweight, dense-haired and very valuable fur varies in colour among different individuals from brownish-black to light brown. The throat area is palest, but not so that one could talk of an actual throat patch. The Sable belongs to the taiga—the coniferous forest of the far north—originally all the way from easternmost Siberia to the very north of Scandinavia, where it was still found in the 1600s. During the following centuries the species was subjected to very heavy hunting, and the range contracted and the population diminished. In 1935 a five-year ban was introduced on both hunting and trafficking in Sable in the whole of the Soviet Union. At the same time extensive restocking was carried out. With that the decline was halted, the population began to grow and nowadays the Sable is again hunted, but with the observance of controls. Its own hunting is directed to a large extent against forest birds. Squirrels are included, as also are small rodents, but these are not so important for the Sable as they are for the Pine Marten. Mating takes place in June–July and the young are born, after long-delayed fetal development, in April–May.

Beech Marten

Sable

Beech Marten

Sable

Wolverine *Gulo gulo*

Body length 70–83 cm, tail length 13–25 cm, weight 9–25 kg.

The Wolverine is Europe's largest species of mustelid. Some individuals are dark brown, almost black, others very much paler. The coat is often bleached by the sun, particularly in the summer. A more or less distinct paler band extends along the side, forwards over the forehead and backwards to the upper part of the bushy tail. The species is powerfully built, short-legged and has big paws. It moves in a gallop and leaves an obvious track, most often paired or triple prints.

The range is circumpolar, and in the Old World the species is found on the tundra or mountain moorland and the taiga, all the way from east Siberia to Scandinavia. It occurs, albeit with a fairly uneven distribution, from northernmost Lapland to south of 62°N in Sweden, where the population has been estimated at 125–150 individuals, and even farther south on the west coast of Norway. At the beginning of the century roughly the same number of Wolverines were shot annually in Sweden as are now estimated to survive there. The species has therefore declined considerably since then. It was placed under protection from 1969, and was for several years after considered to be threatened with extinction. From the mid 1970s the population has, however, recovered somewhat. Occasional Wolverines perform long-distance movements that can take them far down into the lowland wooded areas.

In their breeding areas the Wolverines come into contact with several different habitats: bare mountain, mountain birch forest, sub-montane coniferous forest, and open areas lower down in the wood such as bogs and lakes. In the winter time pregnant females certainly move within each and every one of these habitats roughly in proportion to the habitat's share of the home range. By contrast, they catch most of their food in the coniferous forest.

In the winter the Wolverine lives to a great extent on Reindeer, both animals which it kills itself and carcases which it finds. The latter may, for example, have been killed by other carnivore species or died in accidents. For successful hunting of Reindeer it is very dependent on favourable snow conditions, and on loose snow it is supported far better than the Reindeer: the Reindeer's pressure on the ground surface is eight to ten times greater per square centimetre. The whole carcase is broken into pieces, after which the pieces are carried away and concealed for later use. This has given the Wolverine the reputation for greediness, hence its alternative name of Glutton. The food in summer is less well known, but it probably consists of a wide assortment of smaller mammals and birds mixed with a great deal of vegetable matter.

The young are born in the depths of winter, in February–March. They are usually two or three in number and the den is usually deep down in a hanging snowdrift. Mating has taken place some time between April and August of the previous year, but implantation has not occurred until around, or even after, the turn of the year. The female becomes sexually mature during her second year. Thereafter she has young as a rule every year, but as a consequence of poor food availability breeding may sometimes not take place. The young remain within the female's home range at least until late in the autumn, female young sometimes for longer.

The female's home range varies between 50 km² and 350 km². During the spring it becomes a territory which she closely defends against other females, in particular through constant marking with well-developed scent glands. The male lives within a considerably larger area, 600–1,000 km², and therefore roams within the domains of several females.

Wolverine

The Wolverine has five toes on each foot and a clear heelprint is often visible in the tracks.

Badger *Meles meles*

Body length 67–90 cm, tail length 11–20 cm, weight usually 9–17 kg in males, 6–14 kg in females, with very wide variation between different seasons. Badgers do not hibernate, but in cold climates they become semi-dormant for long periods, feeding on their stored fat. Weights in late autumn may be 3 kg greater than in spring in Britain, much more in northern and eastern Europe.

The black-and-white-striped head, the all-black underside and the shaggy grey back make the Badger unmistakable. The hair on the back and sides, which is used to make shaving brushes, is characteristic. It is sometimes found in tufts on the bottom wires of a barbed-wire fence that the Badger has slipped under but where the gap was slightly too small. These hairs are light-coloured at both the base and the tip, but dark in the middle. The pawprints are also distinctive. They point slightly inwards, are at least as broad as they are long, and have five clawed toes placed in a slight curve. The sets, which may be tens and sometimes perhaps hundreds of years old, have many entrances. They are looked after with great care: sand or earth that has fallen down is dug out, and in the autumn the Badger makes its bed for the winter with dry plant material. This is gathered together into an 'armful' between the forelegs and the chin, after which the animal backs into the set, dragging in the material. Toilet pits—open small holes with droppings in—are often present. The latter are also found at the boundaries of the territory, and the territory-marking purpose of the droppings is reinforced with secretions from the anal glands.

The species is found throughout Europe, except the extreme north and on several of the islands in the Mediterranean. It occurs eastwards through Asia as far as Japan. It has expanded northwards in Scandinavia since the mid 1800s. In Britain and Ireland it is widespread, being particularly common in the south and west of Britain.

The densest Badger populations are found in country where woodland, particularly deciduous, alternates with pasture or cultivated ground and the ground at the same time either is easy to dig or offers natural hollows for sets. The species also occurs in pure wooded terrain. In Britain suburban areas are often used, and sets may be sited on railway embankments and in large gardens.

The food is very diverse, and also varies between different regions, but earthworms are by far the most important items in most places. The Badger consumes most of what it finds during its nocturnal travels—insects, slugs, birds' eggs and the nests of small mammals, including Rabbits which it digs out. Certain individuals seem able to specialise in very odd kinds of food, e.g. Hedgehog. During the autumn vegetable matter becomes more and more significant, and berries, fruit, nuts and grain, particularly oats, are important for putting on fat reserves before the winter.

Both the male and the female become sexually mature at around one year of age, but the majority of females do not have young before they are two years old. This is because of the long period of delay (up to ten months) before implantation takes place. Badgers live in social groups, and if the population is dense not all sows produce young each year. The litter consists of one to five young, born in January–March. Mating, which is prolonged, can take place during any month of the year in Britain, but occurs mainly between February and May. Average mortality during the first year is around 50%.

The social group, which defends a communal territory, varies considerably in composition. Usually one or more adults of both sexes are present, along with yearlings and cubs. The largest male is often the dominant animal. The population density varies considerably with habitat and hence food supply. Between ten and 80 individuals per 1,000 ha are reported from different areas.

The Badger often travels to and from the set along established routes and worn, well-marked paths may be created over lichen-covered boulder country.

The droppings are placed in open pits about 10 cm deep. The pawprint shows marks of five clawed toes placed in a gentle curve shape.

Badger

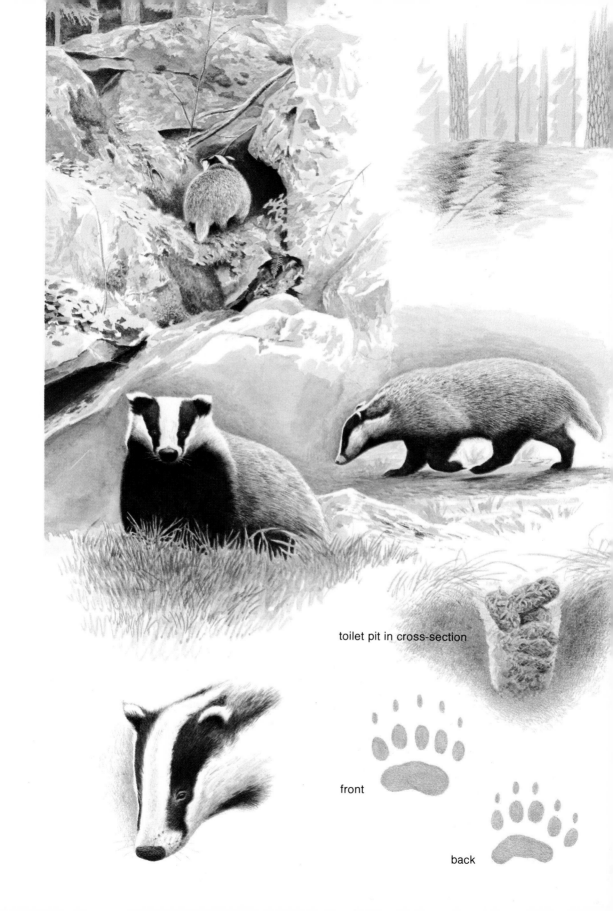

toilet pit in cross-section

front

back

Otter *Lutra lutra*

Body length 53–100 cm, tail length 28–55 cm, weight 3–17 kg.

On shore or sitting on the edge of some ice, the Otter is easy to recognise: it is short-legged, long, slightly stooping, and is rather sluggish in its movements. The tail is long, and tapers evenly from the thick base. Once in the water the species is more anonymous, at least if its size is not apparent. It does not, however, swim so jerkily as the American Mink and on the whole moves smoothly and elegantly. When it is inquisitive—and like the other mustelids it often is—it may slowly rise to the surface from underwater and come to a halt with hardly anything but its eyes and the tip of its nose above the water surface. It can remain in this position and keep watch, for example on whatever has disturbed it. It usually travels in or alongside water, occasionally over land from one open water to another. In clear tracks, impressions of the webbing, which extends right to the very short claws, can be seen. The species moves mostly in bounds of about half a metre in length. In deep snow the length of the bounds decreases, and owing to its short legs the Otter almost slithers along. The tracks then become a broad furrow in which each group of prints forms a crater. Going downhill, the species may travel long distances sliding on its belly. It is possible, as was once believed, that this is done for fun, but the behaviour is also a method of scent-marking. This is otherwise done with droppings (spraint), which are placed in prominent places. The spraint varies, both in shape and in colour, with the composition of the food. It resembles the American Mink's droppings, in appearance as well as siting, but differs in having a 'nice smell'. It has even been said to smell of violets, but this is obviously an exaggeration. The species has several calls, including a shrill whistle which acts as a contact call between female and young.

Otter

The species was once found by water of various kinds—seashores, lakes and watercourses—across almost the whole of Europe. During the 1900s, however, a massive decline has taken place: the Otter has disappeared completely from many areas and become very rare in most others. Populations that suffered reasonably little remain only along the west coast of Scotland, in Ireland and along the Atlantic coast of Norway. In Britain the Otter is now extremely scarce on lowland rivers, although it survives better in the Scottish Highlands as well as on the west coast. The main reasons for the disappearance of this previously common species, both in Britain and elsewhere, are habitat pollution, which has reduced breeding success, habitat deterioration, especially lack of cover and reduction of suitable holts, and human disturbance including hunting and trapping.

The food consists mainly of fish, e.g. eel, perch, pike, burbot, carp and salmon. The composition varies between different waters, and the majority of prey animals are at the most 20–25 cm long. Also included among the prey are small mammals, birds, crustaceans and amphibians. It has been shown that crabs can be an important food for coastal Otters.

The Otter becomes sexually mature at two or three years of age. It appears that the season can fall at any time of year, but it is concentrated in February–April. The litter, which consists of one to five young, is born after 60–62 days' pregnancy, and the young accompany the female for almost the whole of the first year.

The home range for a resident male may comprise up to 40 km of shoreline, and his hunting trips for himself average around 10 km per night.

The Otter frequently places its droppings in prominent sites, such as a rock or a tussock at the edge of the shore, and the droppings have a scent-marking function.

Mongooses and Genet   Family *Viverridae*

The mongooses and Genet are small or medium-sized, short-legged and slim carnivores. Some of them therefore resemble mustelids, while others are spotted and rather like cats. The family also includes the civets, civet being an earlier name for a musk-scented secretion which is released from glands situated in the anal region. The family is found mainly in tropical Africa and Asia and, of the total of approximately 70 species, three occur in Europe. Of these, probably two were introduced.

Genet *Genetta genetta*

The Genet has a body length of 47–60 cm. Apart from its spotted coat, it is recognised by the almost disproportionately long, 40–51 cm tail. The species is found in southwest Europe. In Spain it is locally common, and occasional discoveries—although in some cases probably of animals escaped from captivity—have been made in Switzerland, Germany and Belgium. The Genet prefers rocky terrain and moves about mostly in dense, scrubby vegetation. In Spain the major food is small mammals, mainly mice but locally with a considerable proportion of Rabbits, but birds and insects are also important components of the diet. The species also eats fruit. The droppings are often deposited high up and in the open, not uncommonly on roofs of buildings.

Genet

Egyptian Mongoose *Herpestes ichneumon*

This species, which is roughly the same size as the Genet—body length 50–55 cm—has in the past been called the Ichneumon. The name now used indicates on the one hand what kind of animal it is and on the other something of its geographical origin. It is found in large areas of Africa and bordering parts of Asia. It has recently been introduced to a couple of places in Yugoslavia, including the island of Mljet, and it is probable that its occurrence in the Iberian peninsula is also the result of introductions, albeit a very long time ago. In Europe the species inhabits maquis and other scrubby vegetation, and feeds on a wide assortment of prey in which Rabbits, especially young ones, and reptiles form substantial elements. The species has short jaws, which make it difficult for it to get a grip on and smash larger birds' eggs. It has solved this problem, as have a number of other mongoose species, in a neat way. It holds the egg with its front paws, positions itself with its rear against a rock, and then as it makes a small jump it simultaneously throws the egg underneath itself, between its hindlegs, against the rock.

Egyptian Mongoose

Indian Grey Mongoose *Herpestes edwardsi*

This species is very like the previous one but a little smaller—the body length is about 45 cm. It is found in large parts of southern Asia, and in the 1960s was introduced in an area of Italy south of Rome.

Indian Grey Mongoose

160

Genet

Egyptian Mongoose

Indian Grey Mongoose

Cats   Family *Felidae*

The cats are the most specialised pure flesh-eaters among the carnivores. They have large paws with claws that can be retracted. The canine teeth, which are used for killing prey, are powerful, while the rest of the teeth are reduced both in number and in size. There are barely 40 species in the family, of which three occur in Europe.

Wild Cat   *Felis sylvestris*

The Wild Cat is 48–68 cm long and weighs 3.5–10 kg. It is thus considerably larger than the Domestic Cat (*F. catus*), which otherwise occurs in Wild Cat-like forms. The two species are in fact so closely related that they can interbreed and produce fertile offspring. The best distinction in a brief glimpse is the Wild Cat's thicker, banded tail, which looks almost chopped off at the tip. The species occurs patchily over large parts of central and southern Europe, and in several places its numbers are reported to have increased in recent decades. It also occurs in Scotland, mainly in the north and west, where it is particularly widespread in the Highlands, having benefited from the extensive afforestation that has taken place there. The scientific specific name comes from the Latin *silva*, which means wood, and the Wild Cat lives mostly in forest land, but in particular around natural openings in the forest and in the zone nearest the forest edge. Small rodents form the staple food—in stomach analyses up to 23 Common Voles have been found in one stomach—but much else is included in the diet, e.g. hares, Rabbits, birds and insects. A litter, usually of four young (range one to eight), is born in April–May after the female's pregnancy of 63–69

days. There may sometimes be a second litter in August. The male's home range covers the home ranges of two or more females. The species is a little irregular in its daily activity rhythm, but is most active around dawn and dusk. It often spends the day sunning itself on a thick branch up in a tree. It may also rest for a while around midnight in such places, but in cold weather it often takes shelter in an underground den.

Pardel Lynx *Lynx pardina*

Wild Cat

Pardel Lynx

With a body length of 80–110 cm, tail length of about 12 cm and weight of 13 kg, the Pardel Lynx is smaller than the Lynx. In addition, it has a more pronounced chin-beard and has smaller spots. The two forms are sometimes considered to be races of the same species but are regarded here as separate species. The reason is mainly that during the Pleistocene period, i.e. approaching one million years ago, they had overlapping ranges but they still remained separate, so far as is known without interbreeding. Nowadays the distribution is restricted to a handful of discrete areas in the central and southern parts of the Iberian peninsula. These involve mountainous and lowland regions dominated either by woodland—turpentine pine or cork oak—or by maquis. The number of individuals is small. In the area where the species has been best studied, the Coto Doñana National Park, a population of 20–30 animals is involved. Large prey animals are less important for the Pardel Lynx than for the Lynx, and the main food throughout the year is Rabbits. Some wildfowl are added during the winter and spring, and during the late summer Fallow and Red Deer calves.

Lynx *Lynx lynx*

Body length 80–130 cm, tail length 11–25 cm, weight 18–25 kg.

The Lynx's coat is yellowish-brown in summer but considerably paler in winter: the species' scientific name is related to the Greek *leukos*, which means white or pale. The spotting varies. For a cat, the Lynx is unusually short-tailed. Despite its shortness, however, the tail is unusually striking and, should one see the animal from behind, the swinging tail—accentuated by the black tip—is a good identification mark. The route of the tracks is direct and positive, without the fox's continual embellishments, and the individual pawprint is like a huge enlargement of the usual Domestic Cat's print. It is round, about 10 cm long—in other words as large as the track of a Wolf or a very large dog—and the impressions from the pads are small, smaller than in the dog family. Moreover, the inner one of the two front pads is a shade larger than the outer one, a detail which can be seen well even in slightly indistinct tracks. The Lynx also walks with its toes turned inwards a little. The claws are usually held retracted, but they may be spread out, in order to give a better grip, and they then leave very clear impressions.

The Lynx's pawprint is big and round. The pads are small—smaller than a dog's—and the two front pads are of different sizes. The clawprint is normally not present, but may be visible on surfaces where the Lynx is helped by spreading out its claws in order to get a better foothold.

In historical times the species was found over almost the whole of Europe. The range subsequently contracted, however, and around 1960 the Lynx survived only in parts of Fennoscandia and east Europe, in Karelia—White Russia as well as in and around the Carpathians. Successful re-introductions have subsequently been made in Yugoslavia, Austria, Switzerland, West Germany and France. The Lynx was very heavily persecuted around the turn of the century, but since strict protection measures have been brought in in most countries it has recovered, and has even expanded its range in some places.

The Lynx is essentially a forest animal and thrives particularly well in steep, mountainous terrain. In the Carpathians, for example, it occurs between 150 m and 2,000 m above sea level, but mostly utilises levels from 700 m to 1,100 m.

Hares are without exception the most important prey animals, but the Lynx is an adaptable and skilful hunter and the choice of prey varies greatly between different regions. In Reindeer nurseries in north Scandinavia, Reindeer are the major prey, at least in winter, while the Roe Deer has a corresponding role in south and central Sweden and elsewhere, for example the Carpathians. In areas in Switzerland where the Lynx has been re-introduced the Chamois forms an important food, and from other places, including Poland, many woodland birds are reported to form part of the diet. As in other cats, the hunt consists of a stealthy approach followed by an explosive, brief attack. Large prey are killed with a bite in the region of the throat. This is administered with great precision, and normally brings down the prey more or less on the spot where the attack takes place. The Lynx usually then eats from the whole animal. Before it leaves the prey, it often scratches snow or ground vegetation over at least a part of it, not so that the corpse is covered but such that the scratch marks are well visible. It is absolutely exceptional for the Lynx to bite off the head of Roe Deer or other large prey. A full-grown Lynx requires around 1 kg of flesh per day in winter.

The mating period falls in March–April and the young, usually one to four, are born in May–June. They accompany the female for almost a year and themselves become sexually mature during their second year, at about 22 months of age.

The home range varies in size from a few dozen square kilometres in middle Europe to more than 1,000 km² in north Scandinavia. The Lynx may be affected by fox-mange, but to what degree this may influence Lynx populations is not known.

Lynx

Pinnipedes
Order *Pinnipedia*

The seals and Walrus are usually regarded as forming a separate order of their own, on an equal footing with the carnivores, for example, but were formerly considered to be a suborder within the Carnivora. They breathe with lungs and are therefore dependent on the air's oxygen, but are otherwise closely adapted to a life in water.

Their body is fusiform and endowed with a substantial layer of blubber beneath the skin. This improves the streamline shape, insulates against cold, and provides fuel reserves in the females during suckling and in the males during the mating season. The limbs are equipped with webs between the five fingers/toes and transformed into virtual flippers. The scientific name of the order is in fact a compound of the Latin *pinna*, which means wing or fin, and *pedis*, which is the genitive of foot: fin-footed in other words. The hindlimbs are directed backwards and give the swimming animal speed, the front ones having the function of steering. The outer ear has completely disappeared, which makes it more difficult for the seals when out of water to interpret the direction of a source of sound. By contrast, they have a very good capacity for doing this when underwater. This capacity may even be more developed than is currently known. Some seal species have actually been found to emit very high-frequency sounds, and, since they can also live at depths where they have hardly any use for normal sight, it has been suspected that they have some form of echo-sounder orientation similar to the bats.

The seals can dive to depths of at least 100 m—some arctic species can descend to more than 500 m—and stay underwater for up to 20 minutes. This would not be possible without a number of very special adaptations, which in particular involve economic use of oxygen. They have a comparatively large amount of blood, around 1.5 times more than a terrestrial mammal of equivalent size. In addition, the blood contains an unusually high amount of haemoglobin. When diving, large parts of the circulatory system are shut off and the only organs that receive normal blood supply are in fact the heart and the central nervous system. By this means the blood can circulate more slowly: the pulse in a diving seal beats only five to 15 times per minute, compared with about 70 beats a minute at other times.

Fetal development is delayed in the seals. The egg is fertilised following mating, but then floats free in the uterus for about three months before it is implanted and begins to develop.

The seals probably suffer more than any other order of mammals from the consequences of human activity. Particularly serious are the high levels of the environmental pollutants DDT and PCB which have been found in several different seal species, both in Europe and in other parts of the world. The seals' fat can contain concentrations up to ten times higher than is found in the food. PCB in particular appears to result in serious disorders in reproduction—abortions, premature births, diseased wombs—and may in the long run represent a threat to entire populations of seals.

Walrus *Odobenus rosmarus*

Length up to 4.5 m (male), 3 m (female), weight 700–2,200 kg.

The Walrus has acquired its generic name from two Greek words: *odous*, which means tooth, and *baino*, which means I walk. The name alludes to the species' most distinctive feature, the front teeth in the upper jaw, which are elongated into tusks. These may grow to up to 1.2 m long. The Walrus does not, however, use them for walking with, but it can use them as ice-prods when it hauls itself up out of the water on to the edge of the ice. They are also used as weapons and to dig for food. This wears them down a lot, but they grow almost throughout life.

The range is divided into two parts. One race can be found in the Bering Strait and along the Arctic Ocean coast both east and west of there; another between Greenland and northeast Canada, and also east of Greenland including around Svalbard and Novaya Zemlya. Animals from here occasionally visit the North Sea and waters around the British Isles, and have even reached Sweden (the most recent in 1981). The populations are thought at present to be slowly increasing, but earlier they decreased considerably, one reason being heavy hunting. Starting in the 1950s, however, limits have been introduced on hunting in all the countries where the species occurs.

The main foods are molluscs and bivalves which the Walrus digs up from the bottom mud. For this it uses the tusks as well as the 'moustache', which consists of coarse, very sensitive whiskers. The whiskers are also extremely flexible and can be used for holding a bivalve or mollusc in place while the contents are sucked out. The food also includes fish and crustaceans, and some Walruses may even tackle seals. In the Bering Strait this has been found to happen to a greatly increased extent in association with fast-growing Walrus populations, and also when particular ice conditions have forced Walruses and seals to come into contact with each other more than they normally do. A grown Walrus can consume up to 45 kg of food in one day.

The majority of young are born on the ice in May–June, after the female has been pregnant for around 11 months. They suck until they are getting on for two years old, and may stay with the female for a further one year.

Walrus

Common Seal *Phoca vitulina*

The Common Seal is similar to the Grey Seal but smaller: the male weighs 150 kg at most. In addition it has a proportionately small head, nostrils that are V-shaped and placed close together, as well as a slightly concave muzzle clearly offset against the forehead: there is something in the scientific name, which means 'calf-like'. The species is found in the cold and temperate parts of the North Pacific and Atlantic and neighbouring waters, and from the North Sea the range extends into the southernmost parts of the Baltic, where the population had declined drastically in recent decades and in 1981 was estimated at about 200 animals. There were about ten times as many along the west coast of Sweden at the same period; this represents a distinct increase which began in the mid 1960s when the species was given protection there at the same time as the first seal reserves were established. The favourite habitat is shallow, sheltered waters. The main food is fish, and studies have shown that cod make up a substantial proportion of the diet. The pup is born in June–July on a sandy beach or low island. This means that in some places the species is subject to disturbance when human beings visit these areas for bathing and other recreation. If you come across a pup, it is important to leave it in peace: the female is somewhere in the water offshore, and is waiting only for the chance to come ashore and suckle it.

Common Seal

Ringed Seal *Phoca hispida*

Length up to 1.7 m (male), 1.5 m (female), weight up to 125 kg (male), 110 kg (female).

The Ringed Seal is similar to the Common Seal, but is a shade darker and on the sides has dark spots outlined by more or less distinct white or yellowish-white ring-shaped borders. It also has a weaker dentition than the Common Seal.

This is the smallest and commonest species of seal in arctic seas and also the one that goes farthest north. Separate races, evolved during protracted geographical isolation, are found in the Baltic/Gulf of Finland (*P. h. botnica*), Lake Saimaa in Finland (*P. h. saimensis*) and Lake Ladoga, USSR (*P. h. ladogensis*). The Saimaa race is threatened with extinction, owing mainly to the fact that

Ringed Seal

Common Seal

net-fishing in the lake causes high mortality among the seals, whose numbers amount to only just over 100. In 1981 the Baltic stock was estimated at around 10,000 animals. This population, too, is on the decline; here, the main reason is that a large proportion of the females are so affected by pollutants that they are unable to bear young.

Although it often resorts to bays and fjords, the Ringed Seal also lives in the open sea, especially in winter, and does so even when the drift-ice begins to freeze together. When conditions are very severe, it keeps open a series of breathing and diving holes.

Most of the food is fish. In the Gulf of Finland, Baltic herring is of some importance, but otherwise the Ringed Seal does not appear to concentrate on any particular species or group of species. It also eats bivalves, and during the period March–May two species of crustacean (an isopod and an amphipod) form a very important part of the diet.

The pup is born in February–March at a sheltered site out on the ice. Often the female has first made a virtual cave of snow, and the protection it affords against the sweeping cold arctic winds is of crucial importance for the survival of the young. It wears the white coat of the pup for two to four weeks, sucks for a further five weeks or so, and then enters the water.

Ringed Seal

Harp Seal *Phoca groenlandica*

This medium-sized seal—the male reaches a top weight of 180 kg—is easy to recognise by the dark markings on the face and across the shoulders and sides. The pattern is considerably more contrasting in the male than in the female. Three breeding areas—one off Newfoundland, one around Jan Mayen and one in the White Sea—represent established points in the life of the Harp Seal, but these animals move around in small groups in the Arctic Ocean and neighbouring waters as well. Lost individuals can also turn up in other places as far south as Britain and the west coast of Sweden. Very heavy hunting has taken place, particularly within the breeding areas, and from the 1800s to the end of the 1960s the total population is estimated to have decreased from around 40 million to two or three million individuals. Within the breeding area north of Newfoundland up to 180,000 young were killed each year during the 1960s, but this number has dropped since the hunting season has been shortened. The diet consists of fish and pelagic crustaceans. The Harp Seal has been shown to be capable of descending to depths of as much as 280 m.

Bearded Seal *Erignathus barbatus*

In some languages this is known as the 'Large Seal'—the male can weigh up to 400 kg—but in English the species is generally known as the Bearded Seal owing to the prominent, heavy 'moustache' formed by the whiskers. The species is circumpolar, being found along coasts in arctic waters, and, despite being to a fair extent resident, occasional individuals may sometimes undertake unexpected migrations. Vagrants have occurred in the North Sea and the Skagerrak. The total population in 1964 was estimated at 75,000–100,000 individuals, and there have probably not been any great changes since then. The Bearded Seal's major food in European waters is various bottom-dwelling animals—molluscs, bivalves and crustaceans—which it in part digs up with its foreflippers. These have evolved slightly differently from those of the other seal species in that the third clawed finger is larger than the rest of the fingers. The choice of food is the reason why the teeth of older animals are often very worn. From the Canadian arctic coasts, however, there are reports that 90% of the food may consist of fish.

Hooded Seal *Cystophora cristata*

This is a big seal—the male can weigh up to 410 kg. Its most distinctive characteristic is that on the upperside of the nose the male has a sac of skin, an extention of the nasal cavity, which can be inflated to about the size of a football. The scientific generic name alludes to this: it is a compound of the Greek *kustis* and *phoros*, which indeed mean respectively bladder and carrying. Otherwise the adults are ash-grey with irregular dark blotches. The young pups are uniform blue-grey (their fur in commercial contexts goes under the name of 'blue back'). The breeding sites are situated on the drift-ice from Jan Mayen and westwards to Baffin Island. The Hooded Seals regularly move east from there, including to Svalbard, Iceland and the arctic coast of Norway, with vagrants reaching the British Isles and on isolated occasions even farther south. The world population at the end of the 1970s was estimated at 300,000–500,000 animals. The main diet is fish, but food such as cuttle-fish is also eaten. The Hooded Seal has been met with at depths of as great as 300 m.

Harp Seal

Bearded Seal

Hooded Seal

Harp Seal

Bearded Seal

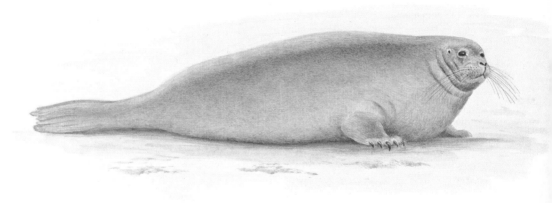

Hooded Seal

Grey Seal *Halichoerus grypus*

Length up to 3.3 m (male), 2.5 m (female), weight up to 315 kg (male), 200 kg (female).

The Grey Seal can often be distinguished from the only other species in English waters by the head profile. This runs in an almost straight line from the top of the head to the nose: in other words it lacks a 'forehead', and the muzzle besides is long. In the same way as the Common Seal has been likened to a calf, so the Grey Seal has been compared with a young pig: its scientific generic name is a compound of the Greek *halios* and *khoiros*, which respectively mean from the sea and little pig. The ground colour is usually grey, the upperside darker, the underside lighter. The nostrils are clearly separated. Particularly in summer, the Grey Seals often join together in herds which spend a lot of time huddled on land. The moult takes place at this time and the species' 'song' is also heard from the herds—long-drawn, rising and falling, very far-carrying cries. The deepest base notes come from old animals, the more barking sounds from the young seals.

The species is found in the Baltic except the very south, and along the coasts on both sides of the North Atlantic. The centre point of distribution is around the British Isles, where the population at the beginning of the 1980s was estimated at about 80,000 animals. The total stock in the Baltic in 1982 was calculated at about 1,200 animals, of which about 750 lived in Swedish waters. This indicates a huge reduction, in earlier years caused mainly by heavy hunting

Grey Seal

172

and more recently by very high levels of certain pollutants interfering with reproduction. A colony of some tens of individuals established fairly recently in the Kattegatt probably originated from the North Atlantic population.

Offshore island groups with smooth flat rocks or rocky, boulder-strewn coasts are the Grey Seals' habitat, but in some areas around the British Isles they make use of sandy shores and tidal flats. Those in the Baltic resort to a completely different habitat when about to give birth: areas with drift-ice that is thick but not too hard-packed.

Research on choice of food includes a Baltic study in which as many as 21 different species of fish were found to be represented in the diet. Baltic herring and cod predominated, and appeared especially important during the mating and moulting periods and when giving birth. The salmonids were also an important food. Adult Grey Seals have been estimated to eat on average 7 kg of fish per day.

The breeding circumstances vary a great deal between different populations. In the Baltic the young are born on the ice in February–March. The female then stays with her pup and suckles it for about one month, after which the mating period follows. Both around the British Isles and on the southwest coasts of Scandinavia, however, birth and mating take place on land in the autumn. When the young is born, it weighs about 10 kg and has yellowish-white fur. When it finishes sucking, its weight has increased to about 60 kg: it has in other words put on nearly 2 kg per day! At this time the pup's fur is shed, and the young acquires the colour of the adult and enters the water.

Monk Seal *Monachus monachus*

Length up to 310 cm, weight up to 400 kg.

The Monk Seal is dark brown with a pale underside. The pale colour may be sharply or diffusely demarcated, and some individuals have only a pale belly patch.

The appearance, however, is of little importance in identification, since the Monk Seal is the only seal species in south European waters. The majority of the population is found in the Mediterranean—in the Aegean Sea, off the coasts of Morocco and Algeria and around Cyprus—but the range extends eastwards through the Sea of Marmora into the Black Sea, and westwards along the Atlantic coast of northwest Africa and from there to at least Madeira and the Canaries.

As a result of a long period of heavy hunting and more recently the massive development of the Mediterranean coasts, probably also disruptions in breeding caused by habitat pollution, the Monk Seal has become very scarce. During the 1970s the total population was estimated at 500–1,000 individuals, and if the decrease continues at the same rate one must expect the species to have become extinct in the Aegean Sea by the year 2000. Exactly how numerous it has been in the past is not known, but the fact that many place names in Greece, Turkey and Yugoslavia are derived from an old Greek word for seal demonstrates that the distribution was once far more widespread.

Extensive sandy beaches were formerly the most important haunts, but the species has been driven away from these to rocky, more remote coasts. The major food is fish of a number of different species, but other groups of animals, e.g. cuttle-fish, are also included. The young are born during the period May–November, often in caves—even ones that have only underwater access from the surrounding world. The survival of young is probably worse here than on open sandy shore.

Monk Seal

Przewalski's Horse

Odd-toed ungulates
Order *Perissodactyla*

The order of odd-toed ungulates is distinguished by the fact that the longitudinal axis of the foot comes in the middle of the third toe. Tapirs, rhinoceroses and horses belong to this order and, even though semi-wild horses as well as donkeys occur here and there in south and middle Europe, the order now lacks wild representatives in our part of the world. In the 1870s the last truly wild Tarpan (*Equus ferus*), a wild horse that was found in steppe regions from eastern Europe east to Mongolia, was killed. The last example in captivity died in 1919. Our Domestic Horse is thought to be descended in the main from the Tarpan.

Even-toed ungulates
Order *Artiodactyla*

In this order the longitudinal axis of the foot comes between the third and fourth toes. The ends of these form hooves. The first toe has disappeared during the course of evolution, while the second and fifth have been reduced to small, short 'dewclaws' which are situated farther back. Most of the world's large and medium-sized vegetarian animals belong to the even-toed ungulates order. Three families in this order are represented in Europe: the pigs; the deer; and the cattle, sheep and goats.

Pigs   Family *Suidae*

Pigs differ from the other families in the order in having only a simple stomach. They also have low-crowned cheek teeth. Both these facts have to do with their being omnivorous; the other families are ruminant vegetarians and have complex stomach systems as well as high-crowned cheek teeth. Only one species is found in Europe.

Wild Boar   *Sus scrofa*

Body length up to 185 cm, tail length 15–20 cm. The weight varies a great deal. In middle Europe the sows weigh 35–150 kg, the boars 40–175 kg. Higher weights, however, are reported from farther east, in the boars up to as much as 320 kg.

The Wild Boar is compact, dark in colour and bristly. The bristliness, however, varies seasonally: the winter coat is much thicker and longer-haired than the summer coat, which has occasionally been likened most closely to week-old chin stubble. The body is hefty and appears to be flattened from the sides, the head large and the legs proportionately short and thin. The Wild Boar is sometimes said to be unmistakable. Distinctive would perhaps be better, for there are cases of the species having been confused with a bear. There are similarities, such as the large head, short thick neck and high withers. The boar's canine teeth in both upper and lower jaws grow throughout life and form upward-pointing tusks. The young are lighter in colour and more or less obviously striped lengthways. The tracks can be difficult to distinguish from those of other species of even-toed ungulates. Prints from the dewclaws, however, are almost always visible, and besides this the Wild Boar walks with its feet turned outwards. The species has various muffled calls. The warning cry, with which the female alerts the young to danger, is a short, gruff grunt.

The range includes the whole of central and most of southern Europe. The species also occurs in North Africa and in central and south Asia as far as the Pacific Ocean. It has also been introduced in North America. In Europe it formerly occurred in the north, too, but was eradicated perhaps mainly through slow intermixing with domestic pigs. It became extinct in Britain during the 17th century and, in spite of attempted re-introductions, no feral populations survive. In the latter part of the 1970s escaped Wild Boars succeeded in establishing vigorous stocks in many places in the southern half of Sweden, and in 1983 there were probably around 300 animals living in the wild there. The species has lately reached Finland through immigration from the southeast across the Isthmus of Karelia.

Particularly in south Europe, the Wild Boar is confined to woodland, deciduous and mixed, and it is extinct in many pure agricultural areas. On the other hand, it does extremely well in cultivated country of varied type provided it has access to cover, such as spruce forest, swampy woodlands or reedbeds. The combination of thick snow cover and deep ground frost prevents the animals from searching for underground food and limits its extension northwards.

The Wild Boar is omnivorous, but the vegetable content of the food far outweighs the animal content. Acorns, beechnuts, hazelnuts and roots of various plants are important, in summer also green plants or plant material. In rooting underground, the Wild Boar in cultivated country comes into contact with potatoes and other root crops and can then cause serious damage. The main kinds of animal food are earthworms, insects/insect larvae and small rodents. In

Wild Boar

an analysis of the stomach contents of Wild Boars that had been shot, remains of small rodents were found in about every third stomach; in another analysis, 900 larvae of cockchafers were found in one stomach. The Wild Boar also eats carrion.

Breeding can take place at almost any time of the year, but normally the season falls in late autumn–early winter. The animals then gather in packs and the boars indulge in quite rough fighting over the sows. After about four months' pregnancy—normally in February at the earliest, in June at the latest—the three to eight young are born. Younger females have fewer young on average than older ones. For the first week the young remain at the birthplace, a rough bundle prepared in advance and usually concealed in dense vegetation. Afterwards they accompany the female until she next gives birth. In at least some populations, some of the females become sexually mature as early as their first autumn.

Wild Boars usually have a fairly fixed daily routine, although this may be less marked in areas where they are not hunted. They sleep away the day, often in some sunny, damp spot, and are then active at night. A female with young can move within a home range of 100–300 ha, while a single boar may utilise even more than 1,000 ha.

At dawn on 7 October 1982, a big male Wild Boar was standing tearing pieces from a cow which the day before had died on the grass steppe in the Coto Doñana National Park in Spain.

Deer Family *Cervidae*

The deer family, together with the cattle, sheep and goats, form the ruminants. Also belonging to this group are some families that lack representatives in Europe, including the camels. The ruminants are usually regarded as a distinct suborder within the order of even-toed ungulates, which also includes the pigs among others.

There are approximately 50 species of deer spread across both the Old and the New Worlds. They vary immensely in size, from the South American Pudu at 7–9 kg to the largest Alaskan Mooses weighing about 100 times more.

The antlers are perhaps what one associates most with the deer. In most species it is the males that wear these, but there are exceptions to this basic rule. In the Reindeer both sexes have antlers, but the cow's are much smaller than the bull's. Two other species—the Musk Deer, which is not, however, found in Europe, and the Chinese Water Deer—lack antlers altogether, and in these both the female and the male are provided instead with tusks similar to those of the Wild Boar.

The antlers consist of bone tissue. Every year the old set of antlers is shed, and a new one grows out at a rate that means the new antlers being fully developed for the rut. While they are growing out the antlers are covered with a skin rich in blood vessels, the so-called velvet. When the antlers are through, the velvet loses its primary function, that of transporting the material with which the antlers are built up. It begins to shrivel up, after which the animal scrapes off the velvet against trees or bushes.

Several species of deer have a prominent rump patch, an area around the anal opening with hairs that are paler than the surrounding hair and which can be erected when necessary. The rump patch then becomes a conspicuous signal. It can act as a warning to others of the species. Some studies, however, indicate that it also acts as a signal to an attacking predator that it has been detected and can therefore break off its hunting attempt.

It has been said in various contexts—including in the advice to Elk-hunters to wear a brightly coloured cap band for safety reasons—that deer are colour-blind. Without in any way belittling this certainly very reasonable measure, it is worth mentioning that experiments made with Wapiti (the name for the Red Deer in North America) have shown that it can distinguish fluorescent orange from other colours. Also, examination of the structure of the eye in different deer species indicates that there are mechanisms for colour-sightedness within the family.

The majority of deer are very important hunting quarries. This means that not only the population density but also the age and sex compositions in many areas are strongly influenced by hunting. The number of individuals may also be governed by other game-preservation measures, such as putting out winter feed. To this it should be added that many species have been the subject of introductions. Sometimes this has involved re-introduction or just minor translocations within or in the proximity of the region where the species occurs naturally, but at other times manipulations have been on a larger scale. In fact, a half of the species of deer living wild in Europe today—five out of ten species—have their origins in other parts of the world.

Fallow Deer *Cervus dama*

Body length up to 160 cm, tail length 16–19 cm, shoulder height up to 110 cm and weight up to 130 kg.

The majority of Fallow Deer are white-spotted on a reddish-brown ground colour in summer, and more uniformly grey-brown in winter. A band down the centre of the back, however, is unspotted and a black stripe runs along the upper side of the almost continuously swinging tail. The rump is white and bordered with black above and at the sides. Some individuals, however, are entirely different in colour, pale greyish-white or dark greyish-black. The antlers, which are shed in April–June and after that promptly begin to grow out again and which are clear of velvet in August–September, acquire a substantial blade when fully developed. The buck's rutting call is a very muffled, almost snoring or belching noise. It has been said that it sounds like something between a tractor and a young pig. A Fallow Deer, when alarmed, may give a short barking call and also bounce away with peculiar, stiff-legged bounds which acts as a warning signal to others of its species.

During the Stone Age the Fallow Deer occurred as a hunting quarry here and there in central Europe, but it seems to have disappeared as early as prehistoric times. It was then re-introduced from Asia during Roman times and the current, extremely fragmented situation is a result of countless introductions and translocations mainly during the Middle Ages and since. In Britain the species is widespread and is the dominant deer in many areas. It is often kept in large parks and estates.

The majority of European populations are found in woodland, deciduous or mixed, with dense undergrowth and surrounded by or interspersed with open ground.

The main food is grass, but much else is included: newly opened leaves in spring, berries in summer and acorns and beechnuts in autumn and winter. The species can cause damage both to crops and to young conifer plantations.

During the rut, which falls at the end of October and in November, the bucks gather together a harem more or less as the Red Deer. After about 230 days' pregnancy, one or two calves are born in June–July. The reproductive cycle seems to indicate that some of the northern populations are not really adapted to the climate to which they are exposed. Wintery weather towards the end of the rut can eliminate some of the bucks, which at that time may be extremely worn out. Similarly, calves born late may have difficulties if the winter is early.

Fallow Deer

Spotted Deer *Cervus axis*

The Spotted Deer is slightly smaller than the Fallow Deer—body length and shoulder height reach at the most 130 cm and 90 cm respectively. Throughout the year the coat has white spots on a reddish-brown base colour, and the species is therefore a little like both Fallow and Sika Deer in summer dress. It is recognised, however, by its well-defined white throat patch, by lack of any black on both the tail and the white rump, and by the fact that the antlers are long and when fully developed have at most three points on each side. The species is found in Asia, including India and Sri Lanka, and has been introduced to zoological parks and hunting preserves in many European countries. It lives in the wild on Istria in Yugoslavia, but may also appear as an escape in other places.

Sika Deer *Cervus nippon*

The Sika resembles the Red Deer but is considerably smaller. The body length is at most 130 cm, the tail length 15 cm, the shoulder height 90 cm and the average weight 64 kg in males, 41 kg in females. The summer coat is reddish-brown with distinct yellowish-white or white spots arranged in rows, the winter coat dark grey-brown with the spots only faint. Hinds with calf retain the summer coat for longer in autumn than those without calf. The rump is white, outlined above and at the sides by a dark border. When alarmed, an animal raises the white hairs, which makes the area of the rump increase in size: a signal to other individuals in the group. The antlers are a little like the young Red Deer's, but have only eight points when fully grown out. Of these, only one on each side points forward. The buck's call during the rut is a peculiar, almost human-like whistle.

The scientific specific name *nippon*, which means Japan in that country's own language, indicates the species' geographical origin. From east Asia it has been introduced into many European countries and established wild populations. In some areas where it has come into contact with Red Deer the two species have interbred.

In contrast to the Red Deer, the highest-ranking buck accepts other subordinate animals of the same sex in the territory during the rutting season. Captive Sika Deer in Sweden have shown a behaviour that can be interpreted only as tool-using, a phenomenon that, so far as is known, is extremely rare in mammals. The behaviour involves the bucks, immediately they have shed their antlers, chewing the end of a stick until it looks almost like a brush. They then 'clean' the holes of the wounds against this brush, a task that may continue for up to 20 minutes. The result is that the holes become completely white and all traces of bleeding are gone.

Opposite: In the Sika Deer, hinds with calf retain the summer coat for longer in the autumn than hinds without calf.

Sika Deer

182

Red Deer *Cervus elaphus*

Body length 165–260 cm, tail length 12–15 cm, shoulder height up to 150 cm, weight up to 255 kg (male), 120 kg (female).

The Red Deer is Europe's largest species of deer after the Elk. The coat, which in full-grown animals may have a hint of spots only in quite exceptional cases, is short-haired and mainly reddish-brown in summer, longer-haired and dark grey-brown in winter. The calf on the other hand has a spotted coat for the first two months. The rump patch is yellowish-white to buff and the tail lacks black markings. The antlers grow out during the spring–summer, are cleaned of velvet in August and are shed in March–April. They never form blades, but points or 'tines', and the stag in his prime has at least ten points in the antlers. Of these, the lowest two on each side are forward-pointing. In winter in particular, the Red Deer peels bark, especially from conifers. The Elk also does this, and the damage is fairly similar but can be distinguished. The Red Deer attacks younger woodland, often 15–40-year-old trees, whereas the Elk attacks trees 30–60 years old; thus, trunks peeled by Red Deer are normally 10–15 cm in diameter at chest height, and those attacked by Elks often more than 20 cm. The marks left by Red Deer are often lower down, below 150 cm above ground compared with 100–230 cm for the Elk. Finally, the chisel-like marks of the front teeth are different in width: the Red Deer's are less than 16 mm, the Elk's more than 16 mm. Other distinctive features worth mentioning include the rutting call—the stag's muffled, far-carrying bellowing call during the mating season.

The species is found continuously within a large part of east and central Europe, and patchily in many places in the rest of our part of the world. It is mainly the influence of man that lies behind this very fragmented picture. The species has been hunted heavily—it has been described as the first European quarry that was systematically put down with firearms—and in many places has first become extinct and then been partly re-introduced. In addition it has been introduced in places where it is not indigenous, even outside Europe, including the USA, Argentina and Australia. In Britain the Red Deer has an erratic distribution, with isolated sightings occurring almost anywhere. In Scotland, however, it is common in open high ground and some herds may number over one hundred.

From the open lofty deciduous forest where it originally belonged, the species has adapted to extremely varied habitat types. In many places it lives in areas where forest of various kinds alternates with cultivated land, but it also occurs on treeless heather moors, in mountains above the tree-line and on grass plains. It benefits from moderate or slight amounts of snow.

During periods when snow is lying, the Red Deer feeds mainly on plants and grass from the ground. It simply kicks its way through small bits of snow, but should the depth increase it searches up among trees and bushes. It then takes leaves, buds, shoots and—as mentioned above—bark, and is not very particular. In a study in the Carpathians, shoots of 36 and bark of 27 different species of trees and bushes were found in the diet. Spruce predominated with about one-third of the food, and the proportion of sallow was also large. Because of its choice of food the species may cause damage, even appreciably so, both in conifer nurseries and on cultivated fields.

The rut takes place during a three-week or so period from the end of August to the beginning of October. The largest stags then assemble large herds of hinds. Other males are kept away by the intensiveness of the rutting call but also by an aggressive reception. Small males normally give way at the mere sight of

Red Deer

the larger animal, but if the rivals are more equal in size a fight often develops. The majority of matings are achieved by those stags that have succeeded in keeping a harem together. The hinds, which in most cases do not become sexually mature until after two years of age (in exceptional cases as one-year-olds), are pregnant for nearly eight months. In May–June they give birth to (nearly always only) one calf. This means that the species is considerably less productive than, for example, both Elk and Roe Deer.

Red Deer can have a slightly different appearance in different regions, and this, together with some variation also in antler and skull measurements, has given rise to much argument over the species' separation into races. At times no fewer than 17 have been distinguished. The nominate race was first described by Linnaeus in south Sweden in 1758, and the species has probably existed in northern Europe since the end of the Ice Age. The size of the home range varies with habitat, season and sex. Studies in the Alps have indicated home ranges during autumn–winter of 50–150 ha, compared with up to 400 ha during spring–summer. On the isle of Rhum in Scotland they are about 400 ha for hinds and 800 ha for stags. Activity, too, varies with the time of year. In the summer the stags can be on the move for 15 hours of the day; during the winter they instead rest for that length of time each day.

White-tailed Deer *Odocoileus virginianus*

The White-tailed Deer is up to 180 cm long and can weigh up to 125 kg, putting it between Fallow and Red Deer in size. Its tail is long (15–28 cm), and on the underside is white like the rump. When the animal is alarmed, the tail is raised straight up, and this white flash then becomes a conspicuous warning signal. The scientific specific name indicates the species' geographical home, but it does not occur only in the State of Virginia but in the greater part of southern North America and in addition in northern South America. In 1934 it was introduced to Finland. It spread and increased in numbers: in 1962 there were about 1,000 animals, while the 'bag' in autumn 1980 amounted to almost 15,000 animals. The reason for this rapid increase is of course that the species ended up in an environment where it thrived, but the White-tailed Deer also has a high reproductive capacity. It usually has two or three calves, compared with normally one in Fallow and Red Deer. At the beginning of the 1980s, however, there were signs that the increase had moderated or perhaps even ceased. The 'bag' dropped, the proportion of young fell and, at least in some areas, the number of animals decreased. At the same time, the species was showing a tendency to move away from open agricultural country to more secluded woodland. In North America the White-tailed Deer has been found to carry a cerebral nematode that appears not to harm the animal itself but which can attack Elks, sometimes with fatal results.

White-tailed Deer

Elk *Alces alces*

Body length up to 290 cm, tail length 4–5 cm, shoulder height up to 220 cm, weight up to 800 kg (bull).

The Elk is the largest deer species, in a class of its own, and competes with the Bison and Polar Bear for the title of Europe's largest land mammal. It probably acquired its scientific name from the Greek word *alké*, which means strength. The legs are grey-white but the rest of the coat is shaggy greyish brown-black all year round. In females the pale colour on the hindlegs extends up the inside in a narrow wedge as far as the underside of the tail, a detail which nearly always makes it possible to tell the sex of an Elk seen from behind. The calf is reddish-brown. It acquires its first antlers as early as the end of its first autumn, but they are not much more than an inch long. Henceforth the antlers begin to grow out in April. They are clear of velvet in August–September and are shed in December–March; younger animals normally bear antlers for longer than older ones. The antlers are essentially of two different sorts, flattened (palmate) or with branched points (cervine). They are most developed when the bulls are eight to ten years old, and then reduce again in size. The Elk gives a very muffled, almost coughing sound which is an anxiety or perhaps rather a warning cry. In addition the cow calls the calf with a subdued whimpering sound, and finally both cow and bull have a nasal, slightly squeaky advertising call during the rutting season.

The Elk is found around the whole of the northern hemisphere, in what are considered to be seven different races. In Europe it is nowadays found only in the far northeast, but in prehistoric times it also occurred in central Europe. It is present virtually throughout Scandinavia, in north Russia and east Poland and across Siberia. In the New World the Elk is widespread in Alaska and Canada, where it is known as the Moose. The Swedish population has undergone very dramatic changes. During the 1700s it declined steeply, no doubt mainly as a result of very heavy hunting, and around 1820 only scattered remnants were left in parts of the north-central lowlands. The stock recovered, however, then increased slowly and irregularly over a long period, at the same time gradually extending its range, but in particular after 1960 what is almost an explosion has been witnessed. The 'bag' in 1960 was a good 30,000 animals. In 1982 the figure was over 170,000, which should mean that the population before the hunting season stood at nearly half a million. The reasons for the increase are many: firstly protection and other direct conservation measures, later the decline of Brown Bears and Wolves together with changes in land-use and stockbreeding, and finally in recent decades changes in forestry as well as modifications to principles of shooting. There is a clear correlation between the number of Elks killed per 1,000 ha and the proportion of new timber growth, and it is therefore to a great extent man that determines the Elk's numbers.

The species originally stems from the northern coniferous forest—the taiga—but has adapted to practically all other wooded environments. It also appears in open country, from farmland to bare mountains, particularly when searching for food.

The Elk derives a considerable part of its food from trees and bushes. In winter the basic food consists of pine shoots, but twigs and bark of aspen, rowan, willow species etc are also included. In summer leaves of various kinds are the main food, but at this time the Elk also grazes *Vaccinium* sprigs and plants from the ground. Many Elks are fond of aquatic plants, e.g. water lilies, which they grab with their head deep beneath the surface. Another food source that should be mentioned is the autumn oat fields. At the end of the 1970s,

Elk

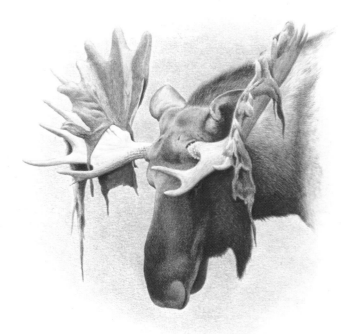

perhaps as a result of greater competition for winter grazing in the increasing populations, Elks began to peel bark from spruce in the manner of Red Deer. A grown Elk consumes up to 10 kg of food per day.

The rut takes place at the end of September in the southern and central parts of Scandinavia, and at the beginning of October farther north. This is tremendously intensive and involves behaviours that do not occur during the rest of the year. The bulls come more and more often in contact with one another, encounters that usually mean the smaller animal standing aside, but which can result in violent trials of strength if the animals are equal in size. Furthermore, they attack trees and bushes with their antlers and kick up rutting holes with the front hooves. The bull urinates in one of these hollows, and then lies down in it. This forms part of his courtship, and the cow may also come and lie down in the hollow. Her calf, too, may do the same incidentally. In the last week before the day when the cow is receptive, she is guarded intensively by the bull, which at that time barely has time to eat. After about 235 days she gives birth, usually to two calves. Young cows normally have only one calf, while triplets occur in only one percent or so of the births. Quads have sometimes been reported but are extremely rare. The cow can still give birth when she is 20 years old. The newborn calf weighs around 10 kg. During its first month it doubles its weight, and thereafter it increases—thanks to the summer's nutritious food—by more than 1 kg per day. This means that at the change-over from August to September it weighs 85–90 kg. The calves accompany the cow throughout the first year, and are chased off by her 10–15 days before she next gives birth.

In the northern parts of the range more than 100,000 animals move between extensive high-lying summer territory and winter feeding areas down in the forests. This may involve movements of up to 70 km. In the winter quarters they are concentrated in much smaller areas, create traffic problems, and leave behind them decapitated young pines and other damage to the forest.

In August/September the male Elk clears itself of velvet, which for several days hangs in shreds around the now fully developed antlers.

190

Muntjac *Muntiacus reevesi*

Muntjac

With a body length of at most 90 cm, a shoulder height of up to 50 cm and an average weight of barely 14 kg in the buck and 12 kg in the doe, the Muntjac vies with the Chinese Water Deer for the title of Europe's smallest species of deer living in the wild. The buck has short antlers, up to 6 cm, that are shed in May/June and have grown out again in October/November and which are placed on greatly elongated permanent projections (pedicels). His canines in the upper jaw are also elongated, not so strikingly as in the following species but nevertheless such that they peep out under the upper lip. The tracks are characteristic in that the hooves are of different sizes. The species' distribution is restricted to southern England, where it was introduced around the turn of the century from southeast Asia and where, particularly since 1950, it has expanded. It lives in dense woodland, deciduous or mixed, and takes food both from the ground and from trees and bushes. It also eats berries, acorns, chestnuts, fruit etc. There is no fixed mating time, but for captive animals more births are reported in summer than in winter. The species is sometimes also called 'Barking Deer' from the loud bark that the buck gives, particularly during the rut. At that time he may carry on for up to three-quarters of an hour, and utter individual barks continuously about every five seconds.

Chinese Water Deer *Hydropotes inermis*

Chinese Water Deer

The Chinese Water Deer is about the same size as the Muntjac—body length is up to 100 cm, shoulder height 60 cm and weight at most 14 kg in the buck and 11.5 kg in the doe. It is characterised above all by its lack of antlers. The scientific specific name alludes to this: it is Latin and means unarmed. Also characteristic are the buck's greatly elongated canine teeth in the upper jaw, up to 80 mm long, which almost have the character of tusks. The Chinese Water Deer, too, is an east Asiatic species. It was introduced at the turn of the century to a zoological park in eastern England, from where it later escaped and established feral populations. These are found in areas of extensive grassland and also brushy woodland, whereas the species is associated with marshland in its original homeland. The main food is grass. The rut takes place in December in

Chinese Water Deer

Muntjac

England and the litter is born in May/June. In east Asia this may consist of as many as six fawns, but in England, at least in captivity, two to four fawns are most common.

Reindeer *Rangifer tarandus*

Body length up to 220 cm, tail length 10–15 cm, shoulder height 85–120 cm, weight 70–150 kg (bulls), 40–100 kg (cows).

Perhaps the most distinctive thing about the Reindeer is that both sexes have antlers. They are fully developed and clear of velvet in September, after which the males shed theirs in December/January while the females, which have slightly smaller antlers, keep theirs right up to May. The calf, too, which acquires antlers as early as its first autumn, wears them throughout the first winter. The summer coat is usually dark grey-brown, the winter coat much lighter, but domesticated Reindeer in particular vary in colour from almost all-white to dark greyish-black. The Reindeer may be heard to make a grunting noise, which is among other things a contact call between female and young and which thus has an important function within the Reindeer herd, and also a characteristic twanging. This is heard from animals on the move and is caused by a small tendon in the foot which is stretched across a brone protuberance. The footprint shows that the front hooves are curved in a marked crescent shape.

The species has a circumpolar distribution in both Old and New Worlds. In north Europe there were originally two races, a mountain one (*R. t. tarandus*) and a forest one (*R. t. fennicus*). Both have gradually been replaced by domesticated Reindeer and been driven back to very restricted areas. The mountain Reindeer is found in southernmost Norway (about 25,000 animals) and also on the Kola peninsula (about 20,000), while wild forest Reindeer survived in Russian Karelia and from there got into neighbouring parts of Finland in the 1950s. The Russian/Finnish stock is slowly on the increase and in 1980 was estimated at up to 5,000–6,500 animals. East of there, on the Russian tundra and taiga, there are around 900,000 wild Reindeer. Domesticated Reindeer have been introduced to the Cairngorms in Scotland, where a herd now lives in a semi-wild state.

Mountain heath, tundra and the northern coniferous forest are home to the Reindeer, and a large proportion of the domesticated Reindeer of Fennoscandia are found in mountains in summer and down in the forest in winter. The species feeds to a large extent on lichen. In the autumn and early winter this includes reindeer moss, although this is mixed with a proportion of grass. Even in deep snow the Reindeer digs down to the ground, but, should the snow become difficult to get through, the epiphyte lichens—lichens living on trees—become more and more important. With the spring and the ground free of snow, twigs and plants of various kinds, as well as leaves and shoots from bushes and trees, will be included in the diet. Towards late summer the Reindeer readily eats fungus.

The rut falls at the end of September–October, and in May, after 220 days' pregnancy, usually only one calf is born. The summer herds consist of females, calves and one-year-old animals, and the bulls do not join them until immediately before the rut. The dominant males then attempt to keep the females together in harem groups.

In the Reindeer herd there is an order of rank: certain animals are dominant over others. The antlers play a large role in the position of the individual in this system, and experiments have shown that an animal that loses its antlers drops in rank.

At the end of the summer, the Reindeer's antlers are fully grown out but still covered in velvet. The males shed their antlers around the turn of the year, the females not until after the winter.

Reindeer

prime bull, autumn

cow, April

bull in velvet, midsummer

Roe Deer *Capreolus capreolus*

Body length up to 135 cm, tail length 2–4 cm (but tail concealed in hair of rump), shoulder height 63–75 cm, weight 18–36 kg.

The Roe Deer is the smallest—and it is tempting to add also the most elegant—of Europe's indigenous species of deer. It is warm reddish-brown in the summer, grey-brown in winter. The white rump, which is more conspicuous in winter dress than in summer, is expanded when the animal is alarmed and then functions, as in some of the other deer, as a warning signal to others of its species. In the doe it is furnished with a small downward-pointing tuft, which usually makes it possible to determine the sex of animals seen from behind. The buck has a small set of antlers with at most three points on each half. They grow out during the winter, are cleaned of velvet in March–June and shed in October–December. Younger animals are usually later than the older ones in this timetable. The newborn fawn is brownish-black, with white spots in longitudinal rows along the back and sides. In areas where Roe Deer are present it is not difficult to find footprints, but in practice they are difficult to tell from prints of other hoofed species of the same size. On the other hand, the scrape marks which the buck makes when he marks his territory by rubbing a scent gland on his forehead against sections low down on thin trunks of trees and bushes are very characteristic of the species. The territory is defended from the time the velvet is lost and through the rut. Fights along territory boundaries are often very intense, sometimes even so intense that occasional individuals are gored to death. A call that is often heard but perhaps is not always associated with Roe Deer is a stifled, repeated bark which both male and female may give if they are alarmed. In addition, a thin, disyllabic, almost whistling noise may be heard from the female during the rut.

The Roe Deer occurs within the greater part of Europe. It is absent from the far north and the Mediterranean islands, as well as Iceland and Ireland. In Britain it is abundant in Scotland, while in England it is found in the south and southwest, commonly in places, as well as in parts of the north and East Anglia. The species is also found in the temperate parts of west and central Asia.

The Roe Deer probably originated in southern deciduous forests with rich plant vegetation, but the species has shown itself to be very adaptable. With the distribution and individual abundance shown by the Roe Deer today in Scandinavia, it is almost hard to believe that about 150 years ago it was practically extinct there. It is found in woods of every conceivable kind, though usually in association with some form of open ground. The species can also live in open terrain—heather moor and agricultural country—where shelter is afforded only by, for example, reeds around a lake or ditches overgrown with weeds.

The Roe Deer has been called the epicure of deer species. Its feeding is concentrated on ground vegetation: in a Polish study, plants represented 80% of the food during the spring and summer. In a wooded region of central Sweden the Roe Deer's food in July consisted of practically nothing but herbaceous plants. Bramble predominated, but as many as 26 different species were included. The majority had been eaten only in very small amounts, i.e. animals had with great discrimination chosen the most nutritious and easily digested plants and moreover picked only the most desirable parts of them. In this case Roe Deer did not attack trees and bushes until towards the winter—and were then probably compelled to by difficult snow conditions—but in many places they also do this in summer. Even in regions with harsh winters, however, the species attempts to dig down to ground vegetation, which in the depths of winter can still form up to 30% of the food. *Vaccinium* sprigs, e.g. cowberry and

Roe Deer

There is a great difference in the
male Roe Deer's appearance between
summer and winter.

bilberry, are important food, especially in spring and autumn, and furthermore Roe Deer eat the berries, in particular cowberries. They are also fond of fungi. Locally, other plants may also make up the diet. The species can, for example, attack top and side shoots of young spruce saplings and thereby cause a certain amount of damage.

The rutting season falls at the end of July–beginning of August. The Roe Deer is the only deer species that has delayed implantation: the fertilised egg does not attach itself in the womb before December or January, and not until then does actual fetal development start. In May or June one to three fawns are then born. The fawn weighs 1.5–2.5 kg, sucks two or three times per day, and for its first few weeks stays on its own for 23 out of the 24 hours of the day. Should one come across a fawn in this situation, it should be left in peace; it has not been abandoned, even though the mother happens not to be seen.

Roe Deer are normally most active around dusk and dawn. They alternate between periods of activity when they feed and move around and periods of rest when they ruminate. The latter are about one hour long in summer but twice as long in winter. This is due to the fact that the twigs etc that make up most of the food at that time are harder to digest and simply require more cud-chewing. The size of the home range varies, one factor being the habitat type. There are reports of home ranges of around 7 ha (England), but also of ranges of about 30 ha in winter and twice as much in summer (France). In males that are not sexually mature they can be even bigger, well over 100 ha. The population density also varies. In pure woodland it can be around 30 animals per 1,000 ha, while in a landscape with alternating woodland and cultivated land it may be three times greater. In winter the Roe Deer freely assemble in groups or even herds. Exceptionally these may include as many as 20 animals, and within the group an established order of rank prevails.

A Roe Deer's antlers when fully developed have at most three points on each.

antlers from younger Roe buck

antlers from stag
of 5–7 years

Cattle, sheep and goats   Family *Bovidae*

The cattle, sheep and goats, together with the deer and others, form the larger group, usually termed suborder, of ruminants. This in turn, together with the pigs among others, makes up the order of even-toed ungulates.

The cattle, sheep and goats originated in Eurasia. A few species resistant to cold found their way successfully across to North America, while considerably more species emigrated to southern Asia and Africa. In the latter part of the world in particular, the family has since evolved a great wealth of forms.

Common to all bovids is the fact that the horns are unbranched and are not shed. They consist of a protuberance from the frontal bone—the core—which is covered by a sheath of keratin. In most species both sexes have horns.

Our Domestic Cattle belong to this family. They are descended from the Aurochs *Bos taurus*, which was found in the wild in the whole of Europe into the 11th century. In the majority of European countries it appears to have become extinct during the 1200s; it survived for longest in the Jaktorow forest in Poland, where the last individuals died in 1627. Man has tried to 're-breed' the Aurochs through interbreeding with various primitive races of Domestic Cattle, and has produced examples which at least show a strong external resemblance to that species. In addition, primitive forms of cattle have survived in several places in Europe and have changed only negligibly since Medieval times. In Britain, the white Chillingham cattle in Northumberland are a good example of this.

A further animal species worth mentioning here is the Water Buffalo, which exists in both wild (*Bubalus arnee*) and domestic (*B. bubalis*) forms in southeast Asia. The domesticated form, however, is used by man in many places in southern Europe, particularly in Italy but also in Hungary and in the Balkans, and may occasionally become almost wild.

The English Chillingham cattle is an example of a primitive form of cattle little changed since the Middle Ages.

Bison *Bison bonasus*

Body length 250–270 cm, shoulder height 180–195 cm, weight 800–900 kg (bull), 500–600 kg (cow).

The Bison, like its North American counterpart (usually known as Buffalo), presents a front-heavy impression. This is due to the coarse, tangled mane, the short broad head, the fringe, chin-beard and humped back, characters that are all more marked in the bull than in the cow.

Originally the species no doubt had a widespread distribution, and during the Stone Age it was an important quarry over large parts of Europe. From Medieval times, hunting then became—at least periodically and in certain areas—the preserve of the king and his retinue. One result of this is that the dramatic decline, both in distribution and in numbers of individuals, is fairly well known. In 1755 the species had gone from Prussia, in 1790 from Hungary, and so on, and the last examples were shot in the Bialowiecza forest in Poland in 1921 and in the Caucasus in 1925. The species would then have been extinct had there not been some remaining in zoological parks. From a stock of some tens of animals, the number of Bisons has increased through controlled breeding, so that it has even been possible for re-introductions to be made. In the Bialowiecza forest, for example, there is now a population of several hundred animals.

The species lives in deciduous forest, or mixed forest dominated by deciduous, preferably with scattered open glades.

The food is gathered both from the ground and from trees and bushes. It therefore consists of grass and plants, but also of buds, leaves and finer twigs.

The animals become sexually mature in their second or third year. The rut occurs in August–September, and in May–June (usually only) one calf is born.

The Bison is a herd animal. The herd usually consists of 10–30 individuals and is led by an old bull. Very old animals, both bulls and cows, often live as recluses.

Saiga *Saiga tatarica*

Body length 120–135 cm, tail length 9 cm, shoulder height 75–80 cm, weight 40–45 kg.

In proportion to its length, the Saiga is both short and a little heavy. This makes it slightly clumsy, an impression which is reinforced by the heavily swollen snout.

Following the last glaciation, the species had a widespread distribution in central Europe. The range contracted, however, and in the middle of the 1700s the western limit was approximately the Carpathians. After that it very rapidly went downhill, mainly because of over-hunting, and at the end of the 1800s the Saiga was considered almost extinct. In 1919 it was placed under protection in the Soviet, and from then on man began purposefully to preserve the remaining fragments of the population. The result was almost astounding. From 1930 to 1960 the number of animals increased from about 1,000 to around 2.5 million, in spite of the fact that from 1950 a careful culling of the population had taken place.

The Saiga lives in semi-deserts and on steppes, and feeds on sparse vegetation which is dominated by grass and salt-resistant plants. A full-grown animal eats up to 1.7 kg dry weight per day in summer and about 0.7 kg dry weight per day in winter. The mating season occurs in December–January and the young, usually two, are born in May–June. The species forms herds which undertake very long seasonal migrations.

Bison

Saiga

Chamois *Rupicapra rupicapra*

Body length 110–130 cm, shoulder height 70–80 cm, weight 30–50 kg (male), 25–42 kg (female).

The Chamois is probably most easily recognised by the contrasting head markings which extend on each side from the ear, over the eye and forward to the muzzle. The pattern is easy to see, even at long range. The horns, too, are distinctive. They are long, almost pliant and strangely bent backwards at the top. In summer dress the animal is pale reddish-brown, but has dark brown, almost black legs and a dark stripe down the back. During the winter the whole body takes on this dark colour. Females and young form groups on their own which in winter may join together and contain up to a hundred animals. The males live more solitarily, but attach themselves to the female groups during the rutting season. The species has a sharp whistling alarm call and also utters other sounds, including a very goat-like bleating.

The largest populations of Chamois are found in the Alps, but the species occurs in isolated populations from the Pyrenees in the west to the Carpathians in the east. In many places, for example in several of the south German mountains and in the Vosges, it is introduced animals that are involved.

The species lives in mountain regions and is well adapted to life in precipitous and rocky terrain. The first part of the species' scientific name comes from the Latin *rupes*, which indeed means rock. In spring and autumn it lives at altitudes around the tree-line; in summer higher, though rarely up to the spheres of the Ibexes; and in winter some way down in the forest.

The food consists mainly of grass and herbs of the alpine meadows, but down in the forest the Chamois may also browse on trees, even conifers. It may then eat both needles and bark.

The Chamois does not become sexually mature until four years of age. The mating season is from the middle of October to the beginning of December, and after a gestation period of 24–26 weeks the female gives birth to (usually only) one young. During the rut, the males mark the territory with scent glands located behind the horns. The display behaviour between the males includes raising of the greatly elongated hairs of the dark back stripe.

The Chamois can vary somewhat in appearance between different populations. Those in the Alps have slightly shorter and heavier horns than those in the Apennines.

Chamois

Musk Ox *Ovibos moschatus*

Body length 200–250 cm, shoulder height 130–165 cm, weight 225–400 kg (females appreciably lighter than males).

The Musk Ox is enormously solid in build. Judging from its appearance alone, it is difficult to believe that it is a close relative of the antelopes, sheep and goats, and the scientific name indicates that zoologists, too, once had difficulty in knowing exactly where it belonged systematically—*ovis* and *bos* mean respectively sheep and ox. It has a heavier coat than any other species of animal. The underfur is dense and the guard hairs are curly and long. On the sides of the body they may be up to as much as 70 cm in length, and they therefore hang down almost to the hooves. The species is well adapted to life in a cold climate: tail and outer ears are completely concealed in the coat. The horns emanate from broad bases in the centre of the crown. The bases are covered by a ridge of hair in younger animals; in older ones they are joined by a deep hairless groove.

At the time of the last glaciation, the Musk Ox had a widespread distribution in Europe and north Asia. During periods of higher temperatures the distribution was then confined to more and more restricted areas in the far north, and 3,000–4,000 years ago the species became extinct in Europe. According to some theories, heavy hunting by nomadic hunters contributed to this. The Musk Ox then survived only in Greenland and along the arctic coast of North America. During the 1900s several attempts were made to re-introduce the species in Scandinavia. The Second World War put a stop to one of these, but another, engineered after the end of the war, was successful. This has given rise to a population around the Dovrefjäll in Norway. From there, five animals wandered across to Sweden in 1971, and these too have done well. The latter group has frequented a large area on both sides of the Norway/Sweden border and has increased in numbers: in 1984 it contained 30 animals.

Musk Ox

The windswept arctic tundra is the species' natural home and the European animals resort to a similar environment in winter, sections with little snow high above the tree-line. In summer they move lower down, to the birch forest or the upper coniferous forest region. The southern limit of distribution of the species seems to be set by the July isotherm of $+10°C$.

In Sweden the food in winter consists mostly of lichens, *Vaccinium* twigs, grass and sedge. In summer it varies more and includes willow, dwarf birch, birch and also many herbaceous plants, e.g. mountain angelica and alpine lettuce.

During the rut, which is in July/August, both courting of females and fighting between the males occur. Usually it is the leading male of the herd that is challenged, and the challenge can lead to a fight which is probably among the most violent in the animal world. It starts with prolonged displaying of horns etc, but then the males slowly back away from each other while swinging their heavy heads from side to side. The distance between them may increase to getting on for 50 m before they stop and rush at each other. The result is a violent collision, but the process may be repeated at least ten times before one party gives up. The gestation period is eight to nine months, the animals become sexually mature at two to four years of age, and the female then gives birth to usually one calf every other year. Deviations from this are perhaps not too unusual. Thus the oldest female in the group that reached Sweden in 1971 gave birth to at least eight, perhaps nine, calves in a period of 13 years.

The Musk Ox is a herd animal. In the summer the herd normally consists of a dozen animals; in the winter the number may increase even to over 50. The species actually has only two enemies, Wolf and man. It has developed a defence behaviour that consists of the herd closing together in a tight group in which the old animals are on the outside and form a front-line against the attacker.

Ibex *Capra ibex*

Body length 130–150 cm, tail length 12–15 cm, shoulder height 65–85 cm, weight 80–125 kg (males), 50–55 kg (females).

In this goat-like animal both sexes have horns. Females and young up to three years old form separate groups which are very sedentary: they may live all year within an area of only about one square kilometre. The males, which are consistently much more mobile, form groups in summer, but during the autumn gradually change to living more and more solitarily. The Ibex is closely related to the Domestic Goat: it can interbreed with it and produce fertile offspring. As a result of such interbreeding, and probably also interbreeding farther back in time with wild ancestors of the Domestic Goat, the species occurs in various forms. The *Alpine Ibex* is, so far as is known, the only form that has not been influenced by such interbreeding. The male's horns are long, heavy, curved like sabres, and on the front edge equipped with parallel ridges; the female's are appreciably smaller. In rocky terrain the brown to brownish-grey colour of the body can easily merge into the background, but if the animal is seen diagonally from below—which is the norm, bearing in mind where the species lives—the pale belly is very conspicuous. In the *Spanish Ibex* the horns are twisted in a slight spiral outwards and upwards, and also lack ridges. This form varies a great deal in other respects: variations include animals with very pale coloration, with a black stripe down the back, and with a more or less pronounced beard. Finally, in the *Wild Goat*, the ancestral form of the Domestic Goat, the horns are evenly semicircular in shape; they have a sharp, almost wedge-shaped front edge, but indistinct widely spaced ridges.

The Alpine Ibex was at one time still found only in the Gran Paradiso National Park in Italy, but successful transplantations have been made from there to many other places in the Alps and the Tatra Mountains. The Spanish Ibex is found in isolated populations in several of the Spanish mountain regions, the most northerly being on the southern slopes of the Pyrenees. In Crete and a few other Greek islands the Wild Goat can perhaps still be found in pure form, but the majority of the goats that live here have during the passage of time become mixed with domestic animals. Domestic Goats that have gone wild are found in several places in Wales, Scotland, Ireland and the Mediterranean.

The Ibexes live all year round in undulating, high-lying mountain districts, often around 2,000 m above sea level or higher. The only time the animal can be seen below the tree-line is in the spring, when groups of males may occasionally descend that far in search of the first verdure. The other forms live at a lower level, but also in steep and rocky terrain.

The major food is grass. Herbaceous plants of various kinds are often included, ligneous plants and lichens more rarely. The nutritional value of the food decreases with altitude above sea. In precipitous terrain their search for food can cause damage from trampling, which may later result in erosion. The Wild Goat and feral Domestic Goats browse more on trees and bushes.

The rut falls in December or at the beginning of January. Following a gestation period of 21–23 weeks, the female then gives birth to usually one but occasionally two young. Reproduction is influenced by the weather conditions, and can drop drastically after a rainy spring when many fetuses are resorbed.

Areas where avalanches have advanced can sometimes offer easily accessible food but are also, on account of the risk of new landslides, dangerous places to feed. Males appear to be more vulnerable to this type of mishap than females.

Ibex

Mouflon *Ovis musimon*

Body length 110–130 cm, shoulder height 65–75 cm, weight 25–50 kg.

The Mouflon is a small wild sheep with a short-haired coat. The ram usually has a white 'saddle' patch which, in combination with dark areas on the neck and upper part of the legs, together with white 'socks', white stern and white muzzle, contributes to its variegated impression. Its horns are heavy, and, in a full-grown adult, twisted almost a complete revolution. The ewe has either a pair of short horny stumps (Corsica) or lacks horns (Sardinia). The tracks are recognised by the fact that the hooves are strongly splayed outwards.

The species is found endemically or at least has long been present in Sardinia and Corsica. From there it has been introduced, mainly as a hunting quarry, in many European countries.

On the two Mediterranean islands the Mouflon sheep lives in steep mountain woods near the tree-line. A large part of its feeding takes place at night on open slopes at considerably higher altitude. In regions where it has been introduced it may also adapt to other habitats, e.g. deciduous wood or extensive pasture meadows.

The Mouflon feeds mainly from the ground and the major food is therefore grass and plants. Leaves and tender twigs, however, are also included and the species may even gnaw bark, particularly in winter.

During the rut, which falls in October–November, the rams fight out intense duels. The lambs, usually only one per ewe, are born after a gestation period of about five months. The ewe becomes sexually mature before she is even one year old, the ram not until its second year of life.

The species is regarded by some as the ancestor of the Domestic Sheep, by others as a species that has long since run wild from Domestic Sheep. In reasonably undisturbed conditions, the ewes and lambs form flocks on their own which keep together throughout the year. The rams join these flocks only during the rut.

Mouflon

Whales
Order *Cetacea*

The whales are adapted to life in water to a greater extent than any other order of mammals. The young are born at sea and the whales are unique in being unable to survive for very long if they are washed ashore.

Their ancestors, however, lived several tens of millions years ago on land, but made their way first down to shallow coastal areas, then more and more out towards the open sea. Possible reasons for this development are that there was fiercer competition for food on land than in the water, that the pressure from large terrestrial carnivores favoured those forms which got by in water, and also that extreme climatic changes could have more devastating effects on terrestrial fauna than on aquatic fauna.

The connection between the whales' aquatic life and their body structure is very obvious. Their shape is extremely streamlined, with a smooth body surface: all irregularities are levelled out by a thick layer of blubber beneath the skin. This blubber also has other functions, including insulation (in this respect it replaces the fur, which has been lost in the whales). Nor does the skin have any sweat glands, but excess heat is released via blood vessels in the blubber layer that can be regulated. Finally, the blubber acts as reserve food, particularly in connection with long migrations or when staying in areas poor in food.

The front limbs are transformed into fins, while all other protruding parts of the body—outer ears, external sex organs and hindlimbs—have disappeared. It is therefore not the hindlimbs that are the whales' organ of propulsion—which it is in the seals—but the tail, which is equipped with a powerful horizontal tail fin (fluke). Using this, even the largest species of whales can reach a speed of 25–30 km per hour.

Living in water places special demands on everything that has to do with breathing, since the whales, like all other species of mammals, are dependent on the air's oxygen. Except in the Sperm Whale, the nasal openings take the form of one or two blowholes high up on the head and these are the first thing that reaches the air when a whale rises to the surface. On diving, they are shut off by reflex action. The blood is extremely rich in red blood corpuscles and is therefore able to carry unusually large amounts of oxygen. During diving, it is also 'shunted' so that organs which have to work hard (heart and nervous system) receive normal blood and oxygen supply, while others (e.g. digestive organs and kidneys) receive reduced supplies and therefore function at low level until the whale returns to the surface again. In addition, the whales are fairly insensitive to an increased content of carbon dioxide in the blood. They also have mechanisms which counter the effects of caisson disease (the bends), the very dangerous condition brought on when the air's gases, in particular nitrogen, are released in small bubbles into the blood as a result of the reduction in pressure that takes

The whales' hindlimbs have evolved regressively, and remain only as insignificant non-functioning remnants of bone.

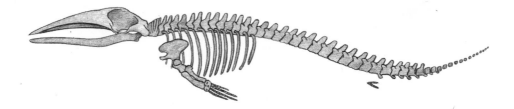

The appearance of the blow varies among different whales. From left to right here, Sperm Whale, Fin Whale, Humpback and right whale are shown.

place on rapid movement upwards from great depths. Thanks partly to this adaptation, some whale species can remain underwater for more than one hour and dive to a depth of more than 1,000 m.

When a large whale has been underwater and comes up after a long dive, it gives a snort. The warm, moist air from lungs and air passages then condenses into a visible cloud, the whale's 'blow'. The shape and angle of direction of this can be a guide in species identification.

Many whale species have strikingly large brains: proportionately they are fully comparable with man's. The development of the brain and the rest of the nervous system is a good reflection of the importance of the various sense organs. Olfactory lobes and olfactory nerves are rudimentary (baleen whales) or lacking altogether (toothed whales), and the whales' sense of smell is indeed insignificant. By contrast, the auditory nerves and a nerve conducting impulses from sensory cells just below the skin in the front part of the head are large and well developed. The same applies equally to the appropriate centres in the large brain. And quite rightly the sense of touch and to an even greater degree the sense of hearing are tremendously important to the whales.

The sense of touch is important particularly in the baleen whales. On the front part of the head they have tactile hairs which are used for locating food at close quarters. The sense of hearing is important in all whales. It is adapted to function underwater and picks up sounds of at least two different kinds. One is ultrasound, which the whales use as an echo-sounder, in other words to navigate and to search for prey. Exactly how this is achieved is not known, but the whales can both detect prey at a very long distance and separate objects which differ only very slightly in size, shape or structure. The second kind of sound includes the calls with which the whales communicate. In a great many species these are extremely variable and complex; the Humpback Whale, for example, sounds almost as if it were singing when it utters long series of whistling, twittering, tooting and blowing sounds.

Some research workers consider that the whales are able—chiefly with ultrasound—even to 'listen in to' each others' bodies and in this way detect disorders or injuries, possibly even state of mind. An injured whale would accordingly be able to get help from others of its species. It has even been argued whether this could be behind the strange events which occur from time to time when several or even many tens of whales, over a day or more, become stranded together on beaches and die. The injured whale would in this case head for land, and the others be so absorbed in their efforts to help it that they would not see the danger in time. Other explanations have also been discussed. One of these is based on careful studies of a situation in October 1982, when 28 Long-finned Pilot Whales were stranded on the east coast of England. They turned out to be heavily infected with a roundworm which was found, among other places, in great numbers in cavities close to the middle ear. There they could possibly interfere with the transportation of sound to the inner ear and in this way impair echo-navigation. The stranded whales would in that case have first all navigated off course. They might also have done this for other reasons. There are theories that the whales had orientated with the help of the earth's magnetism, and at least one comprehensive study supports this idea. This shows that 95% of these mass strandings have occurred at exactly those places on the earth where the earth's magnetic field is of negligible intensity.

In at least some species of whales breeding begins with very extensive courtship ceremonies. Mating itself, which happens belly to belly either horizontally in the water or with the whales rising up partly out of the water, then takes place quickly. The gestation period varies somewhat but is up to a year or more—in the Long-finned Pilot Whale, for example, it is as much as 16 months. In many species, including the dolphins, the young is born tail first, no doubt an adaptation that reduces the risk of drowning. After the birth, the young is led to the surface to take its first breath. Normally it is very probably the mother that does this, but she may occasionally be helped with the job by another female. The young of the largest species are more than 7 m long at birth, and during the next six to nine months they double their length solely on mother's milk.

Many whale species undertake long annual migrations between the cold polar seas, which are rich in food in summer, and warm tropical waters, which are more suitable for breeding. Grey Whales in the Pacific Ocean may in this way travel up to 30,000 km every year.

There is said to be an old Japanese proverb that a dead whale signifies prosperity for seven villages, and whales have been hunted by man since a very long time back. From the start it was eskimos and other primitive people who hunted for their own needs with primitive weapons from land or in inshore waters. For them the whales' flesh, skins, blubber etc were products vital to life. This still applies to a certain extent, even though both weapons and boats have obviously been modernised.

From time to time schools of whales are stranded and die. The reasons for these strandings are not known, but it has been shown that dead whales may be infected with worms in such a way that the animals' echo-navigation may have been interfered with.

Early on, however, another type of hunting also began in which the hunters were not themselves dependent on the prey but sold it. The Basques are said to have been the first in the field. To begin with they hunted right whales off the Spanish coasts, but when things started to get more difficult—as they did as early as the 1500s—they moved up towards Greenland with larger whaling expeditions. During the 1600s the Dutch and the English came in, and in the middle of the 1700s over 250 whaling boats were operating in arctic waters. A characteristic of the activity, however, was that it went in waves. One species or a group of species was hunted as intensively as possible, and, when stocks then diminished to the point that this hunting was no longer profitable, it took time before varieties to hunt next were found, perhaps species a little less big or more difficult to come across. For this reason, the activity had decreased very markedly towards the end of the 1700s.

It started up again, however, this time mainly through the Americans. They, too, went in for right whales first, but changed over to Sperm Whales, which contain oil with slightly different properties from those found in the majority of other species. The oil was used in the mid 1800s primarily as a lubricant and for heating of dwellings, but with the growth of the petroleum industry towards the end of the same century, it quickly lost its importance. With that, hunting of Sperm Whales also declined. It gained renewed impetus, however, during the 1900s when the oil started to be used as a base in the cosmetics industry, and for long periods the Sperm Whale was the most hunted species, measured both in number of individuals and in total weight of the catch. In 1981 a total ban was introduced on catching of Sperm Whales, and with that a stop was put—at least for the time being—to the longest persecution in terms of time that any individual whale species had been subjected to.

Behind this decision and many other regulations concerning whaling is the International Whaling Commission (IWC), which since 1946 has been responsible for the supervision of this activity on the world's oceans. The work of the commission has involved a long drawn-out tug-of-war between blocks of non-whaling and whaling countries. In the latter, Japan and the Soviet Union in particular but also Norway have played important roles.

In this tug-of-war the IWC has succeeded in achieving on the one hand catch quotas for various whale populations—in other words a top limit on the numbers that may be caught each year—and on the other total bans on catching, as in the case of Sperm Whales. The work has, however, progressed slowly, the opposition has been great, and the commission has had to endure much criticism. The catch quotas have been criticised for being based less on biological facts and more on calculations regarding the profitability of the whaling industry, and the protection orders for having been introduced too late, in many cases not until a species had become so few in number that hunting was no longer justifiable economically. In July 1982, however, the IWC took an historic decision: a five-year ban from the 1985/86 season on commercial whaling. Time will show whether this can bring a turn around in the drastic decline for many of the world's species of whales.

The contrast between the traditional whale-hunting by primitive people and commercial catching from ships is tremendous.

Toothed whales
Suborder Odontoceti

The species belonging to this suborder are distinguished by having teeth. The number can vary, however, from two in some beaked whales (which moreover are well developed only in the male) to 120 in some dolphins. All these teeth are of the same type. Furthermore, the toothed whales have an asymmetrical cranium and only one blowhole. The number of species is about 65, the number of families seven. Of these, all except the river dolphins (Platanistidae) occur in European waters.

Dolphins   Family *Delphinidae*

The dolphin family is so diverse that it is sometimes divided into subfamilies. The closest relations are in some of the genera which might make up these separate units. Several common features, however, are found throughout the family. The dolphins are fast. They are also slim, have a narrow, generally prominent snout, and all European species have a large, slightly backward-bent dorsal fin placed approximately in the middle of the back. The teeth are pointed, unlike those of the porpoises which are blunt. The family consists in total of about 30 species, of which ten appear in Europe. Sometimes an eleventh species is also stated to be found here. This is the Spotted Dolphin *Stenella dubia*, which lives along the North American Atlantic coast and which is claimed to have been found once in France. The report has, however, been called in question, since for one thing it appears to be impossible to find out whether the specimen is preserved, and the species is not included here.

Rough-toothed Dolphin *Steno bredanensis*

With a body length of 2.1 m maximum, the Rough-toothed Dolphin is among the small members of the family—in Europe it is the smallest species. It also has a characteristic pattern, with black upperside, white belly and pale, irregular spots on the sides. The snout is drawn out into a point, and the teeth—20–37 in each half-jaw—have a network of fine ridges which gives them a rough surface. The species is found in tropical and subtropical seas throughout the world. It occurs in the Mediterranean Sea, but farther north it has been encountered only a few times.

Striped Dolphin *Stenella coeruleoalba*

This is a small dolphin—the body length is at most 2.7 m. In proportions it is very similar to the Common Dolphin, but it has an elegant, almost graceful pattern of white, grey and blue along the side of the body. The number of teeth in each half-jaw is 43–50, and they are small—only about 3 mm in diameter. The species occurs in schools of 30–40 and is found in tropical and subtropical waters all around the world. It has been reported a few times from Europe, and then only from the southwesternmost part.

Common Dolphin *Delphinus delphis*

This species, in many places the commonest dolphin, reaches a top length of
3 m. It has a clearly defined beak and a contrasting pattern along the side of the
body. As regards the colour of this pattern, there are wide variations between
different areas, but it often contains a bright yellow patch. The species is one of
the dolphins seen most, owing to its habit of accompanying ships. Then it often
plays in the bow-wave, rides on the waves and leaps high above the surface of the
water. It is found in all the world's oceans except in the polar areas, though it
also sometimes visits these as a result of favourable temperatures and thus
feeding conditions. It joins other dolphin species and appears in schools of
hundreds, sometimes as many as 1,000 animals. In such a school the movements are frequently synchronous: the members dive and then surface to breathe
all more or less at the same time. Together with Porpoise and Bottle-nosed
Dolphin, this species has been hunted very heavily in the Black Sea/Sea of Azov.
The highest catch figures were reached during the 1930s, when together more
than a quarter of a million individuals of the three species were taken each year,
with the Common Dolphin the predominant species. Up to 120,000 Common
Dolphins were taken annually. In the 1960s the catch figures were down to
5,000–7,000 per year, and the Porpoise then predominated. It has been
estimated that the combined populations of the three species have during the
last 50 years been depleted from nearly one million individuals to somewhere
near one-fifth of this. Pollution, however, has no doubt also played an important
part in this decrease.

Rough-toothed Dolphin

Striped Dolphin

Common Dolphin

Bottle-nosed Dolphin *Tursiops truncatus*

The Bottle-nosed Dolphin reaches up to 4.1 m long and is thus one size bigger than the smallest dolphin species. It is also plainer in pattern, white below and pale steel-grey above, a colour that quickly darkens, however, in beached individuals. The beak is clearly defined but rather short, not quite reaching the tip of the lower jaw. This has given rise to the scientific specific name *truncatus*, which is Latin and means cut off: the beak looks as if it is cut short. The species is found mainly along the coasts of tropical and temperate seas throughout the world. To the public at large, however, wild Bottle-nosed Dolphins are much less familiar than those in captivity, since the species is far and away the commonest dolphin in dolphinaria. There it is affectionate, playful and tremendously competent at learning to perform tricks of various kinds.

White-beaked Dolphin *Lagenorhynchus albirostris*

The White-beaked Dolphin, which grows up to 3.1 m long, has an extraordinary black and white pattern which varies a great deal among different individuals. The beak, however, is nearly always white, which is the character borne in mind in many languages when naming the species. This applies also to the scientific specific name, which is a compound of the Latin *albus* and *rostrum*, meaning white and nose respectively. Other identification marks are that the back fin is large and bent backwards, and that each half-jaw contains 22–25 teeth with a diameter of around 6 mm. The species is found in the entire North Atlantic and is common in the North Sea. It moves about usually in groups of tens of individuals.

White-sided Dolphin *Lagenorhynchus acutus*

This species is roughly the same size as the previous one—its top length is 3 m—and also resembles it in appearance. It differs in that the beak is black, that a band of colour on the side above the white belly has a tinge of yellow or brown in it, and also that the rear part of the body is relatively deep and narrow—it looks as if it is laterally compressed. In addition, this area is bordered above by a keel running between the back fin and the tail fluke. A skull washed ashore or a stranded individual can be distinguished from the White-beaked Dolphin by having more but rather smaller teeth: 30–40 in each half-jaw, but only about 5 mm in diameter. The species occurs only in the northern parts of the North Atlantic, but moves seasonally between arctic and temperate waters. Summer schools in particular up in the Arctic can consist of up to 1,000 individuals.

Bottle-nosed Dolphin

White-beaked Dolphin

White-sided Dolphin

False Killer Whale *Pseudorca crassidens*

This species of dolphin, which reaches 6 m in length, is a little like both the Long-finned Pilot Whale and the Killer Whale. It is, however, entirely black. It differs from the Long-finned Pilot Whale also in the nine to 11 teeth in each half-jaw being much bigger. It is these, too, that have given the species its scientific name: it is formed from the Latin *crassus* and *dens*, which mean thick and tooth respectively. In cross-section the teeth are circular and around 25 mm in diameter, compared with about half that in the Long-finned Pilot Whale. The dentition is thus very reminiscent of the Killer Whale's, which indicates that the False Killer, too, concentrates to a certain extent on large prey animals. It is found in all the seas of the world apart from the polar areas, but is rare: the species was not described until 1846. It is fast, and has been shown to be capable of swimming at a speed in excess of 55 km per hour (34 mph).

Killer Whale *Orcinus orca*

With a body length in the male of up to 10 m—the female reaches only 5 m at most—the Killer Whale is the largest species of dolphin. The parti-coloured pattern of black and white is characteristic, and in the male the strikingly high back fin is also distinctive; it may grow to as much as 1.8 m. The teeth are like those of the False Killer Whale but are slightly oval in cross-section and even bigger, 25–30 mm in diameter. The species is found in all the seas of the world and generally lives far from land, but is also encountered for example in the Baltic and the Mediterranean. It moves about in schools of at most a few tens of animals and can swim fast, over 60 km per hour (37 mph). The Killer Whale probably lives mainly on fish, but is known more for its habit of attacking larger prey. This involves mostly squid, seals and other dolphin species, but the school may also jointly attack considerably larger species of whales. The species' behaviour in captivity may seem to some extent to contrast with this: captive individuals are easily trained and become very attached to their keeper.

Risso's Dolphin *Grampus griseus*

This species attains a maximum length of 4 m, and is therefore almost the same size as the Bottle-nosed Dolphin. It is also similar in colour, with a white belly and grey back and sides—*griseus* means grey in Latin. The forehead, however, bulges forward almost as on a Long-finned Pilot Whale and the head has a slight yellow tinge. In addition, there are often parallel scars on the sides of the body. These are believed to be bite marks from its own species, which if so suggests a certain amount of aggression within the species. Risso's Dolphin occurs in tropical and temperate seas over the whole world. In Europe it appears regularly around the British Isles, but considerably more rarely north of this.

False Killer Whale

Killer Whale

Risso's Dolphin

Long-finned Pilot Whale *Globicephala melaena*

The Long-finned Pilot Whale grows to a maximum length of 6 m, has a top weight of 3 tonnes, and most closely resembles a Bottle-nosed Whale. In particular, the forehead is arched in the same way and this is alluded to in the scientific generic name. This is a compound of the Latin *globus* and the Greek *kephale*, which mean globe and head respectively. The species lacks the Bottle-nosed Whale's pointed beak, though, and the curved back fin is placed a long way forward. To this may be added the Long-finned Pilot Whale's more variegated colour pattern, particularly below, and its considerably longer flippers, which may be up to a fifth of the length of the body. The species occurs in two geographically isolated forms, usually regarded as different races. One is found in the Pacific Ocean but enters the Indian Ocean and the southernmost parts of the Atlantic; the other lives in the North Atlantic. The Long-finned Pilot Whale is sociable and forms schools of up to several hundred animals. These often come within sight of ships, even in shallow, coastal waters. Because of this the Long-finned Pilot Whale is one of the species most often stranded (page 208). It has also been hunted over centuries—mainly in the Faeroes but also in other places—by the local inhabitants with small boats driving in and killing whole schools in harbours or enclosed, shallow bays.

Porpoises   Family *Phocoenidae*

Six whale species belong to the porpoise family. All are small, short-nosed, dumpy and equipped with around 23 blunt teeth in each half-jaw. Only one species occurs in Europe.

Porpoise *Phocoena phocoena*

The Porpoise reaches no more than 1.8 m in length and is thus the smallest of all European whale species. Only a close relative which lives off California—the Cochito *P. sinus*—is smaller. When briefly glimpsed, and if no idea is obtained of the size, a Porpoise can be difficult to distinguish from small dolphins. The latter, however, have a more pointed snout and a higher, more recurved back fin, and they can also leap right out of the water, which the Porpoise does not do. The Porpoise is found in all seas around Europe and, so far as differences from dolphins are concerned, habitat choice can also be a guide: the Porpoise lives near the coast and groups or small schools frequently make their way towards river estuaries, occasionally even up into larger rivers. This makes it easily accessible for hunters and in some areas it has been very heavily hunted. In the Danish zones, for example, as early as the 1500s up to as many as 3,000 Porpoises were taken, at least in some years; at the end of the 1800s the figure was 1,000–2,000. The stocks in the Baltic and the North Sea are also very severely depleted, but this is to a great extent caused also by factors other than hunting. Living in shallow, coastal waters and on a narrow diet of fish means that the Porpoise is exposed to environmental pollution, mainly DDT and PCB, and on top of this many Porpoises get drowned in fishing nets. In this respect, modern synthetic nets seem to be considerably more dangerous than nets of natural material.

Long-finned Pilot Whale

Porpoise

White whales   Family *Monodontidae*

A whale family that exhibits primitive features with regard to some details of body structure. The cervical vertebrae, for example, are independent and do not meet. The family is found only in the Arctic, and is sometimes considered to have survived there at least partly because it has avoided competition from other whales. It consists of only two species.

White Whale *Delphinapterus leucas*

The White Whale grows up to 5 m long and is therefore approximately the same size as the Narwhal. Adults are pure white, juveniles are grey, and unlike Narwhals it has eight to ten teeth in each jaw. The scientific generic name is a compound of the Greek *delphis*, which means dolphin, together with the prefix *a* and *pteron*, which mean respectively without and wing or fin: the White Whale resembles a dolphin without a back fin. From its circumpolar arctic range the species not infrequently moves southwards, including into the North Sea, where it readily comes close inshore. This is an important quarry for man in the Arctic, and the total stock is estimated at between 32,000 and 58,000 animals.

Narwhal *Monodon monoceros*

The body length in the Narwhal reaches a maximum of 5.5 m. To this can be added (in the male) the tusk, which is usually about half as long as the body and can grow to as much as 3 m. It is the sole front tooth in the left half of the upper jaw, which shoots off in a spiral into an organ which has given the name to the family as well as the genus and species: *monos* and *odous* mean single and tooth respectively, while *keres* is a horn. The male also has a small tooth in the right half of the upper jaw, but in other respects the species is toothless. The tusk provides some of the substance behind the myth of the unicorn, but its biological function is probably only partly known. The males, however, use it against each other during the mating season. The Narwhal, which is found in a circumpolar distribution in arctic seas, regularly moves along the north Norwegian coast, more rarely farther south. It has never been hunted commercially, but is an important quarry for the local inhabitants. This has meant harsh treatment for the Asiatic populations, which are possibly totally extinct, but the population around Canada/Greenland is estimated at around 10,000 animals.

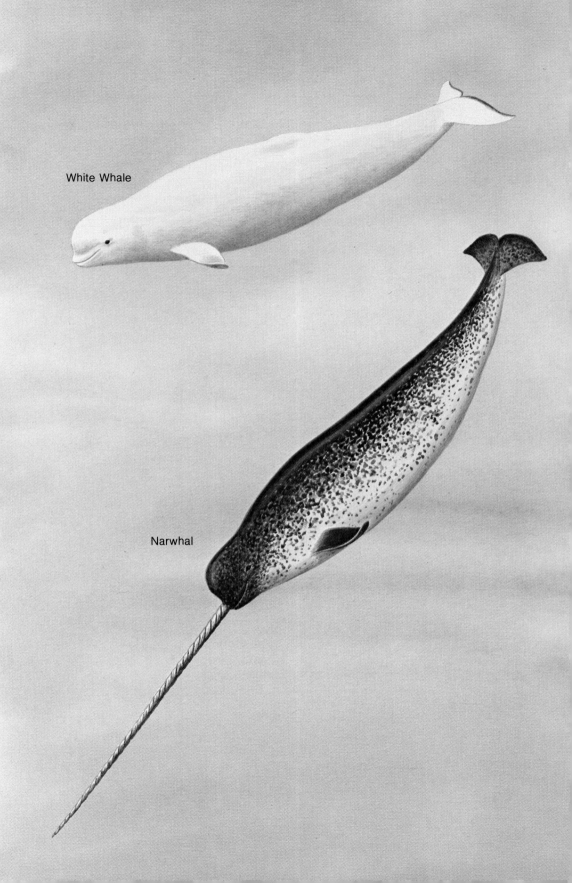

White Whale

Narwhal

Sperm whales Family *Physeteridae*

A small family with species that are very different in size but which have several features in common. Functional teeth are present only in the lower jaw, but they are many: 10–30 in each half-jaw. In the head there is what is known as a 'spermaceti' organ, a cavity filled with waxy oil which among other things has an influence on the animal's buoyancy. It was this very oil that made the sperm whales so desirable for the whalers. The skull is asymmetrical and the blowhole (the nasal openings) is located on the left side. The family consists of three species, two of which occur in Europe.

Pygmy Sperm Whale *Kogia breviceps*

The Pygmy Sperm Whale reaches a top length of 3.5 m, and thus lives up to its name. It also exhibits other differences compared with its larger relative. These include a well-developed back fin and by comparison a considerably smaller head. This latter fact is the background to the scientific specific name, which is a compound of the Latin *brevis* and *ceps* (from *caput*), meaning quite simply short and head respectively. The species is found, but rarely, in tropical and subtropical seas all over the world, and has become stranded a few times on coasts of west Europe.

Sperm Whale *Physeter catodon*

With a total length in the male of normally up to 18 m—in extreme cases to as much as 25 m—and a top weight of 55 tonnes, the Sperm Whale is the largest species of toothed whale. The male is fully comparable in size with the biggest baleen whales. The female, however, is much smaller; she reaches a maximum length of 12 m and weighs no more than 16 tonnes. The most distinctive characteristic of the species is the colossal head, which is almost rectangular and which represents about a third of the animal's total length. The blow is also characteristic. It is directed obliquely forward because the blowhole is not up on the top of the crown as in other whales, but far forward on the head and also on the left side. Females and young animals live in warm seas, mainly between 40°S and 40°N, while older males undertake extensive migrations. There is even an old record from inside Baltic waters, and reports from the Atlantic include one of a male that was marked in 1966 off Canada's east coast and re-captured seven years later immediately off Spain. The food, some of which is obtained at considerable depths—at least in some cases down to 1,000 m—consists for the most part of squid. Even very large ones are taken, and it is common for Sperm Whales to have scars on their body from squids' suckers. No other species of whale has been hunted commercially for a longer period of time than the Sperm Whale (see page 210). The Sperm Whale is not, however, among the most severely affected species, one reason being that hunting has to a large degree been directed against the males. Calculations show that numbers were roughly halved during the time when commercial whaling was going on. For a population which has been reduced to this level, however, it takes a century from the cessation of catching for it to recover to 90% of its original level. In the mid 1970s the total population in the North Atlantic was estimated at around 38,000 animals.

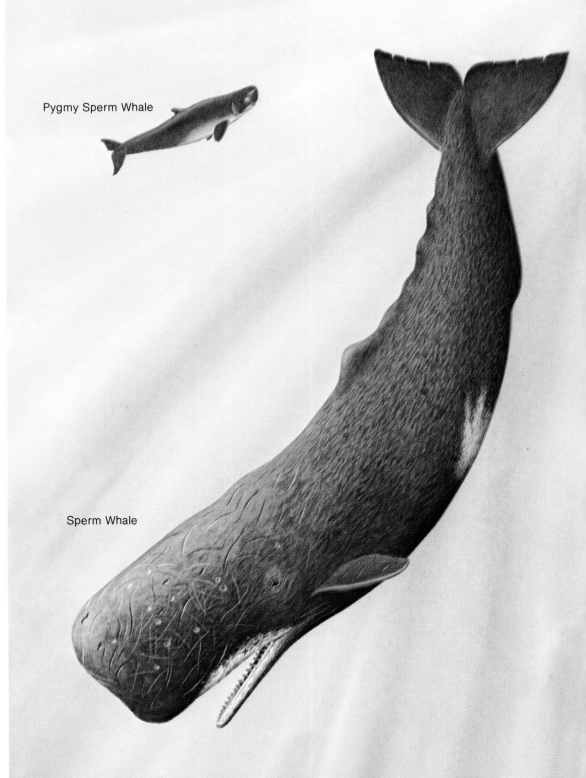

Pygmy Sperm Whale

Sperm Whale

Beaked whales   Family *Ziphiidae*

The family of beaked whales is so named because of the snout, which is protracted into a point. The species are medium-sized (5–10 m), have a triangular back fin placed far back—about two-thirds of the distance between snout and tail—and have a much reduced set of teeth. In the upper jaw there are no teeth at all, in the lower jaw often only two. These may be shaped like small tusks, which is sometimes interpreted as an adaptation for catching cuttle-fish and squid. If this is true, the food probably varies between the sexes since the female's teeth are so poorly developed that sometimes they do not even erupt properly. In addition the beaked whales have two pairs of longitudinal grooves in the skin on the throat.

Sowerby's Whale   *Mesoplodon bidens*

This species grows up to 7 m long. All species in the genus *Mesoplodon* are, incidentally, approximately equal in size and furthermore are relatively similar to one another in appearance. The generic name is formed from the Greek *mesos*, *oplon* and *odon*, which respectively mean the middle, a weapon and tooth, and the teeth are indeed located in the middle of the lower jaw and are probably used by the males as weapons when fighting over the females. The males at any rate often bear scratches along the sides. The specific name *bidens* in fact means simply that it has two teeth. Sowerby's Whale is found commonly in the cooler parts of the North Atlantic and appears regularly in the North Sea.

Gervais's Whale   *Mesoplodon europaeus*

Gervais's Whale is very like the previous species, but a stranded individual can be identified by the fact that the teeth are not located in the middle of the lower jaw but near the tip. The scientific specific name may seem to suggest that this is a European species of whale, but it derives from the fact that the first individual described had stranded itself in north France. The species is found in the warmest parts of the North Atlantic and is probably commonest in waters around the West Indies.

True's Beaked Whale   *Mesoplodon mirus*

Owing to its pale, often rather spotted throat and underside, this species differs slightly in terms of appearance from other *Mesoplodon* species. Moreover, it should not be assigned to this genus literally speaking, since the teeth are placed in the tip of the lower jaw. The species has long been known from the North Atlantic, where strandings happen now and again both on the east coast of the USA and on the west coast of Europe. Recent discoveries in South Africa, however, intimate that the range may be considerably more extensive.

Sowerby's Whale

Gervais's Whale

True's Beaked Whale

Gray's Whale *Mesoplodon grayi*

This, on average the smallest of the *Mesoplodon* species, is either all-dark or dark with a pale, lengthways striped belly. The teeth in the lower jaw are located centrally between the middle and the tip of the lower jaw. It lives in temperate waters in the southern hemisphere, but has been stranded once in Holland.

Blainville's Whale *Mesoplodon densirostris*

This species, too, is very like the other small beaked whales. The back fin is proportionately large, but the only safe specific identification character is that the teeth in the lower jaw on the one hand are strikingly well developed and on the other are placed on a sturdy elevation of bone in the centre of the jaw. The distribution appears to embrace tropical and subtropical seas right across the earth; in Europe stranded individuals have been reported from Madeira and Spain.

Cuvier's Whale *Ziphius cavirostris*

A species that does not grow quite so big as the Bottle-nosed Whale—the length is no more than 8 m—and which also differs from that species in having a profile that is entirely different. It lacks the prominent forehead. The colour can be either uniform grey or darker blackish-brown with pale head and front part of body. The species is found in tropical and temperate seas throughout the world.

Bottle-nosed Whale *Hyperoodon ampullatus*

This species, which is the commonest beaked whale, can grow up to 10 m long. It differs from its closest relatives particularly in the very pronounced forehead, especially in the male. The scientific specific name, which it has got from the Latin *ampulla* and *-atus*, meaning respectively bottle and equipped with, alludes to the fact that the well-defined snout may perhaps be likened to the neck of a bottle. The species is found in the North Atlantic and is well known for its habit of approaching ships, in particular those lying at anchor. It has been hunted since the end of the last century, with one peak in 1890–1900 when 2,000–3,000 individuals were taken each year, and another during the 1960s. The species was then caught more as a by-product of other whale catches and the highest catch figure was barely 700 per year. The total population has been estimated at between 14,000 and 26,000 individuals.

Gray's Whale

Blainville's Whale

Cuvier's Whale

Bottle-nosed Whale

Baleen whales
Suborder Mysticeti

The species within this suborder are, with one exception, large or very large. The exception is the Pygmy Right Whale *Caperea marginata*, which is, however, found only in the southern hemisphere. The baleen whales lack teeth. Instead they have whalebone or baleen, large, triangular horny plates which hang down from the roof of the mouth cavity. These are sited roughly at right angles to the animal's longitudinal axis and are heavily frayed along the inner edge. In these frayed fringes, the food—mostly small crustaceans known as krill, which have a lifestyle like plankton—is strained out of the sea water by the whale swimming with its mouth open into a shoal and then shutting its mouth and squeezing out the water between the baleen plates. Nowadays seven species of baleen whales belonging to two different families appear in European seas. The Grey Whale *Eschrichtius gibbosus/E. robustus* which is found in the Pacific Ocean occurred earlier in the Atlantic, too, but has been missing from there since the beginning of the 1700s.

Rorquals and Humpback Whale
Family *Balaenopteridae*

This family contains five species which are fairly different in size yet have several common characters. They are slim, well proportioned, and fast swimmers. A small back fin is located well behind the animal's middle. Sixty to 90 longitudinal grooves run from the throat backwards, and these enable this area to be expanded considerably in conjunction with taking in of food.

Blue Whale *Balaenoptera musculus*

There is not, and nor so far as we know has there ever been, any animal on earth larger than the Blue Whale. The female, which on average is slightly bigger than the male, is normally 25–30 m, in extreme cases up to as much as 35 m long, and can weight up to 150 tonnes. How then can this colossal animal have acquired the scientific specific name of *musculus*, which means little mouse and which is also the specific name of the House Mouse? Well, this is not known, but the naming is possibly based on a misunderstanding. The Roman author Pliny used the name for a sea creature which Linnaeus believed was the Blue Whale but which was instead probably a pilot fish, a small fish that does not accompany whales but sharks. As far as the Blue Whale's coloration is concerned, there is no great difference between upperside and underside but the whole animal is an even blue-grey or grey with irregular white flecks particularly on sides and belly. The baleen plates are short, broad, and all-black, and the blow is narrow and high—up to 7 m. The species is found in all the oceans of the world, but owing to heavy persecution it has drastically diminished and there are probably small groups left that live in complete isolation from the others of the species. The 10,000 or so Blue Whales that are reckoned to exist in the world's oceans as a whole—of these only a few hundred are found in the North Atlantic—represent approximately 6% of what there were up until the time commercial catching started.

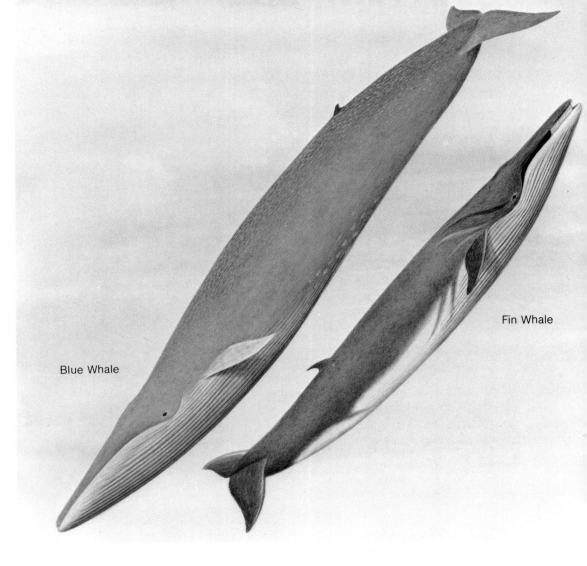

Blue Whale

Fin Whale

Fin Whale *Balaenoptera physalus*

With a body length of normally over 20 m, in rare cases up to 27 m, the Fin Whale is the second largest of all whale species. Like many of the oceans' animals, it is dark above and pale below, but the head pattern is strangely asymmetrical: the right lower jaw is white on the outside, the left one is dark. Also, at least the front third of the baleen plates on the right side are white; the others are grey, often with longitudinal yellow stripes. The species usually dives without showing the tail fluke, and the blow is vertical and shaped like a narrow funnel. The Fin Whale is found in all the world's seas except the tropical ones. North Atlantic animals move southwards in autumn to subtropical waters and breed there during the winter. In the spring the journey is then north again to the food-rich polar seas. During these migrations the species regularly appears in small schools in British waters. It was badly hit by whale-catching, perhaps above all in the southern hemisphere where, over several decades at the beginning and the middle of the 1900s, the numbers were reduced from around 400,000 to about 80,000 animals. In the North Atlantic the population is considerably smaller than this, only a few tens of thousands or less.

Sei Whale *Balaenoptera borealis*

The Sei Whale grows to a maximum length of 18 m and is thus smaller than the Fin Whale, which it otherwise resembles. Its markings, however, are symmetrical and the baleen plates are black with pale fringes. The blow is low, and when the Sei Whale blows it shows less of the head and body than do the other species of baleen whales. The Sei Whale, too, is found in all seas and undertakes seasonal migrations similar to the Fin Whale's between warmer and colder regions. The specific name *borealis* means that it belongs in the north, but there is nothing to indicate that it spends a longer part of the year in polar seas than the Fin Whale—rather the contrary. During the era when whale-catching was directed mainly against Blue and Humpback Whales, the Sei Whale was hardly hunted at all. As the Blue Whale in particular became more and more rare, so the interest in the Sei Whale increased, however, and for a period from the end of the 1940s it became almost the most important target of the whaling industry. Thanks to the catch being subjected relatively early to certain regulation, the decrease was, however, not quite so horrific as in many other species: the 75,000 or so Sei Whales that were reckoned to exist in the world's oceans in the mid 1970s represented at a rough estimate about 40% of the original stocks.

Minke Whale *Balaenoptera acutorostrata*

As the Minke Whale does not reach more than 10 m at most, it is by far the smallest of the baleen whales in the northern hemisphere. A broad white band across each flipper is characteristic and the snout is pointed. This is alluded to in the scientific specific name, which is a compound of the Latin *acutus* and *rostrum*, meaning respectively simply sharp or pointed and snout. The baleen plates are all-white. The species is found in cold and temperate seas right across the world, and moves in coastal waters more than other baleen whales. It also becomes stranded more often than other species and is in addition, like the Bottle-nosed Whale, well known for its readiness in approaching ships at anchor. Because of its 'smallness', the Minke Whale did not become the object of any larger-scale commercial hunting until the bigger species had really begun to decrease. During the final years before the five-year ban (page 210), however, this was the species that dominated the whale catch in terms of numbers. The total population has been estimated at at least 300,000 individuals.

Sei Whale

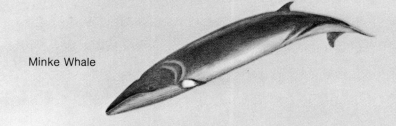

Minke Whale

Humpback Whale *Megaptera novaeangliae*

The Humpback Whale is another of the large baleen whales. It can reach a length of up to 18 m and is the least slim of the family. Very often the word slim is not used at all; instead it is described as heavy or even lumbering. The fact is, however, that the species, even though it swims more slowly than the others of its family, leaps completely clear of the surface of the water both more easily and more often then they do. In so doing it also shows other characters. The colour is black and white in pattern, varying among different individuals but with the tail often strikingly white. The same applies to the flippers, which besides are lumpy and very long, up to a third the length of the body. It is this latter point that has given the genus its scientific name: *mega* means large and *pteron* feather, wing or fin. The baleen plates are black. When the Humpback Whale dives, its back shoots up in an arc high above the surface of the water and after that the tail fluke also pitches up in the air. The blow is short but broad. The species is found in all the world's seas and moves seasonally between warm and cold regions. Where it is possible, the migration route goes through shallow water near the coast. The Humpback Whale was very severely affected particularly by catches in the 1900s, and when, towards the middle of the century, it gradually received some protection—in the North Atlantic commercial hunting was stopped in 1960—it was reckoned that only a few thousand animals were left of a world population that must once have comprised over 100,000 at least. Observations during the 1970s suggest that it has slowly begun to increase again in the eastern sectors of the North Atlantic. A study of the Humpback Whales that live west of Greenland in summer does not indicate any connection with the occurrence of plankton. On the other hand, these Humpbacks appear in the same areas as Great Shearwaters *Puffinus gravis* and obviously live mostly on capelin and other fry.

Right Whales Family *Balaenidae*

The right whales differ from the rorquals and Humpback Whale in lacking a back fin and in having an ungrooved throat and a slightly heavier build. In particular the head is unwieldy. Furthermore, the blow is divided into two and directed slightly forwards. The baleen plates are longer than in any other species—up to 3 m—and black. The right whales acquired their English name because, in the early days of whaling, they were the 'right' whales to hunt. There were several reasons for this: they swim relatively slowly, they often move about in shallow water, and they float after harpooning. The major food is a crustacean, *Calanus finmarchicus*, which is only 3–4 mm long. Two species of right whale are found in European waters.

Black Right Whale *Balaena glacialis*

The Black Right Whale can grow to 21 m in length and thus is not far behind the largest baleen whales as far as size goes. Occasional individuals may have several white spots on the body, but otherwise the species is black with horny pale excrescences on the upperside of the upper jaw. The species is found in cold and temperate seas in the northern hemisphere. A very closely related form in corresponding areas in the southern hemisphere is regarded either as a race of the Black Right Whale (*B. g. australis*) or as a full species (*B. australis*). The early whaling had a very severe effect on the Black Right Whale: as early as the turn of the last century, probably fewer than 10% of the original populations were left. Despite protection from commercial hunting from 1935, no recovery of any note has taken place. In the eastern parts of the North Atlantic it is doubtful whether the species can still be found at all; in the western sectors it is so rare that it is not considered wholly certain that it will survive.

Bowhead Whale *Balaena mysticetus*

Normally the Bowhead or Greenland Right Whale grows to 15–20 m, but it can reach up to 24 m and so is the larger of the right whales. It is similar to the Black Right Whale, but differs in having a white patch on the lower jaw and a proportionately bigger head—about one-third the length of the body. The species is if anything even more northerly than the Black Right Whale and has a circumpolar distribution in the Arctic Ocean. In the same way as for its smaller relative, whaling activity during the 1700s and 1800s had disastrous consequences and the species is nowadays fewer in number than any other species of baleen whale. Despite the fact that the Bowhead Whale, like the previous species, has been protected from commercial hunting since 1935, it shows no sign of increasing and the total population is so small that it has even been questioned whether the species will be able to survive.

Bibliography

Boyle, G.L. (ed.) 1981. *RSPCA Book of British Mammals*. Collins, London.

Brown, R.W., Lawrence, M.J., and Pope, J. 1984. *Animals of Britain and Europe—their tracks, trails and signs*. Country Life, London.

Chanin, P. 1985. *The Natural History of Otters*. Croom Helm, Beckenham.

Clark, M. 1981. *Mammal Watching*. Severn House Publishers, London.

Corbet, G.B. 1966. *The Terrestrial Mammals of Europe*. Foules, London.

—— 1978. *The Mammals of the Palaearctic Region—a taxonomic review*. British Museum, London.

—— and Ovenden, D. 1980. *The Mammals of Britain and Europe*. Collins, London.

—— and Southern, H.N. (eds.) *The Handbook of British Mammals*. 2nd ed. Blackwell Scientific Publications, Oxford.

Ewer, R.E. 1973. *The Carnivores*. Weidenfeld and Nicolson, London.

Freethy, R. 1983. *Man and Beast*. Blandford Press, Poole.

Gotch, A.F. 1979. *Mammals—their Latin names explained*. Blandford Press, Poole.

Hewer, H.R. 1974. *British Seals*. Collins, London.

Kurten, B. 1968. *Pleistocene Mammals of Europe*. Weidenfeld and Nicolson, London.

Laidler, K. 1980. *Squirrels in Britain*. David and Charles, Newton Abbot.

Lawrence, M.J., and Brown, R.W. 1973. *Mammals of Britain—their tracks, trails and signs*. Blandford Press, Poole.

Leatherwood, S., and Reeves, R.R. 1984. *The Sierra Club Handbook of Whales and Dolphins*. Sierra Club Books (Dist. Pandemic Ltd, London).

Lloyd, H.G. 1980. *The Red Fox*. Batsford, London.

Macdonald, D. 1984. *Encyclopaedia of Mammals,* vols 1 and 2. George Allen and Unwin, London.

Matthews, L.H. 1969. *The Life of Mammals,* vols 1 and 2. Weidenfeld and Nicolson, London.

Neal, E.G. 1986. *The Natural History of Badgers*. Croom Helm, Beckenham.

Nowak, R.M., and Paradiso, J.L. 1983. *Walker's Mammals of the World,* vols 1 and 2. 4th ed. John Hopkins University Press, Baltimore and London.

Schober, W. 1984. *The Lives of Bats*. Croom Helm, Beckenham.

Stebbings, R.E., and Griffiths, F. 1984. *Distribution and Status of Bats in Europe*. Inst. of Terrestrial Ecology, Abbots Ripton, Huntingdon.

van den Brink, F.H. 1967. *A Field Guide to the Mammals of Britain and Europe*. Collins, London.

Whitehead, G.K. 1964. *The Deer of Great Britain and Ireland*. Routledge and Kegan Paul, London.

Index